Blue Sky Metropolis

Western Histories
William Deverell, series editor
Published for the Huntington-USC Institute on California and the West
by University of California Press and the Huntington Library

Blue Sky Metropolis

The Aerospace Century in Southern California

Edited by Peter J. Westwick

Published for the Huntington-USC Institute on California and the West
by University of California Press, Berkeley, California, and
the Huntington Library, San Marino, California

Series jacket design by Lia Tjandra
Interior design by Doug Davis
Copyediting by Sara K. Austin and Jean Patterson
Indexing by Jean Patterson
Printed in South Korea by Charles Allen Imaging Experts

Library of Congress Cataloging-in-Publication Data
Blue sky metropolis : the aerospace century in Southern California / edited by Peter J. Westwick.
      p. cm. — (Western histories ; 4)
   Includes bibliographical references and index.
   ISBN 978-0-87328-249-9 (alk. paper)
   1. Aerospace industries—California, Southern—History—20th century.
   2. Aerospace industries—Social aspects—California, Southern—History—20th century. 3. California, Southern—History—20th century. 4. California, Southern—Social conditions—20th century. 5. California, Southern—Economic conditions—20th century. I. Westwick, Peter J. II. Huntington-USC Institute on California and the West.
   HD9711.5.U63C23 2012
   338.4'76291097949—dc23
                  2011042199

Contents

Foreword

This book was launched by an ambitious scholarly effort begun about six years ago. The Aerospace History Project, sponsored by the Huntington-USC Institute on California and the West, aims to collect and interpret documents and reminiscences drawn from Southern California's century of aerospace design and production. This industry forever and fundamentally changed the region, and it continues to do so, though in more subtle ways than at the height of the Cold War. The American embrace of jet engines and jet travel, followed quickly by the space race, was of course a national phenomenon. But its center was in Southern California. Expanding outward and upward from a foundation built upon airplane experimentation and manufacture in the early twentieth century, the aerospace industry transformed the region's economy, culture, demography, environment, and political landscape in ways that scholars are just beginning to acknowledge.

The Aerospace History Project is a modest effort focused on a huge industry. In careful, deliberate steps, the personnel of the project, led by this book's editor, are reaching out to aerospace pioneers, rank-and-file workers, and corporate representatives so that documentary materials and first-person accounts might be preserved. They then organize and make them accessible for analysis by scholars whose interests cross disciplinary boundaries. The project is not the first to focus archival or scholarly attention on the industry and its regional impact. But it is, we believe, an unusually concerted effort, in that our aim is to closely associate the collecting wing of the project with the scholarly scrutiny of the materials we have gathered.

The results thus far have been exciting. This book is one indication of the catalysis we feel fortunate to have experienced and in some ways to have created. A test-flight of the project, this collection of essays, which Peter Westwick has so ably curated and edited, is a way for us to lay critical scholarly groundwork about the industry's impact here in the far West. Each one of these essays is a statement about meaning and significance, just as each is a call for more work. Even as these essays were being prepared, edited, and set in type, the aerospace collections at the Huntington Library were far from static. What was in the archival care of the Huntington a year ago was a fraction of what is there now, and we expect that growth to continue.

It may be too soon to offer synthetic interpretations of the impact of aerospace on Southern California beyond claims of significance and importance. By metrics of demography and economics alone, we know well enough that the industry employed hundreds of thousands of people at its height and that the economic multiplier of aerospace employment and contracts made aerospace every bit the equal of such other industrial giants as oil and Hollywood. Those are easy pronouncements to make, but the repercussions of the impact remain to be studied in scholarly detail.

The prospective disciplinary range of further inquiry is 360 degrees of curiosity. Where (and when, and how) does the economic impact of aerospace stretch toward and connect with the rise of a particular brand of Cold War conservatism, which scholars have tracked to Southern California in the 1950s? How did aerospace manufacture further regional decentralization, and were aerospace plants simply the Cold War iteration of earlier industrial distribution throughout the Los Angeles Basin?

What of architecture? Los Angeles loves its "Googie" architecture, born of automobile and space-age angles, materials, and whimsy. Surely there's more to know about the fundamental role aerospace expansion and aerospace culture played in the rise and excitement of that regional idiom. The cultural strands are direct and tantalizing: How did aerospace secrecy and security wash over into everyday life in Southern California? What does it mean when Daddy—or occasionally Mommy—can't talk about work at home? How does an industrial culture so explicitly tied to technology and engineering fit into a regional culture tied to a world of leisure, the beach, and the Beach Boys? How does Southern California's racial and ethnic diversity intersect with the rise and impact of a giant industry seemingly so white? Where did those aerospace workers live? And, as Peter Westwick reminds us in this book, how is it that they collectively refined, refashioned, and in many ways reinvented the region's leisure and recreational culture? Stereotype insists that we imagine a Cold War California aerospace worker complete with short-sleeved Oxford shirt, pocket protector, and crew cut. But we might just as well find him at Pixar creating algorithms for rendering fuzzy blue monsters on screen as at JPL designing spacecraft.

So many fascinating questions. This book is a start, a smart, good start, on the road to answers. But we of course hope and expect that questions will always outnumber answers, and that the work—the collecting, the processing, the thinking, and the interpreting—will go on. Even if the seemingly infinite horizons of the blue-sky metropolis have contracted a bit, the stories of its making allow us to cross one frontier after another.

Acknowledgments

I must first thank William Deverell and Daniel Lewis, my co-conspirators in the Aerospace History Project at USC and the Huntington Library. Bill and Dan very early recognized the importance of documenting the history of Southern California aerospace, and they have directed the resources of USC and the Huntington to the archival project with boundless intellectual enthusiasm and good humor.

I must also of course thank the contributors to this volume, many of whom have helped the project's archival efforts as well; Sherman Mullin in particular has guided us to crucial historical papers and oral-history candidates. A number of fellow historians, scholars, and writers have offered encouragement and advice, among whom I must single out Joe Bassi, Soraya de Chadarevian, Martin Collins, Erik Conway, Fred Culick, David DeVorkin, Michael Gorn, Mike Gruntman, Reynal Guillen, Richard Hallion, Art Hansen, Gretchen Heefner, Matthew Hersch, Volker Janssen, Roger Launius, Peter Neushul, Curtis Peebles, Ken Phillips, Trudi Sandmeier, Allan Sekula, Steven Strom, Rick Sturdevant, Harry Waldron, Jason Weems, and James Young. I also thank several archivists at other aerospace institutions, in particular Julie Cooper, Katrina Pescador, Alan Renga, and Bonita Smith.

At the Huntington Library, Steven Koblik and David Zeidberg provided leadership and support from the start of this project. We also thank the Huntington's aerospace archivists, Brook Engebretson and Emily Wittenberg, and photograph curator Jenny Watts and assistants Erin Chase and Suzanne Oatey. At USC, Dean Howard Gillman likewise has steadily backed our efforts. We have also benefited from USC's Science, Technology, and Society program and thank its director, Andrew Lakoff. We profited in particular from the discussions at an STS-sponsored workshop, "Designing the Technological Future: The Landscape of Science in Postwar California," held at the Huntington in March 2011. We also thank Kim

Matsunaga for administrative support at the Huntington-USC Institute on California and the West.

This volume was enabled by generous funding from Margaret and Will Hearst, whom we thank deeply. Susan Green, Sara K. Austin, and Jean Patterson at the Huntington Library Press, and Kim Robinson at the University of California Press, guided the manuscript to publication with remarkable patience and editorial acumen.

Some of these papers originated in a conference at the Huntington in 2007, titled "Rocket Science and Region: The Rise, Fall, and Rise of the Aerospace Industry in Southern California," funded by the John Randolph Haynes and Dora Haynes Foundation; we thank in particular Haynes Foundation trustee Willis B. Wood Jr. for enlightened interest and support. The Huntington-USC Aerospace History Project is supported by the National Science Foundation (grant number 0957382) and by the Northrop Grumman Foundation.

As always, I thank my wife Medeighnia and sons Dane and Caden for their forbearance and refreshing distractions.

PETER J. WESTWICK

INTRODUCTION

A century ago, a quarter-million people flocked to a grassy field in Los Angeles over a ten-day period. They came to see a brand-new technology that promised to define the young century. The event was the Los Angeles International Aviation Meet of January 1910, the first such gathering in the United States, and it stoked interest in aviation in Southern California. A *Los Angeles Times* reporter declared it "one of the greatest public events in the history of the West."[1] The judgment is fair in retrospect. Over the next hundred years, the aircraft and aerospace industries transformed Southern California from a collection of quiet agricultural groves into a sprawling high-tech nexus on the Pacific Rim. Southern California as we know it would not exist without aerospace. Throughout the twentieth century, millions of people flooded Southern California to claim aerospace jobs, forever reshaping the political, cultural, and physical landscape in the process. They came first to build airplanes; the aircraft business, already thriving in Southern California by the 1920s, became a network of vast plants by the Second World War, each of which might employ a hundred thousand people. Many firms made the transition from making airplanes to making spacecraft, an evolution represented by the neologism *aerospace*. By the 1980s Southern California was home to about 40 percent of the United States' missiles-and-space business and to one-third of the nation's aerospace engineers, a remarkable brain drain across the American continent. The industry as a whole employed close to a half million people in the region.

Southern Californians learned to live with sonic booms, security clearances, test-rocket firings that flashed and echoed in the foothills, and an economy tied to the vagaries of defense spending. In doing so, they helped provide one of the defining symbols of modern technological culture in the twentieth century.[2] They mass-produced sophisticated

1

technologies in support of national security in World War II and the Cold War, from propeller-driven airplanes and bombers to strategic missiles, spy satellites, and stealth aircraft. They built commercial aircraft and, later, communications satellites that connected distant continents and impelled globalization. Finally, their fundamental contributions to the civilian space program, including the triumphant Moon landing and the robotic exploration of the solar system, challenged and transformed the human imagination.

The essays in this volume explore the many ways aerospace and Southern California intertwined. Despite its recognized centrality to California and American history, what scholars have called the "aerospace capital of the world" has attracted surprisingly little attention.[3] Among the many surveys of American aerospace, and biographies and histories of prominent figures and firms, few consider the specific context of Southern California.[4] This book begins to fill the void. It brings together writers with diverse perspectives, from anthropology to the history of science and technology, labor, business, ethnicity and gender, architecture, and the environment. Although this book's general theme is the centripetal formation of the aerospace economy, it provides no single, overarching conceptual framework. Rather, the essays that follow highlight a diversity of approaches, a breadth made possible by the complexity and importance of the aerospace industry; connected by the subject itself, these essays tell us a great deal, and they invite us to look and dig deeper.

The book's scope is deliberately broad. Chronologically, the essays range from the 1910 air meet to the present, a century of activity. Geographically, they look beyond the Los Angeles basin to chart the influence of aerospace from Vandenberg Air Force Base north of Santa Barbara, south to San Diego along the coast, and inland to the Antelope Valley and Mojave. The definition of aerospace is equally inclusive, ranging from aircraft to spacecraft, from airframe manufacturers to machine-tool suppliers, and from traditional aerospace corporations to the alt-space movement. Together the essays illuminate not only why the aerospace industry developed where and how it did, but also its diverse impacts on the surrounding society.

The essays address two fundamental open questions about the industry. Why did Southern California become a focal point for aerospace? And what were the consequences of this concentration for the region, the nation, and for aerospace itself? Posed the first question, most people just answer: the weather. Yes, Southern California sunshine allows year-round flying and outdoor construction of large aircraft. But many other places in the United States have nice weather, and almost all aerospace work was, in the end, conducted indoors. Understanding Southern California aerospace is not just a matter of meteorology. Rather one must consider, among other things, the region's long history of civic booster-ism, by newspaper publishers, real-estate developers, and Hollywood moguls; the investment in local universities that supplied research, test-ing facilities, and technical labor; open-shop rules in the labor market; local military installations; and a culture of expansive imagination and entrepreneurialism.

The second question is equally important. What did it mean for the aerospace industry to do much of its work in a particular place? The air-plane has revolutionized modern society, connecting the most distant corners of our planet. As much as the airplane helped drive globaliza-tion and diminish the differences between places and cultures, however, it was very much the product of a specific locale. Did Southern Califor-nia leave a distinctive stamp on aerospace technology? Aerospace engi-neers would of course deny that the laws of physics or engineering are affected by place, but historians have recently examined the possibility that technologies may reflect the place of their production in other ways.[5] Is there a distinctive Southern California style of airplane or spacecraft? Could Stealth aircraft, say, have been built anywhere else, and would they look different if they had been? One might speculate that Southern Cali-fornia attracted a particular sensibility, one attuned to the imaginative possibilities of flight. California historian Kevin Starr has long described the state as a land of dreamers; did the blue-sky California environment encourage the combination of vision and technical know-how captured by *imagineering*, a neologism from that other local industry?[6]

The geographical concentration of specific industries has ample his-torical precedent (think of, for example, Lyonnais silks, Alsatian calico, Swiss watches, or Detroit automobiles) and significant advantages, since mutually independent producers can capitalize on a common labor mar-ket and a network of suppliers and services. There has been much recent interest in various high-tech versions of this phenomenon, such as Route 128 near Boston, Bangalore in India, Novosibirsk in Russia, Tsukuba in Japan, and, especially, Silicon Valley.[7] Almost all of this research, except for that of the geographer Allen Scott, ignores Southern California as per-haps the premier example of a high-tech region.[8] Southern California aerospace was one of the main employers of scientists and engineers in the United States, one of the main consumers of science and engineering re-search, and one of the main producers of advanced technologies, which would affect fields far removed from aircraft and spacecraft. It introduced a major manufacturing industry into a new social and cultural context, away from the traditional industrial heartland in the nation's Northeast. It also provided an early model of high-tech agglomeration, with characteristics shared by later high-tech regions such as a common technical labor market and connections to local universities, and a network of electronics fabricators, close-tolerance machine shops, and other specialized suppliers.

Aerospace certainly wrought fundamental changes on Southern California itself. Some of the essays here highlight the social and demographic transformation driven by the rapid growth of the aerospace community, which helped to double the region's population between 1920 and 1940 and doubled it again from 1940 to 1960. Aerospace affected the balance between white-collar engineering jobs and manufacturing, and hence the socioeconomic makeup of Southern California. As Zuoyue Wang's chapter in this volume points out, the industry both reflected and shaped the local labor pool, in this case one marked by the presence of Asian Americans, who because of historical links to the Pacific Rim created a vibrant community in the region. Similarly, D. J. Waldie's evocative essay examines what Ernie Pyle called the "Aviation Okies," the hundreds of thousands of Southern migrants who flocked to work in aircraft plants and helped to give Los Angeles culture a decidedly Dust Bowl inflection.

Those migrants from the southern plains and the South gave Los Angeles the highest concentration of white Protestants among the twenty largest U.S. cities in 1960.[9] As that statistic suggests, aerospace also shaped the region's religious landscape. Along with the influx of "Aviation Okies," the relative scarcity of Catholics in science and engineering diminished the local Catholic presence. It may not be coincidence that the Air Force based its first ballistic missile office in an abandoned Catholic parish in Inglewood. Indigenous American tribes meanwhile saw their traditional sacred sites pressed into service as Air Force bases and test ranges. Dwayne Day's article examines one such intersection, between local Chumash traditions and missile launch pads at Vandenberg Air Force Base. Encounters between native tribes and the U.S. military—and between indigenous societies and modern technological systems—are not new in the American West. Adding to the now-familiar accounts of earlier centuries, historians have considered twentieth-century episodes—for instance, the opposition of Shoshone tribes to MX strategic-missile bases in the Nevada–Utah Great Basin.[10] Day's example adds to this long history of cross-cultural assumptions and appropriations.

M. G. Lord's essay highlights the industry's circumscribed gender roles, and the frustrations of generations of women excluded from the decidedly masculine realms of aerospace. Although women workers earned jobs and recognition in World War II as "Rosie the Riveters" in aircraft plants, they found themselves again excluded after the war, especially as the industry shifted from manufacturing to research and development. The limited presence of women in the American engineering profession affected their influence in the industry, and despite the feminist movement, the aerospace technical community remained a largely male bastion for much of the twentieth century.[11] By the 1990s, however, gradual inroads had increased opportunities for women in aerospace and begun to break down gender constraints.

Aerospace also reflected and shaped Southern California politics. The aircraft industry took root and flourished in the region in part because it was an open-shop citadel. Los Angeles, in particular, had a long history of antagonism toward the labor movement, led by civic leaders and the *Los Angeles Times*. Local strike busting left what Carey McWilliams long ago called the lingering "political pathology of Los Angeles," which made the city "the paradise of the professional patriot and the red-baiter."[12] As Anita Seth documents here, the unionization of aircraft plants proceeded fitfully against this backdrop; it was further hindered by the fact that aircraft production was largely devoted to the military and strikes could be viewed as a threat to national security.

Aerospace reinforced a general conservative political orientation in Southern California. The region reversed the usual class migration pattern: instead of working-class immigrants, the initial waves consisted of well-off easterners, followed only later by middle-class midwesterners and finally laborers. As McWilliams put it, "the rich came first"—a pattern that gave the area a conservative cultural and political cast.[13] When large numbers of poorer immigrants did come, many hailed from conservative areas of the South; the "Aviation Okies," for example, brought the working-class, traditional values of white evangelicals.[14]

The Cold War regime of security clearances and classified information may have further reinforced this orientation. Anthropologist Mihir Pandya's essay examines the implications of the classified community that developed Stealth aircraft in Southern California. In addition to maintaining the usual secrecy about proprietary information common to any competitive industry, aerospace was subject to government secrecy rules to protect national security. Tens and eventually hundreds of thousands of aerospace workers had official security clearances and had signed agreements forbidding them from discussing their work with family, friends, or even colleagues. Secrecy contradicts the ideals of democracy as well as science, and limits both political oversight and technical collaboration and peer review. Where it is pervasive, it can have broader social effects as well. Among other things, the security clearance process, with its detailed questionnaires and investigations, encourages social and political conformity (for instance, by discriminating against homosexuals), and may have added weight to conservative political inclinations in Southern California.

The intertwining of political, economic, and cultural conservatism in the industry raises a question of cause and effect: Did aerospace thrive in Southern California because of existing conservative inclinations, or did the middle-class, classified world of the Cold War defense industry encourage conservative politics? For example, were Aviation Okies carriers of conservatism, or left-leaning populists who were only turned rightward by the suburban conformism of Southern California in the 1950s?[15] The answer probably lies in the middle: in its resistance to unions, its welcoming of Aviation Okies, and its adaptation to the Cold War defense industry and its security regime, Southern California aerospace both drew on and encouraged conservative political tendencies.

Aerospace, however, is far from conservative in a technological sense. Patrick McCray's article traces an ideological strand in Southern California that merged conservative politics with technological futurism. Southern California had long attracted visionaries—architect Richard Neutra perceived "a people who were more 'mentally footloose' than those elsewhere." Carey McWilliams noted that Southern California's embrace of visionary nonconformism included a particular scientific and technological bent shared by the necromancing rocket scientist Jack Parsons; L. Ron Hubbard, who "magicked" with Parsons and went on to found Scientology (whose very name betrays scientistic aspirations); and the "I AM" movement, about which McWilliams asked, "will some future historian regard this Buck Rogers phantasy as the first cult of the atomic age?"[16] The thriving sci-fi community in Southern California, from Robert Heinlein, Ray Bradbury, and Hubbard in the 1940s through Larry Niven and Jerry Pournelle more recently, tapped this vein of technological futurism. As McCray highlights, this visionary impulse continues to prosper in today's alternative-space sector, also known as "alt-space" or "NewSpace," in which technological and economic entrepreneurs challenge mainstream aerospace firms from the fringes in Mojave (Burt Rutan's Scaled Composites) and from the very heart of the industry in Hawthorne (entrepreneur Elon Musk's SpaceX).

This view sheds light on the relationship between Southern California and Northern California, which most state residents view as distinct entities. In the common perception, Southern California is conservative and defense oriented, while Northern California is home to flakes and nuts. Thus, for example, Northern California's counterculture nurtured the freewheeling technophiles of Silicon Valley; the so-called California Ideology combined hippie counterculture with yuppie entrepreneurialism and turned the personal computer and the Internet into tools of personal liberation.[17] (And Silicon Valley, as McCray notes, incubated many alt-space entrepreneurs.) But Southern California also had its own cohort of technological visionaries, who helped create the aviation industry and more recently have embraced alt-space. This strand of technological futurism, advanced at times more from the margins than the mainstream, tempered the Southland's conservative political tendencies. McCray shows that this Southern California version of the California Ideology merged left-wing counterculture with right-wing libertarianism to create a pro-space movement with a distinctively left-coast flavor.[18]

Why did aerospace concentrate in Southern California and not Northern California? The north offered many resources, including manufacturing infrastructure, early airfields, and strong research universities, and while its weather was perhaps not as good as Southern California, it was certainly better than in the Northeast. But the presence of industries there perhaps softened the urgency to create new ones. Certainly Los Angeles boosters invested much energy into bringing the first air show in the United States to the south, and there it served to jumpstart an aviation sector. Nevertheless, Northern California did play a role in aerospace, as Glenn Bugos points out with his perspective from Silicon Valley. And, he shows, aerospace shaped Silicon Valley in turn, with aerospace procurement underwriting investment in electronics manufacturing. Southern California's connections to Silicon Valley suppliers may have increased as the industry's emphasis shifted from airframes to avionics and electronics.[19]

Sherman Mullin discusses this "rise of the coneheads" and the waning of the "tin-benders" in his piece on Robert Gross, the longtime head of Lockheed, which highlights as well the tension between finance and engineering—between aerospace as a business and as an arena for technological creativity. Mullin's piece also comments on Lockheed's diversification strategy, demonstrating that Lockheed's embrace of missiles and space saved the company financially when its core aircraft business soured. The Lockheed case helps to illuminate why the space business came to be dominated by aircraft firms, how *aero* became linked to *space*.

Although building spacecraft drew on some of aviation's technical disciplines and infrastructure, it required new know-how and suppliers, for example in chemistry for rocket fuel, and entailed a shift from mass production to one-off or small-batch manufacture. Some aspects of spacecraft production benefitted little from a Southern California location, and some of Southern California's original attractions, including open-shop labor, open space, and cheap land, were scarcer by midcentury. As a result, some aerospace firms sought out other locales: in the 1950s Lockheed located its space business in Sunnyvale in the Silicon Valley, and Aerojet opened a new rocket plant in Sacramento. Southern California did retain several attractions for spacecraft manufacturers, however, including local universities, a skilled labor market and network of suppliers, and the culture of technological futurism, and much of the nation's missiles-and-space business, as we know, ended up in Southern California.

The technological creativity of aerospace engineers filtered into Southern California society and culture. The development of infrared sensors for missile guidance and tracking later revolutionized astronomy, a scientific discipline that also had a strong local presence, with observatories at Mount Wilson and Palomar Mountain. Aerospace also developed the infrared sensors and information processing technologies that underpinned the Los Angeles Police Department's high-tech policing philosophy and aerial surveillance.[20] Telecommunications coding theory first pursued for the deep-space program later provided the basis for cellular telephones, itself now a vibrant industry in the region.

A primary point of access to the heavens—first the skies, and then space—Southern California also had an open route to the national imagination through popular culture. The movie business had strong connections to the aircraft industry from the outset. As my article demonstrates, these could lead to surprising technological intersections, including the development of computer-generated animation. Other convergences of aerospace and pop culture appear in pursuits especially identified with Southern California. Hot-rod car culture used airstrips for early races and later drew on aerospace engineers and suppliers to build exotic exhaust manifolds and custom camshafts.[21] Consider as well surfing, another touchstone of California culture. Two of the most influential figures in surfboard design over the last century had aerospace backgrounds. Robert Simmons studied engineering at Caltech, worked for Douglas Aircraft during World War II, and applied his knowledge of aerospace materials and advanced hydrodynamics to make several key advances in surfboard design. Tom Morey joined postwar Douglas to work on composites as a process engineer before turning to surfboards and later inventing the boogie board, which opened up surfing to a mass market.[22]

Connections to aerospace also emerge in highbrow intellectual and cultural endeavors. In addition to the thriving local science-fiction community, writers from Joan Didion to Thomas Pynchon (who started out as an aerospace technical writer) have mined Southern California aerospace for their work.[23] In design and the visual arts, aerospace contributed visual idioms such as the streamline aesthetic, and Charles and Ray Eames, who built experimental gliders during World War II, used fiberglass and resins from local aircraft suppliers in their work.[24] Stuart Leslie's article details how aerospace and architecture intersected in Southern California, examining the architect William Pereira's integration of California themes—open spaces, lush landscaping, water—with space-age accents in his aerospace aesthetic, evident in the striking photographs that accompany Leslie's article.

Leslie's piece also highlights how local universities influenced aerospace and vice versa. City planners worldwide are currently trying to replicate the model of high-tech development based on corporate "research parks" built around universities. Long before Stanford and Silicon Valley, or MIT and Route 128, Southern California's aircraft industry was drawing on Caltech and other local universities as sources of research, testing facilities, and technical labor.[25] As Leslie demonstrates, aerospace firms backed the creation of new University of California campuses, defined their curriculum, and influenced their built environment through aerospace architecture.[26] Leslie echoes the historian Matthew Roth in challenging popular and scholarly stereotypes of Southern California as an aesthetic wasteland.[27] In his survey of industrial archeology subtitled "Who Will Love the Alameda Corridor," Roth calls for a detailed examination of the material culture of industry, a call that Leslie answers here.

Roth also warns against adopting the narrative of development and decline familiar from manufacturing centers of the American Northeast, but one might indeed see Southern California aerospace as a "rise and fall" story. The end of the Cold War in particular led to the shedding of hundreds of thousands of jobs, as firms shuttered plants and relocated headquarters to Washington, D.C. As in earlier rounds of layoffs, for instance in the early 1970s after the end of the space race, aerospace workers who thought they had lifetime job security got a rude awakening, and their personal resentments percolated through Southern California society. The 1993 film *Falling Down*, in which Michael Douglas plays a pink-slipped aerospace engineer who resorts to violence, updated the old story of imperial expansion and domestic collapse. The Rodney King riots of 1992 and the Lakewood "Spur Posse" high school sex scandal were in part an expression of this post–Cold War economic dislocation.[28]

The aerospace era in Southern California has not ended entirely. The industry still has a large local footprint, albeit in new sectors such as alt-space and remotely piloted vehicles, with new corporate players (such as SpaceX, Scaled Composites, and AeroVironment), and in new locations beyond the Los Angeles basin, in particular in the Antelope Valley, where Lockheed's celebrated Skunk Works now resides.[29] Leslie notes, however, that as aerospace retools and relocates, much of its physical history is disappearing, converted to other industrial uses or leveled by the wrecking ball. Leslie urges the preservation of aerospace's architectural legacy, what Didion called "the cathedrals of the Cold War."[30]

As Wade Graham's article demonstrates, however, the physical legacy of aerospace may long outlast the industry itself, through its impact on the environment. Groundwater pollution by rocket fuel is just the most publicized inheritance, and cases of disease and deaths attributed to pollution have brought home to the afflicted individuals and Southern Californians generally the possible consequences of living with aerospace. Although lawsuits and federal remediation efforts still struggle to assign dollar figures to aerospace environmental damages, the costs—human and ecological—may prove incalculable.

Looking at the environment in its broadest sense, Graham shows how the aerospace presence shaped the engineering of Southern California. For example, the heavy rains that flooded Los Angeles aircraft plants in 1941 turned flood control into an issue of national security and helped justify flood control projects in the Los Angeles basin; aerospace demand for electricity meanwhile helped spark hydroelectric development. The aerospace metropolis extended its reach far into the American West, funneling electric power, water, and other resources from surrounding areas into Southern California to support the industry, developing ever-expanding suburbs, and eventually exporting residents. Graham presents a space-age version of the interdependent urban–rural ecology that William Cronon described for nineteenth-century Chicago, with jets and spacecraft instead of pork bellies.[31]

The essays are grouped into thematic sections, each with a brief introduction that makes connections across essays. We have encouraged overlap and tolerated occasional repetition in the hopes of highlighting intersections across disparate themes. A photoessay based on images recently deposited at the Huntington Library opens the proceedings with an overview of the first half-century of Southern California aviation, introducing themes and issues that resonate across the ensuing essays, which cover later periods. Next comes a section on "The Human Element," with the evocative, first-person accounts from Waldie and Lord. Then comes "The Work," in which Mullin, Seth, and Pandya detail what all these aerospace workers were actually doing. A section on "Culture" follows, with the essays by Leslie, Westwick, and McCray examining aerospace's technological, aesthetic, and ideological influences. The essays in "Communities" by Wang and Day explore intersections with local ethnic groups, and the final section on "Geography" includes Bugos and Graham considering the broader footprint of aerospace in California and beyond. The afterword, written by historian Philip Scranton, in addition to highlighting the oft-neglected topic of manufacturing engineering, points to other promising areas for future research. More broadly, Scranton notes the need for critical voices in aerospace history, accounts from "unbelievers" who question the costs of such enterprises.

Historical perspective on Southern California has often divided into two views, "sunshine" and "noir," or utopian and dystopian.[32] This book provides both sunshine and noir: Southern California as a source of extraordinary technological creativity and economic opportunity, and also as a place where the powerful exploit the underprivileged and plunder the environment. The builders of the Blue Sky Metropolis sought to slip the surly bonds of Earth, and transcend the failings and foibles of modern society. But aerospace was also, after all, a human enterprise, ever grounded in the realities and complexities of history.

notes overleaf

NOTES

1   Don Berliner, "The Big Race of 1910," *Air & Space/Smithsonian*, January 2010.

2   Robert Wohl, *The Spectacle of Flight: Aviation and the Western Imagination, 1920–1950* (New Haven, Conn.: Yale University Press, 2005).

3   Ann Markusen et al., *Rise of the Gunbelt: The Military Remapping of Industrial America* (New York: Oxford University Press, 1991).

4   Exceptions include Roger Lotchin, *Fortress California, 1910–1961: From Warfare to Welfare* (New York: Oxford University Press, 1992); Allen J. Scott, *Technopolis: High-Technology Industry and Regional Development in Southern California* (Berkeley and Los Angeles: University of California Press, 1993).

5   David Livingstone, *Putting Science in Its Place* (Chicago: University of Chicago Press, 2003); for Southern California, see Harvey Molotch, "LA as Design Product: How Art Works in a Regional Economy," in *The City: Los Angeles and Urban Theory at the End of the Twentieth Century*, ed. A. J. Scott and E. W. Soja (Berkeley: University of California Press, 1996), 225–75.

6   Kevin Starr, *Material Dreams: Southern California through the 1920s* (New York: Oxford University Press, 1990); *Endangered Dreams: The Great Depression in California* (New York: Oxford University Press, 1996); *The Dream Endures: California Enters the 1940s* (New York: Oxford University Press, 1997); *Embattled Dreams: California in War and Peace, 1940–1950* (New York: Oxford University Press, 2002).

7   Henry Birnbaum, "Japan Builds a Science City," *Physics Today* 28, no. 2 (February 1975): 42–48; Manuel Castells and Peter Hall, *Technopoles of the World: The Making of 21st Century Industrial Complexes* (New York: Routledge, 1994); P. Cooke and K. Morgan, *The Associational Economy: Firms, Regions, and Innovation* (Oxford: Oxford University Press, 1998); Paul R. Josephson, *New Atlantis Revisited: Akademgorodok, the Siberian City of Science* (Princeton, N.J.: Princeton University Press, 1997); Robert Kargon, Stuart W. Leslie, and Erica Schoenberger, "Far Beyond Big Science: Science Regions and the Organization of Research and Development," in *Big Science: The Growth of Large-Scale Research*, ed. Peter Galison and Bruce Hevly (Stanford, Calif.: Stanford University Press, 1992); Christophe Lécuyer, *Making Silicon Valley: Innovation and the Growth of High Tech, 1930–1970* (Cambridge, Mass.: MIT Press, 2005); Stuart W. Leslie, "Blue Collar Science: Bringing the Transistor to Life in the Lehigh Valley," *Historical Studies in the Physical and Biological Sciences* 32 (2001): 71–113; Annalee Saxenian, *Regional Advantage: Culture and Competition in Silicon Valley and Route 128* (Cambridge, Mass.: Harvard University Press, 1994); Rosemary Wakeman, "Dreaming the New Atlantis: Science and the Planning of Technopolis, 1955–1985," *Osiris* 18 (2003): 255–70; Margaret Pugh O'Mara, *Cities of Knowledge: Cold War Science and the Search for the Next Silicon Valley* (Princeton, N.J.: Princeton University Press, 2005).

8   Scott, *Technopolis*. Scott suggests that Southern California, by incubating post-Fordist systems of flexible production that then propagated through capitalist economies, was in fact a critical forebear of later high-tech regions.

9   Harold Meyerson, "Y'all Don't Come Back," *LA Weekly*, 7 September 2006.

10   Matthew Glass, "Air Force, Western Shoshone, and Mormon Rhetoric of Place and the MX Conflict," in *The Atomic West*, ed. Bruce Hevly and John M. Findlay (Seattle: University of Washington Press, 1998), 255–75. See also Joseph Masco, *The Nuclear Borderlands: The Manhattan Project in Post–Cold War New Mexico* (Princeton, N.J.: Princeton University Press, 2006), on the Los Alamos nuclear-weapons laboratory and neighboring Pueblo nations.

11   Sherna Berger Gluck, *Rosie the Riveter Revisited: Women, the War, and Social Change* (Boston: Twayne, 1987); Margaret W. Rossiter, *Women Scientists in America: Before Affirmative Action, 1940–1972* (Baltimore: Johns Hopkins University Press, 1995); Pamela E. Mack, "What Difference Has Feminism Made to Engineering in the Twentieth Century?" in *Feminism in Twentieth-Century Science, Technology, and Medicine*, ed. Angela N. H. Creager, Elizabeth Lunbeck, and Londa Schiebinger (Chicago: University of Chicago Press, 2001), 149–68.

12   Carey McWilliams, *Southern California: An Island on the Land* (Salt Lake City: Gibbs Smith, 1983), 283, 292–93.

13   Ibid., chap. 8.

14   James N. Gregory, *American Exodus: The Dust Bowl Migration and Okie Culture in California* (Oxford: Oxford University Press, 1989).

15   For the latter view: Peter La Chapelle, *Proud to be an Okie: Cultural Politics, Country Music, and Migration to Southern California* (Berkeley: University of California Press, 2007).

16   McWilliams, *Southern California*, 265; Mike Davis, *City of Quartz: Excavating the Future in Los Angeles* (New York: Verso, 1990), 54–62; Neutra quoted in Harvey Molotch, *Where Stuff Comes From* (New York: Routledge, 2003), 171.

17   Fred Turner, *From Counterculture to Cyberculture: Stewart Brand, the Whole Earth Network, and the Rise of Digital Utopianism* (Chicago: University of Chicago Press, 2008); see also Andrew Kirk, "Free Minds and Free Markets: Counterculture Libertarians, Natural Capitalists, and an Alternative Vision of Western Political Authenticity," in *The Political Culture of the New West*, ed. Jeff Roche (Lawrence: University Press of Kansas, 2008), 281–309.

18   See, e.g., "Our New, Spaced-Out Governor," *Los Angeles Times* editorial, 5 August 1977; Joseph Lelyveld, "Jerry Brown's Space Program," *New York Times Magazine*, 17 July 1977; Miles Beller, "Q&A" with Newt Gingrich, *Los Angeles Herald Examiner*, 13 April 1982.

19   I thank Henry Rowen for this suggestion. See also *The Silicon Valley Edge: A Habitat for Innovation and Entrepreneurship*, ed. Rowen et al. (Stanford: Stanford Business Books, 2000).

20   Mike Davis, *City of Quartz: Excavating the Future in Los Angeles* (New York: Verso, 1990), 250–53.

21   Robert C. Post, *High Performance: The Culture and Technology of Drag Racing, 1950–2000* (Baltimore: Johns Hopkins University Press, 2001).

22   Peter Neushul and Peter Westwick, "Aerospace and Surfing: Connecting Two California Keynotes," in *Where Minds and Matters Meet: Technology in California and the West*, ed. Volker Janssen (Berkeley and San Marino, Calif.: University of California Press and Huntington Library, forthcoming).

23   Joan Didion, *Where I Was From* (New York: Knopf, 2003); Thomas Pynchon, "Togetherness," *Aerospace Safety* 16, no. 12 (1960): 6–8.

24   Anne Collins Goodyear, "The Effect of Flight on Art in the Twentieth Century," in *Reconsidering a Century of Flight*, ed. Roger D. Launius and Janet R. Daly Bednarek (Chapel Hill: University of North Carolina Press, 2002), 223–41; Anthony M. Springer, *Aerospace Design: Aircraft, Spacecraft, and the Art of Modern Flight* (New York: Merrell, 2003); and Paola P. Antonelli, "Economy of Thought, Economy of Design," *Abitare*, May 1994, 243–49.

25   Richard P. Hallion, "The Impact of the California Institute of Technology on American Air Transport and Aeronautical Development, 1926–41," appendix 1 in *Legacy of Flight: The Guggenheim Contribution to American Aviation* (Seattle: University of Washington Press, 1977).

26   Convair and General Atomic staff helped design science and engineering curricula at the University of California, San Diego; San Diego State University; and the University of San Diego. Marvin Stern, interview by Finn Aaserud, 1 May 1987, Oral History Interviews, OH31355, Niels Bohr Library & Archives, American Institute of Physics, College Park, Md.

27   Matthew W. Roth, "IA and the 20th Century City: Who Will Love the Alameda Corridor?" *Industrial Archeology* 26, no. 1 (2000): 71–84.

28   Didion, *Where I Was From*, 131; David Beers, *Blue Sky Dream: A Memoir of America's Fall from Grace* (New York: Doubleday, 1996); D. J. Waldie, *Holy Land: A Suburban Memoir* (New York: Norton, 1996); see also Allan Sekula, *Aerospace Folktales* (Vienna: Generali Foundation, 2005).

29   William Deverell, Daniel Lewis, and Peter Westwick, "The End of the Aerospace Century," *Visiting Bloggers* (blog), *LA Observed* website, 7 January 2010, http://www.laobserved.com/visiting/2010/01/.

30   Didion, *Where I Was From*, 136.

31   William Cronon, *Nature's Metropolis: Chicago and the Great West* (New York: Norton, 1992).

32   Starr, *Material Dreams; Endangered Dreams; The Dream Endures; Embattled Dreams*; Davis, *City of Quartz*.

PETER J. WESTWICK

PHOTOESSAY:
AN ALBUM OF EARLY SOUTHERN CALIFORNIA AVIATION

A erospace history is rich in material culture but also in visual culture, since the emergence of aviation technologies overlapped the proliferation of photography. The Huntington Library has several collections comprising thousands of photographs that document early twentieth-century aviation in Southern California. This photoessay draws on those collections to introduce important themes from this early history; since many of the essays in this volume concentrate on the industry's heyday from World War II through the Cold War, these photographs provide context for later developments. Consider this a menu of short visual appetizers—amuse-yeux instead of amuse-bouche, so to speak—to whet appetites for the longer, more digestive essays that follow.

A dirigible flight in Pasadena, with the Raymond Hotel in the background, 13 October 1918 (photCL 402 [1D]). Harold A. Parker Studio Collection of Negatives and Photographs, 1889–1949.

Launching the Aerospace Century: The 1910 Air Meet

In January 1910 Los Angeles city boosters organized the first international air meet held in the United States. Local sports promoter Dick Ferris got support from Harry Chandler's *Los Angeles Times* and William Randolph Hearst's *Los Angeles Examiner*, financial backing from the Los Angeles Merchants and Manufacturers Association, and a $50,000 pledge from Henry E. Huntington.[1] The meet, held on an empty field in Dominguez Hills, attracted 226,000 spectators over ten days—quite a crowd, considering the city's population was about 320,000—and launched the airplane business in Southern California. Famous fliers liked what they saw in Southern California and stuck around to build planes; city fathers liked what *they* saw and looked to aviation as the future of Southern California.

The 1910 air meet did not generate interest out of thin air, so to speak. Balloons and dirigibles had a long history in Southern California. Thaddeus Lowe led the Union Army Balloon Corps in the Civil War before moving to Pasadena; Roy Knabenshue then made Pasadena a center for balloon and dirigible flights after the turn of the century, and was a prime mover behind the 1910 meet. But although ballooning had to some degree prepared the way, Southern California was not an obvious site for the meet. The city's boosters pressed for it in part to highlight the advantages of the region's climate, made evident in an outdoor event in the dead of winter. They also viewed airplanes as scientific and engineering marvels, as symbols of technological modernity.[2] Such images had special resonance at that time in the West, a region self-consciously forward-looking, happily unburdened by history (or so they thought). Boosters in Los Angeles, and in many other western towns battling a provincial image, embraced the airplane so ardently because it represented the technological future.

Opposite, top: French aviator Louis Paulhan soars over the Dominguez Field grandstand in 1910 (photCL Pierce 6253). *Opposite, bottom*: Paulhan makes a record-breaking flight to 4,600 feet in 1910. The balloon in the background advertises the young *Los Angeles Examiner* (photCL Pierce 6298). C. C. Pierce Collection of Photographs, ca. 1840–1930.

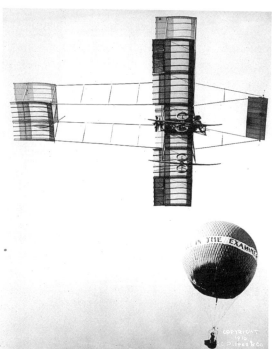

Triumph and Tragedy

Early aviation was not for the faint of heart. It promised great rewards but also grave danger, sometimes separated by only a moment. Early aviation photograph albums abound with heartbreaking photos of hearty, confident young men at an airplane's controls, followed by scenes of twisted wreckage where they met their death.[3]

The two photographs opposite chronicle the final days of Arch Hoxsey. Part of the Wright brothers' exhibition team, Hoxsey and fellow pilot Ralph Johnstone were known as the Heavenly Twins for their aerial exploits. Hoxsey, Johnstone, and other record-setting pilots were celebrities of the time, appearing in a series of "champion athlete" trading cards from Mecca cigarettes. The top photograph shows Hoxsey being carried off the Dominguez airfield on 26 December 1910, to the cheers of a crowd of 75,000, following a record-breaking flight to 11,474 feet.[4] The bottom photograph shows the scene five days later, on the last day of the year, after Hoxsey augured in from seven thousand feet. He was dead at the age of twenty-six. His fellow Heavenly Twin, Johnstone, had died in a crash a month before at twenty-four.

In addition to the threats to life and limb, the aviation business entailed financial risk. Aviation history is littered with the remains of failed firms; even the companies that survived sometimes went through several bankruptcies before succeeding. Aviation's sheer physical danger and uncertain commercial prospects attracted the same sort of people who helped populate the American West: risk-takers and entrepreneurs, individuals attracted by the romance of the enterprise and not afraid of death or ruin. This romantic, idealistic perspective seems to contradict the embrace of technological modernity that helped catapult aviation interest in Southern California. But much of western history is about the intersection, or reconciliation, of these two themes: romantic, even heroic individualism and modern technological systems. Aviation history thus provides a valuable window on the West.

Opposite, top: Arch Hoxsey at Dominguez Field,
26 December 1910 (photCL Pierce 6308)
Opposite, bottom: Hoxsey crash site, 31 December 1910 (photCL Pierce 6314).
C. C. Pierce Collection of Photographs, ca. 1840–1930.

Female Fliers

Both the heroic and technological aspects of the American West were often thought of as masculine realms. Flying attracted women as well as men, as the first photograph here, opposite top, of two anonymous enthusiasts around 1915, suggests. Female pilots were soon matching skills with men, barnstorming in exhibitions, setting speed and altitude records, and stunt flying for movies. But aviation's association with physical danger and mechanical technology meant flying was in its early years a mostly male enterprise. As of 1929, just 34 of the 4,690 licensed pilots in the United States were women, and the first Women's Air Derby, held that year, was mocked by men as the "Powder Puff Derby."[5]

Amid the general emancipation of women in the 1920s, however, women were starting to overcome contemporary prejudices with a mixture of grit and glamour. In Southern California, Florence "Pancho" Barnes, a pastor's wife and granddaughter of the patrician Lowe family of Pasadena (of ballooning fame), hobnobbed with Hollywood stars and had fashion photographer George Hurrell shoot her pilot's license picture, yet could carouse and curse harder than any male aviator. Barnes's hard-charging character contrasted with the most celebrated female flyer and fellow Southern California resident, Amelia Earhart. Earhart took her first flight in late 1920 in Los Angeles and within a year was flying exhibitions in a local "Air Rodeo" (an event that again linked aviation with a romantic image of the West).[6] Earhart presented a glamorous public face but knew her way around an airplane, and an aircraft plant. In the photograph opposite bottom, Earhart takes a break on the Lockheed factory floor in the early 1930s. These women's individual styles—Barnes's rough-and-tumble bluster and Earhart's androgynous image—might be viewed as accommodations to the "man's world" of aviation; but above all they were ambitious, independent women pursuing their goals without compromise and creating space for other women to join them.

Opposite, top: Two women flyers, ca. 1915 (photCL402 [1320]).
Opposite, bottom: Amelia Earhart on the Lockheed factory floor, early 1930s (Christen 1463). Harvey Christen Collection.

The Roaring Twenties and the Crash

The first decade of flight was mostly recreational or military, but in the 1920s commercial aviation emerged. Airlines carried airmail under contract with the U.S. Post Office and seated passengers alongside the sacks of mail. As commercial carriers sprang up, aircraft builders rushed to provide their planes. Again, Los Angeles city boosters saw the future in aviation; local businessman E. J. Clapp declared in 1926: "There is going to be a Detroit of the aircraft industry. Why not here in Los Angeles?"[7] Lindbergh's famous transatlantic flight in 1927 sparked a stampede of investment in aviation, and by 1928 Southern California boasted over twenty-five airframe and aircraft-engine manufacturers.[8]

Passenger flight catered to the wealthy, an expanding market in the Roaring Twenties. In the photograph opposite, a hostess serves tea on a Transcontinental Air Transport flight. TAT specialized in first-class service; a one-way cross-country ticket cost $350, or around $4,000 in today's dollars, an acceptable expense for business executives but few others. The picture was taken on 19 October 1929. Ten days later the stock market crashed.[9]

The Great Depression replaced scenes of luxury with images of hardship, and the aviation industry, along with the rest of the economy, entered a tailspin. (TAT was bankrupt in a year.) All too often, aviation was suffering from literal crashes as well: twenty years after Hoxsey's smashup, airplanes were still going down at an alarming rate. The dubious safety record put another damper on the growth of airlines and took some of the glamour out of flying. On the rainy, foggy evening of 20 January 1930, a Maddux Air flight from Agua Caliente crashed in a bean field south of San Clemente. The pilot had been following the headlights of cars on the coast highway through the fog and caught his wingtip on the ground when he banked to turn. The crash killed the two pilots and all fourteen passengers—each one, according to one account, a prominent resident of Los Angeles.[10] The rash of accidents eventually spurred the development of federal air safety regulations.

Opposite: A hostess on a Transcontinental Air Transport flight, 19 October 1929 (photCL Whitt 2850 [2974]). "Dick" Whittington Studio Collection of Negatives and Photographs, 1924–1948.

Aviation, Oil, and Hollywood

Aviation intersected and reinforced two other engines driving Southern California's growth in the early twentieth century: oil and Hollywood. Oil companies refined aviation fuel and provided early venture capital; the aviation pioneer Glenn Martin started his first aircraft business, in Los Angeles in 1912, with backing from oil money.[11] Southern California oil firms, such as Union Oil and Gilmore Oil, supported the fledgling enterprise by sponsoring air races and individual pilots in return for airborne advertisements. A fitting symbol of these interactions, the Dominguez Hills airfield itself sprouted wells after the discovery of oil there.

Oil money also helped finance early Hollywood films, which in turn provided venture capital for aviation. Hollywood heavyweights such as Cecil B. DeMille, Syd Chaplin, and Thomas Ince were airplane enthusiasts and operated airfields, and early flyers, including Martin, Glenn Curtiss, and, later, Pancho Barnes did stunt flying for movies.[12] It is no coincidence that Southern California attracted early filmmakers, who were testing the limits of a new medium for communication and expression, as well as early aviators, who were testing the limits of a new medium for transportation. Both industries expressed a belief in imagination and technical ingenuity, and both provided a foundation for the regional economy for the next century.

Hollywood also played an important role in propagating the romantic image of flight. The first Academy Award for best film went to *Wings*, in 1927, the first of many films about heroic aviators. Such movies connected flying to another long-standing symbol of the American West. In *The Right Stuff*, Chuck Yeager raced horses through the California desert and then rode rocket planes through the sky. In *Top Gun*, another film set in Southern California, the call sign of Tom Cruise was, yes, "Maverick." Aviators, in short, were the cowboys of the twentieth century.

Opposite, top: Western Gasoline truck at Glendale airport, 1928 (photCL Whitt 2795 [2718]).
Opposite, bottom: Movie cameras at March Field in Riverside, 1937 (photCL Whitt 2944 [2860]).
"Dick" Whittington Studio Collection of Negatives and Photographs, 1924–1948.

From Rural Airfields to Suburban Development

Despite its growth thanks to early aviation, Hollywood, and oil, Los Angeles in the first decades of the century still had plenty of open space. With so much ground to cover between, say, Santa Monica and Pasadena, the airplane offered an alternative to the emerging automobile culture, and Los Angeles city boosters backed air travel as an early basis for mass transit. By 1929 there were fifty-three landing fields within thirty miles of Los Angeles City Hall. The biggest ones kept their distance from downtown to take advantage of cheaper real estate as well as wider takeoff and landing corridors, and because the noise and dust—and danger—of airfield activity recommended distance from any neighbors.[13]

The large fields became centers of gravity for the aviation industry. There was Grand Central Air Terminal in Glendale, where Douglas "Wrong Way" Corrigan learned to fly; Clover Field in Santa Monica, created in 1922 and named for World War I pilot Greayer Clover; and Mines Field, established in 1928 with the backing of the Los Angeles Chamber of Commerce, keen for a municipal airport. The photograph, opposite top, of peacefully grazing sheep shows Mines Field, now LAX. In a typically Southern California twist, it was not named after a pilot, politician, or its owners, but instead after a real estate agent, William Mines, who represented the sellers.

The locations of these airfields help explain why the aircraft industry came to be concentrated in El Segundo, Santa Monica, and Glendale/Burbank, since aircraft plants accreted around airfields. Real estate developers then built planned communities such as Lakewood and Westchester, featured in the photograph opposite bottom, around aircraft firms, in a new model of suburban growth centered on satellite industrial centers instead of downtown. This was not, as the historian Greg Hise has shown, the result of haphazard suburban sprawl, but rather a deliberate, planned effort to build up residential areas around aviation factories.[14] Within a few decades these developments helped transform the Los Angeles basin from a pastoral landscape to an industrial metropolis of suburban communities.

Opposite, top: Mines Field, now LAX, in the 1930s (photCL Whitt 2865a [2789a]).
Opposite, bottom: Houses under construction on tract in Westchester, 1942 (photCL Whitt 0826).
"Dick" Whittington Studio Collection of Negatives and Photographs, 1924–1948.

Bird's-Eye Views

Aviation intersected that other key California occupation, real estate. The photograph opposite top, from around 1926, comes from an album touting a real estate development called "California Income Estates," east of Sacramento. The Rudd brothers, John and Bert, acted as fiscal agents for the development; they were partners in a Los Angeles real estate firm with an office on Vermont Avenue and a thriving business selling land in the San Joaquin Valley. To survey these expansive properties they acquired a fleet of airplanes. Company letterhead touted the Rudds as "California's Colonizers."

The Golden State would indeed be colonized by aircraft—not so much through aerial real estate surveys as by the aerospace economy. In one sense, however, the Rudd brothers were on to something. Aerial photography, first from nineteenth-century hot-air balloons and then from airplanes, provided a new way of seeing the world, as the photograph opposite below suggests. The wide-open spaces of the American West particularly captivated early flyers—the Southwest was Charles Lindbergh's favorite landscape—and continue to beckon aerial photographers. Popular accounts by early airplane pilots and passengers of this new perspective convey their sense of revelation, in the literal sense: that is, of bringing something previously hidden into view.[15] If picturing a place is a way of claiming it, "of converting the terrain into territory," as William L. Fox has asserted, then perhaps aerial perspective provided a way for Americans to colonize California in the American imagination.[16]

Opposite, top: "Rudd Brothers Aeroplane Fleet," ca. 1926
(Album 111 [California Income Estates]).
Opposite, bottom: Aerial photograph of Pasadena and
Mt. Wilson from the southwest, 1932 (COPC 78).
Carnegie Observatories Photo Collection.

RUDD BROTHERS   AEROPLANE FLEET ———
FIRST TO USE AEROPLANES IN REAL-ESTATE SUBDIVISION.

World War II and Southern California

Historians continue to argue over World War II's place as a historical turning point for Southern California. Some see it as a major watershed, a qualitative shift, while others see only a quantitative change: an already big aviation industry just got bigger. According to the latter, wartime expansion was not the cause of the region's aviation industry, but an effect of its established presence.[17] No one denies, however, that the war led to tremendous growth. Aircraft manufacture became the largest industry in the world, much of it centered on Southern California. Airplanes were mass-produced in vast assembly-line factories with 100,000 workers each; Southern California aircraft plants employed 2 million people, who built 300,000 planes over the course of the war. The top photograph opposite shows a shift change at Lockheed, where wartime employment peaked at over 94,000.

The war also brought new groups to prominence in Southern California aircraft plants. These included the Dust Bowl migrants who came to the region in the 1930s and found work in aircraft plants—the "Aviation Okies" described by D. J. Waldie in this volume. Women also joined the aviation workforce as "Rosie the Riveters" in wartime defense plants. By 1944, women made up over 40 percent of the aircraft production workforce in Los Angeles, and at some plants their proportion was much greater, for example approaching 90 percent at Douglas.[18] The bottom photograph opposite shows a worker at Solar Aircraft in 1943 making airplane exhaust manifolds.

Demobilization at the end of the war reversed many of these trends. Southern California aircraft plants shed hundreds of thousands of workers, including women; by 1948 the proportion of women in Los Angeles's aircraft industry had dropped from 40 percent to 12 percent. This is often viewed as a permanent loss, but subsequent Cold War remobilization and the recovery of the aircraft industry, which would soon expand into aerospace, allowed some renewed inroads by women starting in the early 1950s. In 1951, for example, amid a major buildup for the Korean War, Lockheed advertised for women who had worked in wartime

Opposite, top: Shift change at Lockheed in wartime (Christen 6640). Harvey Christen Collection.
Opposite, bottom: A woman machines manifolds for airplane engines at Solar Aircraft Co. in 1943 (photCL Whitt 3069). "Dick" Whittington Studio Collection of Negatives and Photographs, 1924–1948.

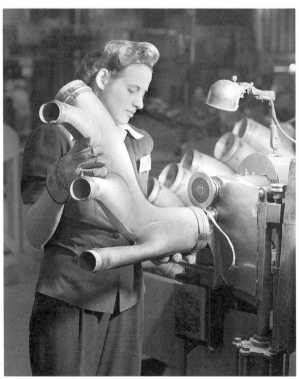

factories and in that year almost doubled the number of women in its Burbank plant, to almost 20 percent of its workforce. However, this did not approach the proportions of the war years, and some things did not change: when the company asked for candidates to ride on the Lockheed float in the 1953 Rose Parade, 141 female employees submitted photos of themselves in bathing suits, and a lucky five were chosen.[19]

NOTES

1   Dick Ferris, "The People's Air Meet," *Out West: A Magazine of the Old Pacific and the New* 3 (January 1912): 70–72; Don Berliner, "The Big Race of 1910," *Air & Space/Smithsonian,* January 2010. There is no evidence that Huntington actually fulfilled his pledge.

2   Kevin Starr, *Material Dreams: Southern California through the 1920s* (New York: Oxford University Press, 1990), 115.

3   For example, see the photograph album of Jack Niblack, chief of police of Signal Hill in Long Beach, photCL 482, Huntington Library, San Marino, Calif.

4   "New Hoxsey Record; Rises 11,474 Feet," *New York Times,* 27 December 1910.

5   Lauren Kessler, *The Happy Bottom Riding Club: The Life and Times of Pancho Barnes* (New York: Random House, 2000), 69.

6   Air Rodeo program, 17 December 1921, reprinted in David Hatfield, *Los Angeles Aeronautics,* vol. 2, *1920–1929* (Inglewood, Calif.: Northrop Institute of Technology, 1973), 80.

7   Greg Hise, *Magnetic Los Angeles: Planning the Twentieth-Century Metropolis* (Baltimore: Johns Hopkins University Press, 1997), 117.

8   Starr, *Material Dreams,* 117.

9   Daniel Rust, *Flying Across America: The Airline Passenger Experience* (Norman: University of Oklahoma Press, 2009), 56. This photograph suggests we need to revise the accepted view that airline stewardesses did not appear until 1930, when United hired Ellen Church.

10   Description with accompanying photograph, photograph album of Jack Niblack.

11   John B. Rae, "Financial Problems of the American Aircraft Industry, 1906–1940," *Business History Review* 39 (1965): 99–114.

12   Shawna Kelly, *Aviators in Early Hollywood* (Charleston, S.C.: Arcadia Publishing, 2008).

13   Rust, *Flying Across America,* 29.

14   Hise, *Magnetic Los Angeles.*

15   Tom D. Crouch, "'The Surly Bonds of Earth': Images of the Landscape in the Work of Some Aviator/Authors, 1910–1969," in *The Airplane in American Culture,* ed. Dominick A. Pisano (Ann Arbor: University of Michigan Press, 2003), 201–18; Rust, *Flying Across America,* 81–85.

16   William L. Fox, *Aereality: On the World from Above* (Berkeley, Calif.: Counter-point, 2009), 7.

17   Gerald D. Nash, *The American West Transformed: The Impact of the Second World War* (Bloomington: Indiana University Press, 1985); Paul Rhode, "The Nash Thesis Revisited: An Economic·Historian's View," *Pacific Historical Review* 63 (August 1994): 363–92.

18   Sherna Berger Gluck, *Rosie the Riveter Revisited: Women, the War, and Social Change* (Boston: Twayne Publishers, 1987). On women at Douglas, see Peter La Chapelle, *Proud to be an Okie: Cultural Politics, Country Music, and Migration to Southern California* (Berkeley: University of California Press, 2007), 101.

19   Ben Rich, "Lockheed in 1951," December 1976, Ben R. Rich papers, series 3 (speeches), box 4, Huntington Library.

SECTION I
THE HUMAN ELEMENT

We begin with two memoirs by D. J. Waldie and M. G. Lord, writers who grew up amid Southern California aerospace but were not themselves part of it. These essays provide a personal perspective on the vast, amorphous aerospace industry, bringing a human element to this highly technological enterprise and linking it to social history.

Waldie has spent his life and career in the suburb of Lakewood, an aerospace community built around the nearby Douglas aircraft plant and populated by "Aviation Okies." These shop-floor workers were captured in the character of Riley the riveter, subject of the popular TV series *The Life of Riley*. Riley does not exactly fit the popular image of the "Greatest Generation," but such workers indeed provided the U.S. military its technological muscle in the Cold War. Waldie's elegiac tone may seem an odd note on which to start this volume, but his deeply personal account of the social costs of aerospace resonates through the ensuing essays. And his tale brings to life an age that many Southern Californians, especially youth and recent immigrants, no longer remember. Just as an earlier generation forgot its maritime history—that nineteenth-century world of ocean travel and the shipbuilding that enabled it—Southern California aerospace threatens to fade from popular memory.

Lord's essay similarly sheds an ambivalent light on the salad days of the U.S. space program, not only illuminating the toll it took on her own family but also highlighting the exclusion of women from the space race. But Lord sounds a more optimistic note as well. Southern California aerospace is not dead, she tells us; initiatives such as the Ansari X Prize support the thriving alternative-space movement, or alt-space, which is also the subject of Patrick McCray's essay in this volume. Lord notes that the post–Cold War space program differs in two respects from the old space race: the alt-space movement is mostly civilian, not military; and it has made room for women, thanks to the feminist movement that coincided with the space race.

LOST IN AEROSPACE

I've lived my whole life in Lakewood—a place built to house fabricators of the future. It's a future now past. This is not to say that my Los Angeles suburb has no future, only that it's not the future for which Lakewood had been made.[1]

More than half a century has passed in what was supposed to be "The City of Tomorrow, Today" when it was thrown up on the lunar-gray soil of 3,500 acres of former lima bean fields in a nondescript corner of Los Angeles County. No one then questioned the paradox of locating tomorrow within the confines of a perfectly ordinary tract-house development. And tomorrow, when it finally did arrive, wasn't what the residents of "tomorrow's city" had been told to expect. They'd been told that the future would be sleek, edged in shining chrome, protectively enclosing like the cockpit of a jet fighter, and armed for confrontation with the Soviet Union and its allies. (How a grid of suburban streets, blue-collar lives, and boxy houses would have fit into that future was never made entirely clear.)

My suburb came into existence near the beginning of the Age of Aerospace. Lakewood has now seen the end of that age. What will be the meaning of that optimistic and terrifying time? What lingering impression will the Age of Aerospace have made on our imaginations? What is the durability—if any—of its effects on Los Angeles?

Tomorrow's Past

The huge assembly buildings of the Douglas Aircraft Company stood not far from where I live. Most of those buildings are gone now. The 260 acres where bombers and then airliners were built have been readied for redevelopment. Most of the ground has been cleared. The construction of low-rise units of office and industrial space has begun. The last of the assembly buildings may come down in two or three years, when production of the C-17 military transport ends on the site's eastern side. The C-17 will be, almost certainly, the last large aircraft built in California. In a kind of geographic symmetry, the former Douglas plant (later McDonnell Douglas and then Boeing) is only a short drive from the Dominguez Rancho, site of the 1910 Los Angeles International Aviation Meet, where flight in California began.

The Douglas plant in Long Beach opened on the eve of war in 1941 and employed an estimated 50,000 workers (87 percent of them women)[2] by war's end. Douglas began the postwar era as the largest aerospace employer in the state, but it wasn't alone. By 1965, fifteen of the twenty-five largest aerospace companies in the nation were concentrated in California. Most of them were in Los Angeles County, in an industrial belt that ran from El Segundo to Long Beach to downtown Los Angeles, and from Burbank to the eastern end of the San Fernando Valley. Through the 1960s to the end of the Vietnam War, aerospace manufacturing in Los Angeles employed more than 250,000 workers. Even at the Cold War's end in 1990, aerospace employed 130,000 workers countywide, which was more than half the state's entire aerospace workforce.[3] By 2009, just 37,000 workers were employed in aerospace manufacturing in Los Angeles County.[4]

The workforce of the Age of Aerospace was as much a product of the industry as the jets and rockets themselves. At the inception of the age— in the midst of World War II, in fact—the image of that new workforce was being fabricated alongside Douglas, Lockheed, Boeing, and Northrop bombers and fighters. The aerospace workforce had to be imagined into being because its size was so great, and the sources of labor so diverse, the materials and purposes so new, and their location in "tomorrow" so insistently asserted. The aerospace workforce had to find both formal and informal self-images in order to project itself into the future that places like Lakewood seemed in such a hurry to reach.

For my neighbors in working-class Lakewood, one pervasive image of the aerospace worker was Chester Riley, the innocent and hapless hero of *The Life of Riley*, a long-running comedy series that began as a vehicle for Groucho Marx in 1944, spawned a popular motion picture in 1949, and became one of television's most successful shows between 1953 and 1958. Riley's exclamation of impotent indignation—"What a revoltin' development this is!"—became one of the best-known catchphrases of the period.

Riley first appeared, with the blackest of Groucho Marxist irony, as the hapless father of "The Flotsam Family." Essentially a big-hearted lug, Riley was defense industry flotsam, already adrift in the first days of aerospace, along with his nuclear family. Riley became the prototype—the proof of concept—for Ralph Kramden, Fred Flintstone, Archie Bunker, and the more recent working stiffs of episodic TV. Today, with even greater irony, Riley's successor as a model technical worker is two-dimensional Homer Simpson.

A lot of my neighbors in Lakewood worked at the Douglas plant after the war. A lot of them wore Riley's work uniform of a khaki shirt and pants, not much different from the military uniforms many had worn in the Pacific and Korea. In the unlikely event that any of them thought they represented the "greatest generation," they had only to look to Riley to see what much of America thought of them. But Riley lacked one defining characteristic of my neighbors. William Bendix, who played Riley, was a wonderful character actor, but when he opened his mouth, it was Brooklyn that spoke. Riley, to be true to life to my neighbors, should have spoken with the drawls and twangs of Oklahoma, Arkansas, Missouri, west Texas, and Tennessee.

Space Age Fabrications

By 1945, an estimated 610,000 migrants from the South[5] had moved to California to find work in defense industries. Many of them were like Steinbeck's Joad family from *The Grapes of Wrath*, completing a migration that led from the Dust Bowl, to the labor camps of California's Central Valley, to Hawthorne or Lawndale or Torrance, by way of an aircraft plant. In 1941, columnist Ernie Pyle called them "Aviation Okies."[6] Well below the level of the engineers with slide rules, among the riveters with a high school education, these "Aviation Okies" gave Los Angeles aerospace a distinctive culture with its own style of music, its own language and food preferences, as well as its own politics, class resentments, and racial antagonisms. Workers from the South gathered at places like Price's Foothill Club on the edge of Signal Hill, the Riverside Rancho in Silver Lake, and the Palomino in North Hollywood. They listened to bands that specialized in melancholy laments.[7] *Billboard* magazine, in describing their music preferences, called them "khaki and overalled Okies."

I grew up among "khaki and overalled Okies" and saw them whip-sawed by cycles of boom and bust driven by defense contracts and aircraft orders. I watched Douglas workers go out on strikes that frightened their sons and daughters and threatened marriages and mortgage payments. I listened to their complaints about the men who supervised them at Douglas—an organization that seemed to be composed of dense layers of managers in short-sleeved white shirts who had a disturbing inability to manage.

The Life of Riley was broadcast on Friday nights when I was a boy. I watched the show on a big black-and-white RCA TV. I watched the *Disneyland* series on Wednesday nights. In 1955, Disney's "Man in Space" and "Man and the Moon" programs, and later, "Mars and Beyond," presented cartoon images of the world of tomorrow—orbiting platforms and multistage rockets that would take boys like me to the Moon and to colonies on Mars.

The cartoon figures on the Disney shows resolved the technical problems of tomorrow with slapstick humor or Technicolor grandeur. In between the cartoons was an earnest, serious man, a little like Riley in body type, and with a funny accent, too. Disney's spokesman for the future was Wernher von Braun. Von Braun, in his roles as affable seller of space flight, counselor to presidents, and master rocketeer, appeared utterly unlike the aerospace workers I knew, except in one way: von Braun, the former aristocrat, had adopted a protective coating of born-again southern-ness after finding a home, far from Peenemünde, Germany, in Huntsville, Alabama. Perhaps that was a further example of aerospace fabrication.

Later, I learned that the Rileys—Chester, Peg, Babs, and Junior—weren't the only "flotsam family" who had been adrift. Von Braun's team of engineers and technicians, who had designed and built the "vengeance weapons" that fell on London, Amsterdam, and Antwerp, had cast themselves loose as well in the waning days of the war. The von Braun family included men like his assistant Dieter Huzel and fellow engineer Bernhard Tessmann. By early April 1945, the two men had successfully stashed 14 tons of plans and rocket parts in a disused iron mine in Germany's Harz Mountains while von Braun and the remainder of his team zigzagged through the collapsing Reich. On 2 May, von Braun made contact with elements of the United States' 44th Infantry Division.

I worked at the local commuter college in the mid-1970s assisting Dr. Patrick Griffin, a historian and documentary filmmaker, in a project called "War from the Air" for the *Nova* science series on PBS. With that project done, Griffin began another *Nova* episode, "Hitler's Secret Weapon," using National Archives footage of V-2 rocket tests. Griffin ended his documentary with an image of von Braun that even guileless Riley would have been able to interpret. Von Braun, in his careening about Germany looking for Americans to surrender to, had been in a car accident. His arm and shoulder were broken. When Army personnel arrived to collect von Braun and the others in May 1945, they brought along a film crew. Because of the accident, von Braun was filmed wearing a heavy cast and an elaborate arm brace. But he also wore a broad and knowing smile for the movie camera. Despite his recent crackup, von Braun knew that he was still on the stairway that led to the stars.

By February 1946, von Braun and his team, including Huzel, were in the United States as part of the federal government's Operation Paperclip. By January 1947, Huzel was working at Fort Bliss, Texas, and a little later at North American Aviation (NAA) in Los Angeles, in its Rocketdyne division. (Rocketdyne was created specifically to transfer V-2 technology to the U.S. military, and Huzel became a full-time NAA employee to coordinate that effort.)

According to Huzel's 1962 memoir, von Braun regretted that his dreams of space flight had to be realized first as military hardware. But, as he had told his team in Peenemünde, the V-2 bombardment of London in late 1944 was a sad demonstration of the fact that "important new developments get nowhere until they are first applied as weapons."[8]

Unfailing Cooperation

I met Dieter Huzel through Patrick Griffin's V-2 documentary. Huzel was an energetic older man then, about the same age as my father. He was another image of the aerospace worker, but completely unlike Chester Riley. Huzel was the image of a competent, disciplined, and largely anonymous engineer. Riley couldn't be trusted with anything more complicated than the care of his family. Huzel was given security clearance for the most secret of the future's most dangerous possibilities. It was less of a future, it now seems, for good-hearted lugs like Riley, or even for the middle managers of Douglas, and more of a future for the former members of the German rocket team.

Huzel didn't look like the astronauts who had gotten us to the Moon, although he had helped to get them there. He didn't look like a hero of the Cold War, but his work would help deliver multiple 20-megaton warheads to targets in the Soviet Union, if that was the president's wish. He didn't look like one of Hitler's willing henchmen, either.

As a key member of the propulsion design teams for the Redstone, Jupiter, Atlas, and Saturn rockets, Huzel continued to weaponize the future, even as von Braun continued in the equally important task of producing the Disney version of tomorrow for NASA. These were the two strands of fabrication in the Age of Aerospace in Los Angeles—at one end of the plant were defense department projects aimed at the Soviet Union; at the other end was the Apollo command module aimed at the Moon. What wove the two strands together was a system of command and control in which thousands of men who were supposed to be like Dieter Huzel directed the work of tens of thousands of men who were feared to be like Chester Riley.

For von Braun, the Rileys hardly mattered, and the sole value of all the Huzels was their single-mindedness. "Great numbers of professionals from many walks of life, trained to cooperate unfailingly, must be recruited. Such training will require years before each can fit his special ability into the pattern of the whole," von Braun wrote in his preface to *The Mars Project* (1953).[9] The target of the Age of Aerospace had never been London or Moscow or even the Sea of Tranquility. It had always been the fabrication of a new kind of industrial worker who could be commanded to make tomorrow inevitable. Tomorrow served none of them—not even von Braun—as well as any of them had hoped it would, leaving all of them jilted by the future.

Embedded in Los Angeles's aerospace culture are these contradictory images of men's work and their usefulness. Over at Douglas, competent, untroubled men like Huzel were committed to serving von Braun's idea of the future. Out on the factory floor, men like Riley riveted together large parts of a tomorrow they believed had come with their houses and the crabgrass in their lawns. And other, lesser men with clipboards managed only to threaten the men on the assembly line with obscure company regulations or cajole them into serving goals they themselves did not know. The managers at Douglas had nothing else to offer, least of all the meaning of their work, until the work evaporated in the rounds of layoffs that cut the Douglas workforce by nearly 30,000 between 1990 and 1994. In the end, the laid-off managers in white shirts were as befuddled and clueless as the laid-off Rileys in khaki. Tomorrow, it turned out, didn't reveal much difference between their clipboards and Riley's rivet tool.

During the war, columnist Ernie Pyle[10] wrote admiringly, but with a flinty realism, about the "little routine men" of America who were fighting to win a future they thought would belong to them. Pyle, who knew them best, thought that their anonymous efforts would add up to a postwar victory that would be visible to everyone, like raising the flag on Iwo Jima's Mount Suribachi. Later, it would be a Thor rocket lifting off from Cape Canaveral. The "little routine men" believed President Kennedy when he said that victory for them would be harnessed to a rocket. Joan Didion, in *Where I Was From*, bleakly concluded that their faith had been false. Those poorly fabricated men, she argued, made up an "artificial ownership class"[11] whose possession of a small house on a small lot in a working-class suburb of Los Angeles was unreal, unearned, and just another situation comedy of the Cold War.

Naturally, my neighbors and I disagree. In Lakewood, aerospace gave us a precarious everyday life, and periodically aerospace took it away. And now aerospace in Los Angeles County is mostly gone, although the houses remain and the lives in them. None of my neighbors asked in the 1950s what their "city of tomorrow" would be fit for if tomorrow's assumptions were falsified. Perhaps the persistent ordinariness of places like Lakewood is the only answer.

Coda

Dr. Griffin recruited Joe Johnston, a student in California State University Long Beach's industrial design program, to redraw some of the V-2 plans that Huzel had so carefully hidden for von Braun. Soon after, Johnston was recruited by filmmaker George Lucas. Johnston ultimately became an art director at Lucasfilm's Industrial Light & Magic and one of the key concept artists for the first *Star Wars* trilogy. Near the end of the Age of Aerospace in Los Angeles, the promised tomorrow—like so much flotsam—had drifted from Peenemünde to a galaxy far, far away.

The Foothill Club became a salsa and reggaetón dance club when Douglas employment waned. After switching to rock and funk in the 1980s, the Palomino closed in 1995. KZLA, once the dominant country-music station in Los Angeles, abandoned the format in 2006. "We apologize for any inconvenience this may cause," was the station's last web posting.

This essay is adapted from a paper presented in August 2007 at "Rocket Science and Region: The Rise, Fall, and Rise of the Aerospace Industry in Southern California," a conference sponsored by the Huntington-USC Institute on California and the West. Abridgements have appeared as "Lost in Aerospace" in *Huntington Frontiers* (Fall/Winter 2007) and as "The Death of Riley" at the KCET website, www.kcet.org/local.

notes overleaf

Notes

1   Lakewood's story is told at the City of Lakewood's website, http://www.lake woodcity.org/about_lakewood/community/lakewood_history/default.asp.

2   For the percentage of women working at Douglas, see Susan Faludi, *Stiffed: The Betrayal of the American Man* (New York: William Morrow, 1999). Faludi details the effects of layoffs on the middle managers of Douglas in chap. 2, "Nothing but Big Work: From Shipyards to Space, the Closing of the American Job."

3   For the number of employees, see the Employment Development Department website, www.labormarketinfo.edd.ca.gov. On the relative size of the aerospace workforce, see James Dertouzos and Michael Dardia, *Defense Spending, Aerospace, and the California Economy* (Santa Monica, Calif.: RAND, 1993).

4   "Manufacturing: Still a Force in Southern California," report by the Los Angeles County Economic Development Corporation (2011), p. 45, table 26, "Employment in the Largest Manufacturing Sectors in Los Angeles County"; http://www.laedc.org/reports/Manufacturing_2011.pdf.

5   For the number of southern migrants to California, see James N. Gregory, *American Exodus: The Dust Bowl Migration and Okie Culture in California* (New York: Oxford University Press, 1989).

6   Kevin Starr, *Golden Dreams: California in an Age of Abundance, 1950–1963* (Oxford: Oxford University Press, 2009), 26.

7   Peter La Chapelle, in *Proud to be an Okie: Cultural Politics, County Music, and Migration to Southern California* (Berkeley: University of California Press, 2007), examines the southern qualities of Los Angeles through the medium of country music. His view of the persistence of "Okie culture" emphasizes the malleability and present endurance of that culture. His book is the source for the reference to "khaki and overalled Okies" (80). KZLA was still broadcasting a country-music format when *Proud to be an Okie* was published.

8   Dieter K. Huzel, *Peenemünde to Canaveral*, introduction by Wernher von Braun (Englewood Cliffs, N.J.: Prentice-Hall, 1962), 119.

9   Wernher von Braun, *The Mars Project* (Urbana: University of Illinois, 1953; reprint, 1991), 2.

10   For Pyle's assessment of the "little routine men" he saw fighting in France and the South Pacific, see Faludi, *Stiffed*, chap. 1, "The Son, the Moon, and the Stars: The Promise of Postwar Manhood."

11   Joan Didion, *Where I Was From* (New York: Knopf, 2003).

COLD WARRIOR'S DAUGHTER

I am the daughter of a Cold War rocket engineer. Although my father was a civilian, we lived like a military family. Each morning he donned his uniform—short-sleeved shirt, skinny necktie, plastic pocket protector—and drove off to ply his brain, which is to say, his weapon, in the all-consuming fight against Soviet Russia.

Mother and I stayed home. If a wife had a brain to ply, she did so in the house, or volunteered with, say, the Girl Scouts, a paramilitary organization that promoted cleanliness, piety, and obedience to patriarchal authority.

In 1962, I was six years old. I remember a spat between my parents about whether women should be allowed to fly in space. Astronaut John Glenn, freshly returned from his triumphant orbit, had declared this a bad idea in his testimony before the House of Representatives' space committee. "The men go off and fight the wars and fly the airplanes and come back and help design and build and test them," he said. It's just a "fact of our social order."

My mother was oddly ticked about this. She herself had a degree in chemistry but quit work to keep house for my father—an endorsement of the "social order," if ever there was one. She instructed me that being a Catholic wife and mother was the highest of callings. Yet she empathized with that woman pilot from the hearing—Jerrie Cobb, I now know her name to be—and those other women who aspired to blast off. They had trained; they could do the work. Did Glenn have any right to ground them? And besides, rumor had it that the Russians planned to launch a woman.

"Well, of course," my father countered. "The Russians are savages. They have no decency. No respect for life. They sent up a dog, remember? And they killed it—intentionally. We're better than that. We brought Sam, our monkey, back."

"Then we sent up *Miss* Sam, and brought her back." My mother smiled. "We're very fair when it comes to the animal kingdom."

My father scowled. "What if a woman died up there? What if she suffocated?"

My mother said nothing, but her look suggested that quick suffocation in space might be preferable to slow suffocation in this house.

"Can you imagine the public relations disaster?" he continued.

My mother walked over to the dining-room table, where I had spread out my homework, pencil case, and space-themed metal lunch box. The box was my favorite accessory. It depicted an orange-and-ochre planet-scape bustling with rovers, rockets, and people in space suits—a thriving extraterrestrial colony. I maintained ardently that the figure in the shapely pressure suit was a woman—not some midget guy with a cinched waist. My mother chose this moment to agree with me.

The gauntlet had been thrown down, but my father ignored it. He lifted the lunch box and examined the figure in question. Then he addressed me rather than my mother: "You could be right. This scene takes place a long time in the future. Things may be different then."

Ten years later, in 1972, things were indeed different—though not in the way the lunch box had predicted. My father was broken, as was his treasured "social order." His wife, whom he had, in fact, cherished, had been dead for two years. But from 1967 to 1970, throughout her battle with cancer, he was largely absent from her side. He was an engineer on Mariner Mars 69, a critical space mission, and in his rock-hard world of emotionless masculinity, missions always came first.

He never doubted the urgency of his work—and especially, the urgency of the Apollo program, the crown jewel in the Cold War space effort, which had landed a man on the Moon. Yet here it was, 19 December 1972, and Apollo was over. The last mission splashed down. No new one would launch.

Technically, the Cold War ended in 1989, when the Berlin Wall fell. But we had won its decisive battle twenty years earlier, when Neil Armstrong planted his pressurized boot in the lunar soil. The entire world had watched that moment. Now nobody cared about the Moon, or what we did up there—motor around in a dune buggy, whack a golf ball. The lavish party was over. My father felt confused and betrayed, as did the other legions of men who had won the space race. For the first moment in years, he had time on his hands—time he wished he could have spent comforting his dying wife.

I, too, had changed in those ten years. Grieving for my mother, angry at his absence, I hardened into a feminist. In high school, I read many books, including Betty Friedan's 1963 classic, *The Feminine Mystique*. She identified the malaise from which my educated mother had suffered, long before her fatal cancer. It was "the problem that has no name," chronic unhappiness and a lack of self-worth inherent in a system that ignored female intelligence. Worse, Friedan discovered, market researchers had confirmed the existence of this problem and, rather than solving it, used it to manipulate women into buying products. I was angry, too, at the weird polarization of the genders—the way the "social order" demanded that men think and women feel. I blamed it for squelching my father's latent tenderness, which had robbed me of parenting.

By 1972, feminists had gained visibility—Bella Abzug was elected to Congress; Friedan's book was a bestseller. And they had begun to get results. Congress passed Title IX, an amendment to the educational code, which said that an educational institution that receives money from the federal government cannot discriminate based on sex. Title IX was not just about sports, though it led to girls playing on boys' teams and athletic scholarships for women. The law precluded discrimination in admittance to classes, extracurricular activities, and benefits.

For girls my age, the world had cracked open. We scrambled to avail ourselves of opportunities, fearing they might again be taken away. In 1973, I entered Yale University, which until 1969 had been exclusively male. That September, men on campus outnumbered women two to one. But the symbolic victory was ours. We had planted a foot—indeed, a high-heeled Frye boot—in the door.

Because it affected education in science and engineering, Title IX made an impact on aerospace culture. For aerospace contractors to co-educate their workplaces, universities had to produce women engineers, which, before Title IX, many were slow to do. But there was only so much the law could accomplish. It specifically exempted "educational institutions training individuals for military services or for the merchant marine"—a reflection of the nation's long-standing aversion to women in battle.

Of course, in 1958, when NASA was chartered, its whole raison d'être was its *civilian* identity—removing space flight from the purview of the armed services. In actuality, however, NASA was more military than the military. Its astronauts were military pilots, "single-combat warriors," as Tom Wolfe called them in *The Right Stuff*. Its budgets were initially as high as the heavens it wished to penetrate. After the Apollo program, the space agency began to lose both its generous funding and its military veneer. But until the late 1990s, it divided its projects into "manned" and "unmanned" missions, rather than using the inclusive adjectives— "human" and "robotic"—that it employs today. Not until 1983 would an

American woman be permitted to fly in space (Sally Ride). And not until 1995 would a woman command a mission (Eileen Collins).

For women to achieve equality as astronauts, scientists, and engineers, space exploration must be divorced from the military. It must be truly civilian: financed by private individuals for private individuals. Doubtless, the U.S. government will continue to maintain a presence in space—if only for national security reasons. But in the same way that the airline industry opened the skies to nonmilitary pilots and passengers, so, too, will private space entrepreneurs unlock the zone beyond the Earth's atmosphere to a greater variety of explorers. In 1972, given the price tag for space missions, the idea of private funding was preposterous. The only private entity with that kind of money was the Vatican or the Mob. But in the 1990s, two things happened: the Cold War formally ended and the economic landscape shifted. The so-called tech bubble placed billions in the hands of private entrepreneurs. One of them was Anousheh Ansari—an Iranian American woman who had come to this country as a teenager, learned English, studied engineering, and founded Prodea Systems, a billion-dollar Internet company.

Although Ansari had dreamed of flying in space, she did not go the NASA route. She believed in private space flight and invested in it. In 2004, she cofinanced the Ansari X Prize, a $10 million purse for the first nongovernment organization to launch a spaceship into suborbit twice in two weeks. (Before her contribution, Peter Diamandis, the space activist who founded the prize in 1995, had been struggling to fund the purse in full so the competition could take place.) In 2006, she bought a tourist seat on a Russian flight to the International Space Station.

I did not pursue a technical career, but I remained fascinated by space flight—following space missions the way that other people followed sports. I was amazed at the stubborn persistence of dated gender roles in the technical community. In the mid-1990s, when women engineers finally broke the glass ceiling, or, in any event, pushed it higher, I traveled from my home in Manhattan to Los Angeles to write a book about the Jet Propulsion Laboratory (JPL), the organization that had once stolen my father away. I wanted to meet the women who were changing things and see whether the men had changed, too. But I discovered that to understand the 1990s, I had to look back to World War II, the crucible from which Glenn's "social order" had emerged.

Because my mother had died when I was fourteen, I never had a chance—adult to adult—to ask her about World War II or about why she had quit graduate school in chemistry to work in the personnel department at a public utility. But as part of my research, I asked her best friend, Betty Nolan, who, like my mom, had grown up in New Orleans, earned an undergraduate degree in chemistry, and wound up at New Orleans Public Service. During World War II, Betty told me, she had been recruited to work as a chemist in the New Orleans branch of a national paint manufacturer that made "retreating compound," a green waterproofing substance for tents. But when the war ended, she was laid off, with this backhanded "letter of recommendation": "We had to let Miss Nolan go because of her outstanding performance," her boss wrote. Her next job would have to have been production supervisor in a factory—"not a suitable job for a woman."

Betty's experience was not unique. In her landmark book, *Women Scientists in America: Before Affirmative Action, 1940–1972*, historian Margaret W. Rossiter describes the way in which women were dragged into scientific jobs during the war and shoved out as soon as it was over. Yet not all women left because they were forced. Many veterans had returned in pieces: shell-shocked, alcoholic, unable to recover from the horrors they had witnessed. And some women relinquished their careers to prop these sad men up. The men had, after all, won a horrible war, and they were now forced to fight another: a war of appearance, concealing their torment behind a stoic facade. Women became emblems of maternal nourishment. Dior's New Look dress dominated fashion. It was girded at the waist, accenting feminine curves. As a metaphor, the dress was particularly resonant, for it had a soft, pillowlike bust where a shattered man could rest his head.

Throughout popular culture, wives struggled to care for their broken husbands. In William Wyler's powerful movie *The Best Years of Our Lives* (1946), a wife fights to keep her husband, whose combat experiences have left him closer to his buddies than his family. In Sloan Wilson's penetrating novel *The Man in the Gray Flannel Suit* (1955), a vet finds greater solace in alcohol than in his marriage. And in J. D. Salinger's ominous short story "A Perfect Day for Bananafish" (1948), a selfish wife ignores her husband's pain, driving him to suicide.

Glenn may not have been a deep thinker—he had to scrape together correspondence credits for the college diploma that the astronaut program required. But he was a decent man. He lived by the code of chivalry implicit in the "social order." He was a protector, a rescuer. As a military man, he was comfortable within a chain of command, yet he stood up to his NASA bosses when the agency's policy hurt his family. Before his historic flight, when his wife, Annie, who had a severe stutter, was hounded by reporters, he ordered NASA to make the press back off.

Other men in the space program were not so chivalrous. They were crude and gratuitously demeaning. Wernher von Braun, the ex–Nazi SS officer who had connived to become the public face of American rocketry, fell into this category. In 1962, the same year Glenn testified before the congressional committee, von Braun was asked during a talk at the University of Mississippi whether NASA would ever fly women astronauts. Yes, he said. On a future mission, NASA planned to "reserve 110 pounds of payload for recreational equipment."

Whether they behaved like Lancelots or louts, men in technical fields often feared women—or, in any event, feared their biology. In his nonfiction book *The Life and Death of a Satellite* (1966), Alfred Bester, best known for such picaresque, male-oriented sci-fi novels as *The Stars My Destination* (1956), described how women's tiny hands could be useful in assembling the little parts that men had designed for satellites. However, he added, "Women are not permitted to work on delicate components during their menstrual periods. Engineers dare not run the risk of subjecting the components to the extra acidity of women's skin at those times of the month." Bester never questioned the inanity of this proscription. I did—in almost every interview I conducted for my JPL book. And without exception, every engineer and scientist called it embarrassing nonsense, without any basis in fact.

At JPL, physicist Marcia Neugebauer is best known as the first woman chief scientist on a robotic mission, Ranger I, which went to the Moon. But she also spearheaded a change in JPL's fear-based policy on maternity leave, which had been codified, she said, "by the Caltech medical staff, who had never seen a pregnant woman before." In the 1950s, when Neugebauer had her first child, women had to disappear *without pay* three months before their due dates and not return until three months after. Perhaps, she joked, the Caltech doctors worried that women might to go into labor or, worse, give birth in the ladies' room, while on the job. But by the 1960s, when a pregnant colleague on whose work Neugebauer relied declined to leave, Neugebauer fought for her—and the policy changed.

Fear also held back women pilots. The military worried that they would fly poorly during their periods, even though nothing of the kind had been documented. Fear may also have grounded the so-called Mercury 13, Jerrie Cobb and the other women pilots who had trained to be astronauts—not because they did poorly on tests, but because they did well. The last thing the male astronauts wanted was a crackerjack woman pilot who could withstand more physical discomfort and medical torture than they could.

The women trained in a rogue program devised by space physician William Randolph Lovelace, director of the Lovelace Foundation for Medical Education and Research in Albuquerque, New Mexico. It was largely financed by Jacqueline Cochran, a wealthy aviatrix. At a certain point, however, if women were to fly in space, they would need to train on the specialized equipment designed for the Mercury 7 astronauts. And when the guys refused to share, the women took their case to Congress—where Glenn's testimony quashed their future.

In 1998, NASA announced plans to launch an old person on a shuttle flight, to study how aging affected function in a weightless environment. Feminists thought this would be a great occasion to give Jerrie Cobb, who was then sixty-seven years old, the chance she had been denied, and they campaigned on her behalf. But despite the many transformations wrought by feminism in the thirty-six years since Glenn's testimony, the dated "social order" prevailed. At age seventy-seven, for a second time, Glenn was blasted into orbit.

Glenn may have won that dogfight, but his worldview was fast becoming antique—museum material, like the F4U Corsair he had flown in World War II. By the late 1990s, Title IX and similar legislation had opened many doors for women. Feminist ideas percolated through scientific and technical communities. Men no longer shunned what had been regarded as "women's work"; in 2010, Caltech astronomer Mike Brown, for instance, devoted much of his book on planet hunting—*How I Killed Pluto and Why It Had It Coming*—to his involvement in caring for his newborn daughter. At JPL, women project managers, lead scientists, and chief engineers became almost commonplace. To me, however, the greatest measure of progress on gender equity was what I heard from male engineers, especially those in two-career couples. They told me what I wished my dad had said: They refused to work around the clock because they wanted to see their kids. And their wives, too, had responsibilities at the lab.

Nor do science-minded girls lack for role models. The girl geek has become enshrined in popular culture—a decisive measure of social transformation. Not only does toy manufacturer Mattel make a software engineer Barbie doll (with glasses and a tiny computer), but *The Big Bang Theory*, a popular sitcom on television, features a woman neurobiologist.

To comic effect, she is every bit as nerdy and socially maladroit as her male counterparts—two physicists and an engineer.

The aerospace industry was born in Southern California, flourished during the space race, and foundered after the Cold War. It is, however, again ascendant—reinvented—thanks in part to the small, private aerospace companies headquartered there. Hawthorne-based Space Exploration Technologies (SpaceX), for example, scored a triumph in 2010 with the successful launch of its Falcon 9 rocket, designed to slash the price tag for reaching orbit—an essential first step to opening space to travelers not affiliated with the government. Although the firm was founded by Internet entrepreneur Elon Musk, Gwynne Shotwell, its president, often serves as its public face—an emblem, perhaps, of the key role women will play in the new, truly civilian space age.

In terms of symbolism, however, no achievement can trump what occurred on 29 September and 4 October 2004: *SpaceShipOne*, a passenger craft built without government money, executed two suborbital flights within two weeks to win the Ansari X Prize.

How vividly I remember that first flight. Hours before sunrise, thousands gathered at the airport in Mojave, California—a cruel, rocky oven at midday, but as mystical and otherworldly as a Chesley Bonestell planetscape in the frail dawn light. The acrid smell of jet fuel hung over the tarmac. To reach the viewing stands, onlookers had to trudge past dozens of abandoned jetliners—beached metallic whales—stored in the dry, clear desert to avoid the ravages of snow and rain. Many spectators had parked their RVs near the airport. Some had spent the night partying; the campground felt like Burning Man or Woodstock. Like kids, many had been too keyed up to sleep.

With *SpaceShipOne* lashed to the bottom of its fuselage, the mother ship, called the *White Knight*, taxied down the runway and took off. When it reached an altitude of 46,500 feet, the smaller craft detached, firing its rocket engine. No matter what happened next, history would be made.

For feminists in the crowd, of course, history had already been made. Anousheh Ansari—a *woman*—cosponsored the award, and her name blazed forth from the authorized signs and placards that blanketed the airport. Her name shimmered on baseball caps, T-shirts, and coffee mugs that vendors hawked everywhere. When space activist Peter Diamandis founded the X Prize in 1996, it had not a single woman on its board of directors. Now it owed its solvency to a woman.

True, engineer Burt Rutan designed the winning craft; Microsoft cofounder Paul G. Allen bankrolled it, and pilot Mike Melvill pulled it out of a scary, unplanned roll on its glide back to Earth. But without Ansari's money—the fruit of *her* technical accomplishments—they would have had no arena for their exploits.

After the postflight press conference, I headed back to Los Angeles, where I was now living. (The JPL book had drawn me back to the West Coast, and I had decided to stay.) My parents were not alive to witness this momentous flight, but my mother's friend, Betty Nolan, was. Betty had no children of her own. We had grown close through our many conversations while I was writing my book. And as soon as I left Mojave, where cell-phone coverage was terrible, I pulled to the side of the road and dialed her number.

Betty immediately grasped the powerful symbolism of the flight. We joked that it would have left my father deeply conflicted. He would not have loved Ansari's name everywhere. But he would have adored the triumph of private enterprise, or as one wag put it on a hand-lettered sign: "*SpaceShipOne / GovernmentZero.*"

Virgin Atlantic Airways founder Richard Branson spoke at the press conference, I told Betty. He's starting a "spaceline"—Virgin Galactic—that will sell tickets on suborbital flights within the next ten years.

She laughed and asked me whether I planned to book a seat.

"Are you kidding?" I blurted. "Tickets are $100,000 a pop."

"Never say never," she said. But on a freelance writer's budget, "never" seemed apt.

The following summer, after a sudden skirmish with bone cancer, Betty died. I felt bereft. I thought of our conversation after the X Prize flight, and of all our other conversations, and I wondered if they had been as meaningful to her as they were to me. When her will was read, I got my answer: Betty had left me the price of a Virgin Galactic seat.

SECTION II
THE WORK

What were all the workers who flocked to Southern California aerospace factories doing? Yes, they were building planes and spacecraft. But they were also doing a job: they built these things to make money. The essays in this section address what aerospace work entailed and what that meant for the workers and, by extension, for Southern California.

Sherman Mullin combines biography with corporate history in his essay on Robert E. Gross, Lockheed's chairman from 1932 to 1961. Gross differed from other early aerospace leaders in that he came from finance, not engineering. Aerospace firms are often portrayed as the domain of blue-sky engineers who pushed the technological envelope; it is easy to forget that these firms were also populated by hardheaded business leaders seeking to maximize profits and shareholder returns. And while history focuses on the success stories, not every firm managed to balance financial discipline and technological creativity. Mullin also observes an irony: financial considerations shaped Gross's strategy of diversification, which helped this major firm survive but also started a centrifugal trend that diluted the presence of aerospace in Southern California.

Anita Seth reverses the optics to provide a view of labor, though that frame includes the corporate boardroom. Like their companies' leaders, the industry's hundreds of thousands of aircraft workers were also trying to make money—in this case for themselves and their families, not just the firm. Seth's view suggests that Gross was exemplary, but not unique, in his attention to the bottom line. For Gross and other aerospace executives, increasing profits meant riding herd on production costs, including labor. Seth's comparison of labor–management relations at Lockheed and North American confirms Mullin's view that Lockheed had better union relations, and that it was seeking to anticipate and preempt labor strife (though not always successfully); North American, by contrast, took a harder labor line. Mullin's key point is relevant here: Gross wanted to keep Lockheed in commercial aviation, not defense, but failed; in World War II and the Cold War, Lockheed turned to military contracts to survive and thrive. This move had major implications for the workers in Seth's account, setting them apart from employees in other sectors: in an industry dedicated to military work, strikes were seen as a threat not only to the bottom line, but also to national security.

The tens of thousands of airplanes churned out during World War II marked the peak of mass production. Blue-collar manufacturing did not go away during the Cold War; workers still assembled aircraft in Southern California. But they never produced them in such quantities as during World War II, and missiles and spacecraft were built in even smaller batches. In the postwar period white-collar engineers assumed a larger role than blue-collar production workers. These engineers were largely nonunionized, despite occasional activism, and hence the industry returned in a way to the open shop.

Mihir Pandya sheds light on the work world of these white-collar engineers, especially its prime characteristic of secrecy. Mullin's point about commercial aviation is relevant here, too: one way in which aerospace differed from other industrial sectors was its connection to national security, which made its work subject to classification. The vast classified world, by its very nature, has often escaped scrutiny. Pandya circumvents classification barriers by taking an anthropological approach, gaining insights through personal interviews instead of through documents, which remain largely inaccessible. Anthropologists have shed light on the classified world of nuclear weapons labs; Pandya brings a similar focus to such top-secret realms as Lockheed's Skunk Works, whose origins and technological achievements Mullin's essay describes from personal experience.

Pandya highlights the effects of secrecy, not just on the workers themselves but also on their families, returning us to the human element described in the essays by Waldie and Lord. He also considers the implications for our view of the Cold War. Many Americans at the time perceived the Cold War as an existential threat to the nation. Why, then, is the Cold War not memorialized like other U.S. wars? In part, this is because the Cold War, thankfully, remained cold and did not involve combat—except in proxy conflicts, and the Korean and Vietnam Wars. But equally influential is the fact that, as Pandya points out, much of the Cold War was conducted out of sight—in nuclear weapons laboratories, reconnaissance-imaging centers, and, to a large degree, Southern California aerospace firms. This pervasive secrecy, whose reach and influence historians are just starting to decode, helps explain the curious elision of the Cold War from American public memory.

ROBERT E. GROSS AND THE RISE OF LOCKHEED:
THE CREATIVE TENSION BETWEEN ENGINEERING
AND FINANCE

Robert E. Gross was chairman of Lockheed Aircraft Corporation
from June 1932 until his death, in September 1961. This period saw
major changes in the aerospace industry, from the Great Depression through World War II to the Cold War. Gross's life and career, so
intertwined with the history of Lockheed and Southern California, sheds
much light on this history. Gross and Lockheed typified aerospace in several respects, but also differed from other firms and executives in ways
that illuminate important themes.[1]

Like his contemporaries in the upper echelons of aerospace firms,
Robert Gross was a self-confident risk taker throughout his career. But,
unlike them, he was not an engineer; Gross came from a financial background. His financial acumen helped steer Lockheed through its turbu-
lent startup years and the Great Depression. His longevity as CEO and
Lockheed's financial success on his watch stand in sharp contrast to the
records of the founders of Lockheed, Allan and Malcolm Loughead, and
also those of the initial leaders of many competing companies, including
William Boeing, Glenn Martin, John Northrop, Donald Douglas, and
several others, who in the end were either forced out of their companies
or walked away in disgust. And these are the companies that survived
the initial growth of the industry; far more numerous are the failed, for-
gotten firms from early American aviation. Many of these early firms
were started by pilots, mechanics, and engineers, whose enthusiasm for
flying and building airplanes led them into the business. Gross shared
their enthusiasm but tempered it with a keen eye for the bottom line. His
career illuminates the balance between engineering and finance in the
aerospace business, and the tensions between blue-sky engineers, who
want to push technological boundaries, and bottom-line businessmen,
who had to deliver affordable products to customers or go bankrupt. It
also illustrates the competing influences of civilian and military markets

in early aviation. As a lifelong Republican, Gross opposed a large federal role in the economy, such as that exemplified by the defense industry, and initially he resisted having Lockheed bid for military contracts and sought to concentrate on the commercial aviation market. But with the coming of World War II and then the Cold War, his patriotism and commitment to national security—aligned with considerations of the bottom line—persuaded him to accept military contracts, a decision that led to Lockheed's tremendous growth in this period.[2]

Starting Out

Robert Ellsworth Gross was a Yankee, born in West Roxbury, Massachusetts, on 11 May 1897, the first child of Robert H. and Mabel Gross. The family was financially well-off and close-knit; Robert H. Gross was the president of the New River Company, a large coal firm, and took his son with him on business trips. In June 1915 Gross was admitted to Harvard; after a brief break when he enlisted in the U.S. Army in 1918, he graduated in 1919 with a liberal arts degree. Although an average student academically, with little interest in science or mathematics, he developed a deep interest in the humanities.[3] After graduation he went to work for the Boston investment-banking firm Lee Higginson, where he advanced rapidly thanks to successful investments during the Roaring Twenties. Nearly a decade in investment banking gave him valuable financial and business experience.

By 1928 Robert Gross was a successful Boston investment banker, happily married to the former Mary Palmer, and the devoted father of their young daughter, Marion Palmer Gross. Four years later Gross was chairman and treasurer of Lockheed Aircraft in Burbank, California. These few years included a financial failure that wiped out a major portion of his net worth and the stock market crash of 1929 that plunged the nation into the Great Depression. Gross weathered these trials because of his innate optimism and a bold, risk-taking entrepreneurial streak—a characteristic he shared with many early aviation leaders—but also because of his financial connections and experience.

Gross took the first bold step even before the crash. In 1928, he resigned from Lee Higginson. The year before, Gross had paid a visit to Stearman Aircraft in Wichita, Kansas, run by self-educated engineer Lloyd Stearman, to evaluate the company's request for venture capital. This visit triggered an interest in the aviation business that would last the rest of his life. When Lee Higginson's partners declined his recommendation that they invest in Stearman, Gross invested $20,000 of his own money. The previous years had seen the start of commercial airmail contracts and passenger service; commercial airlines were springing up to transport packages and people, which gave aircraft builders a potential civilian market beyond private recreational pilots. With his younger brother Courtlandt, Gross also organized the Viking Flying Boat Company in New Haven, Connecticut, to manufacture a licensed version of a French-designed seaplane. He invested $200,000 in Viking. Slammed by the Depression, Viking faltered and Gross took a large personal financial loss. In 1931 Gross left his brother in charge of the ailing Viking company and looked for other aviation opportunities. He soon found one in Walter Varney, owner of the struggling Varney Speed Lines in San Francisco. Varney asked Gross to provide financial advice and commissioned Stearman to design a larger, faster replacement for the Lockheed Orions in Varney's fleet. In the fall of 1931 the three men organized the Stearman-Varney Corporation, aimed at building a single-engine, all-metal aircraft.

Gross meanwhile had an eye on Lockheed Aircraft in Burbank, which seemed headed for bankruptcy. Lockheed had a complicated twenty-year history.[4] In 1912 the brothers Allan and Malcolm Loughead, self-educated engineers, had started their first aviation business in San Francisco. They built a large seaplane called the Model G and sold sightseeing trips from the air around the San Francisco Bay. In 1916 they moved to Santa Barbara and started their second venture, the Loughead Aircraft Manufacturing Company. They found new financial backing and developed a very large twin-engine seaplane, the Model F-1, but their attempts to sell it to the Navy failed. They next designed a biplane, the S-1. For this project they had hired a bright, self-educated engineer named John K. Northrop, who designed a unique manufacturing method based on laminating multiple layers of wood strips in a mold, a process suited to volume production. The end of World War I, however, had flooded the market with surplus military aircraft, and S-1 sales foundered. In 1919 Malcolm left the aircraft business; his brother Allan continued solo, organizing a new Lockheed Aircraft company in December 1926 (with the new name Americanizing the spelling of their surname).

The new firm set up shop in Hollywood, and Northrop's team designed a new aircraft, called the Vega, with a unique laminated-wood fuselage and a single high-strength wing. In search of a larger manufacturing space, in 1928 Lockheed moved to an empty factory in rural Burbank. The location would benefit from the recent opening of the Grand Central Air Terminal next door in Glendale, and also from proximity to Caltech in Pasadena, which had opened an aeronautical lab in the 1920s with funding from the Daniel Guggenheim Fund, providing a prime source of engineering labor and research data from its wind tunnels.

In 1929 majority shareholder Fred Keeler sold Lockheed Aircraft to the newly formed Detroit Aircraft Corporation, a holding company. Founder Allan Lockheed, who strongly opposed the sale, walked out the door, and Detroit Aircraft selected Carl Squier, a former Army pilot and born salesman, to replace him as general manager.[5] That fall the stock market crashed, and by the spring of 1932 Detroit Aircraft had disintegrated and Lockheed Aircraft was bankrupt. By that time Lockheed planes were well known in the United States, with 197 aircraft sold from 1927 through 1931, many of them flown by famous aviators, including Charles Lindbergh, Amelia Earhart, and Jimmy Doolittle.[6] But the U.S. economic bubble had burst, and even this surge of success could not save Lockheed.

In June 1932 a small group of investors led by Robert Gross purchased Lockheed in bankruptcy court for $40,000. None of the money came from Gross. Apparently his losses on the Viking Flying Boat Company and the stock market crash of 1929 had left him in poor financial condition. Of the purchase price, $10,000 was put up by Cyril Chappellet, a recent Stanford graduate, Army Air Corps cadet, and commercial airline pilot.[7] He joined Lockheed as chief administrative officer and also served as a director. Gross became the chairman and treasurer and was compensated with stock.

The new owners acquired the lease to the small Burbank plant, a modest inventory of factory equipment and spare parts, proprietary manufacturing tools for Lockheed wood aircraft, and detailed aircraft design drawings. Two talented individuals also came with the purchase: Squier, who took over the sales department, and Harvey Christen, a motivated young mechanic and jack-of-all-trades. Christen learned about aircraft on the job, becoming the first of many manufacturing engineers and production managers who would move up from the shop floor into management.

Meanwhile, Hall Hibbard, who had a master's degree in aeronautical engineering from MIT and had worked with Gross at Stearman and Viking, joined Lockheed and soon became chief engineer. Hibbard hired a creative and self-confident engineer named Clarence L. "Kelly" Johnson, fresh from the University of Michigan with a master's degree in aeronautical engineering. Hibbard and Johnson represented a trend toward engineers who came to work with advanced degrees from new programs in aeronautical engineering. At the same time, Christen's career shows that

the aviation industry still had room for individuals whose practical engineering and manufacturing expertise derived from the shop floor, not the
classroom.[8] These individuals concentrated in manufacturing, as distinct
from design; their stories are less known because most aviation histories
have focused on design engineering, neglecting the equally important role
of manufacturing engineering and production management.

Gross helped select Lloyd Stearman as the firm's first president,
based on his aircraft design experience. Stearman, however, was a self-
trained engineer, not a manager or finance man. By late 1934 Gross
reached the painful conclusion that he had to force Stearman's resigna-
tion.[9] Never accused of lacking confidence, Gross decided he would be
president as well as chairman, a position he would hold for the next
twenty-two years. Hibbard, Johnson, Chappellet, Squier, Christen, and
Gross's younger brother Courtlandt would be with him at Lockheed for
the rest of his life. Many of them served with Gross as "inside directors"
on the company's board, most of whose seats were filled by Gross's direct
subordinates. This stability and continuity, rare in the early aircraft business, contributed to Lockheed's success. Company leadership was never
challenged by the investors or bankers who provided the large loans necessary for plant expansion, equipment, and operating capital. In this regard Gross was fortunate. Many of his contemporary aircraft-industry
CEOs often lacked skill in raising capital and could not rely on board
support. John Northrop had serious problems with his board and ultimately left the company he had founded. The Lockheed approach served
all parties well for decades before failing shareholders during a near bankruptcy in the 1970s, when an outside board was installed.

Gross focused on the civilian airline market. Chappellet recalled,
"We never thought of ourselves as growing into a large manufacturing
business. We had always thought that we might get two or three thousand in our employ, but surely that would be as far as we'd go, and our desire was in the commercial passenger carrying business."[10] In 1933 Gross
decided that single-engine wooden airplanes were obsolete for commercial airlines. Despite the Depression, the aircraft industry began expanding steadily in the 1930s, fueled by the growth of commercial air
travel and airlines. Aircraft manufacturers capitalized on academic aeronautics programs turning out engineering graduates, bigger wind tunnels refining aerodynamic knowledge, affordable aluminum alloys, and
more reliable, powerful engines.

Gross approved the production of a twin-engine, twin-tail aluminum
aircraft called the Lockheed Model 10 Electra. It carried ten passengers

Figure 1. Amelia Earhart posing with a Lockheed Model 10 Electra. Courtesy of Lockheed Martin.

and initially sold for $55,000, well below the price of a Douglas DC-2 or a Boeing 247D, the primary competition. Lockheed sold the first Model 10 in 1934; early customers included four U.S. airlines,[11] ten overseas airlines, and several private customers, including Amelia Earhart (fig. 1).[12] The Model 10 was followed by the smaller, cheaper Model 12 Electra Junior and the larger Model 14 Super Electra. Investment in these new aircraft initially resulted in a loss of $191,000 in 1934, on revenues of $563,000. However, they rapidly enabled profitable growth at Lockheed, which achieved sales revenues of $2.1 million in 1935. Gross's financial management skills and intense focus on cash flow were a major factor.[13] In this regard he differed from Allan Loughead, Donald Douglas, Glenn Martin, John Northrop, the McDonnell family, and several other contemporary aircraft-industry leaders, whose financial management skills were marginal at best and ultimately led to major problems in their companies.

Gross's investment-banking experience was critical in the 1930s. To obtain the capital to design and build new aircraft, he periodically issued new stock, arranged bank borrowings, borrowed money from his father, and arranged a $150,000 loan from the federal government's Recon-struction Finance Corporation, a Depression-era creation of the Hoover administration. As his reluctant acceptance of this last loan suggests, Gross, though a politically conservative Republican and no friend of fed-eral programs, was also pragmatic. He was also no friend of labor unions, but concluded that Lockheed would end up with a union workforce. He and Chappellet preferred the AFL over the CIO, believing that the AFL was less militant and noting that Boeing had signed a contract with them. Lockheed signed its first union contract with the AFL International As-sociation of Machinists in 1937 and thereafter enjoyed relatively stable relations with labor, providing good wages and growing fringe benefits.[14]

The War Years

In 1938 the British government turned to the United States to augment British aircraft production and ordered 200 highly modified Model 14s, which the British called Hudson bombers. As Lockheed engineer John Duffendack recalled, "for us the war started in 1938, when the British or-dered the Hudsons."[15] The $25 million Hudson contract required large amounts of financing for capital investments and working capital, which further tested Gross's financial ability. It also helped Lockheed sales jump from $10 million in 1938 to $35 million in 1939. A profit of $3 million in 1939 allowed the company to offer its first dividend to shareholders.

In his 1939 annual report to employees noting these gains, Gross lamented their source: "It is a strange and tragic fact that the airplane, which has done much to eliminate international barriers and foster peaceful commerce between nations, is now a leading factor in a war of violence and destruction. No conceivable gains can possibly justify the havoc and destruction of war." Despite the business success of the Hud-sons and the start of World War II in Europe, Gross still focused on com-mercial airliners. In 1938 he approved a new four-engine commercial aircraft known as the Constellation or, more familiarly, the "Connie." Al-though Trans World Airlines (TWA), with majority shareholder Howard Hughes, had been the lead customer for this aircraft, during World War II the Army Air Force stepped in and the Connie became the C-69 military transport.

As the story of the Connie suggests, it proved impossible to keep Lockheed out of the war. In 1936, even before the Hudson contract, Lock-heed had started designing a new twin-engine fighter for the U.S. mili-tary. Lockheed won the contract in 1937 and flew a prototype XP-38 Lightning two years later. The P-38 became Lockheed's major production program, and by the end of the war almost 10,000 P-38 Lightnings had come off the Burbank line.[16]

Despite the initial plans to keep Lockheed small, World War II turned Lockheed and several other aircraft firms into giant companies. From sales of $10 million in 1938, Lockheed revenues grew to almost $700 million in 1943. Lockheed produced over 19,000 aircraft from 1939 to 1945, with production peaking at 5,864 airplanes in 1944 alone.[17] The Lockheed line turned out P-38 Lightning fighters, Hudson bombers, Lodestar transports, PV-1 Ventura patrol bombers, and PV-2 Harpoon patrol bombers; Lockheed also built 2,750 B-17 bombers designed by Boeing. To build all these planes Lockheed hired and trained employees at a breakneck rate. Starting from 7,000 employees at the end of 1939, by May 1941—well before the United States entered the war—Lockheed was up to 28,000 employees, with 18,000 working the day shift and 10,000 on the night shift. By early 1944 employment reached 94,000. Lockheed hired as many as 2,500 employees per month, mostly recent high-school graduates, and many of them women.

Training these employees entailed a vast array of evening classes at local high schools; UCLA, USC, and other colleges set up technical training programs. At any one time several thousand trainees were enrolled in classes on blueprint reading, welding, machining, tool-and-die making, electrical assembly, and so on, all to enable inexperienced employees to fabricate parts and assemble them into complete airplanes. This also required the manufacturing engineering organization to produce clear, simple documents and a wide array of special tools, from simple sheet-metal drilling templates to large, precise assembly jigs, and to develop supervisors capable of on-the-job training of new hires.

The World War II expansion occurred in a rapidly changing Los Angeles metropolitan area. The population of Southern California had grown rapidly in the 1930s, thanks in part to Dust Bowl refugees, many of whom found jobs in aviation. The wartime defense industry provided a magnet for additional migration, and Lockheed's hiring spree helped Burbank's population explode between 1940 and 1950. Lockheed also established feeder plants at several locations in the region, including Bakersfield, Fresno, Pomona, Taft, Santa Barbara, and downtown Los Angeles, and a separate new organization was set up to plan, schedule, and control this outside production, which ran around the clock, seven days a week.[18]

In 1943 Gross established another separate organization with long-term impact on Lockheed, U.S. national security, and aerospace technology. This was a small group formed to develop, in deep secrecy, the XP-80 jet fighter for the Army Air Force. Gross gave Kelly Johnson total authority over all aspects of the project: staffing, design, manufacturing, purchasing, and testing. This authority and tight secrecy allowed Johnson's group to institute simplified design, procurement, and manufacturing procedures, avoiding the detailed procedures needed for mass production by relatively low-skilled employees. Johnson's group, known jokingly as the Skunk Works, designed and built the XP-80 in 143 days, but the war ended before production models entered combat.[19]

The Hot War Ends, The Cold War Begins

When the war ended Lockheed employment fell drastically, from the wartime peak of 94,000 to 14,500 by the end of 1947. Southern California's aircraft industry entered a tailspin, with several hundred thousand employees laid off and several of Robert Gross's executive colleagues forced out of their jobs. Within two years, however, the emerging Cold War began changing the aircraft business climate. In March 1947 President Harry Truman announced what became known as the Truman Doctrine, which established the containment of Communism as a basic tenet of U.S. foreign policy and military strategy. In July 1947 Truman appointed an Air Policy Commission, known as the Finletter Commission after chairman Thomas Finletter, which urged military aircraft procurement to sustain the industry as a national resource. Finally, in September 1947 the U.S. Air Force became a separate military service within the newly established Department of Defense. As a result military aircraft procurement became increasingly centralized, with more direct congressional involvement and Defense oversight. Under Robert Gross, not always happily, Lockheed adjusted to this new environment, for example by creating a permanent Lockheed office in Washington to provide closer connections with government officials and military officers.[20]

During the war, Lockheed had indeed developed a formidable engineering organization in both advanced design and detailed production design. The Constellation entered commercial airline service immediately after World War II, finally satisfying Gross's goals. The military, however, also provided a major market, with the Air Force using it as the C-121 transport. The Navy also purchased a fleet of Constellations. Out of the 856 Constellations built from 1943 to 1959, 58 percent went to commercial aviation and 42 percent to the military. The P-80 (later redesignated as the F-80) also continued in production until 1951 and was the basis for two derivative aircraft, the T-33 jet trainer and the F-94 Starfire jet interceptor. The T-33 became Lockheed's most successful program of the 1950s, with 5,691 planes built. The F-94 was a two-seat, all-weather interceptor designed by the Skunk Works.[21]

Not all Lockheed ideas succeeded. The Model 89 Constitution was a huge four-engine double-deck transport developed under a Navy contract during World War II. It was a big, beautiful airplane, but it was designed to use four 5,500 horsepower engines, which never materialized. Lockheed delivered two underpowered aircraft to the Navy in 1949, but they operated for only three years. The Model 75 Saturn, an initiative Gross strongly supported, was developed as a twin-engine feeder airliner that could carry fourteen passengers. Intended to be a relatively low-cost airplane, its selling price turned out to be $100,000. It could not compete with the glut of World War II surplus aircraft, and the Saturn program was terminated in 1948 with a loss of $6 million. Two other programs, the Model 33 and Model 34, known as the Little Dipper and Big Dipper, similarly failed in the low-cost, light aircraft market amid the surfeit of surplus planes.

Robert Gross continued to focus on sales to commercial airlines by developing improved versions of the Constellation, competing with newer versions of the Douglas DC-7. The first deliveries of Super Constellations to airlines started in 1951, but military aircraft sales continued to exceed commercial aircraft sales by a large margin. By this time Gross had become strongly committed to supporting U.S. Cold War initiatives and had accepted the fact that the company could not be successful with only commercial aircraft business.

Politically and philosophically Robert Gross was a Republican. Despite the fact that much New Deal legislation benefited Lockheed directly, he was privately opposed to government activism during the Roosevelt years and afterward. His political philosophy, however, mattered little when it came to war and foreign policy. Gross devoted his considerable energy from 1938 to 1945 to winning World War II. In the Cold War, although not a supporter of President Harry Truman, Gross strongly supported the Truman Doctrine and containment of Communism. He backed Dwight Eisenhower in the elections of 1952 and 1956. After John F. Kennedy defeated Richard Nixon in the 1960 presidential election, however, Gross again revealed a pragmatic, nonideological bent: "Although I am a Republican and likely to remain one, I have been quite impressed with President Kennedy personally since he took office. I feel that most of the problems he has are ones he inherited from the Republican administration."[22]

As it turned out, 1947 was Lockheed's lowest postwar year, with employment down to 14,550, just 361 aircraft delivered, and a net loss of $2.5 million on revenues of $135 million.[23] By 1949 Lockheed was growing again. Employment increased to 16,700 and deliveries to 500 aircraft, and net income was $5.5 million on sales of $118 million. The Korean War greatly accelerated this growth. When the war started abruptly in June 1950, the Soviet MiG-15 fighter began outperforming the F-80, and the F-86 jet fighter from North American Aviation replaced it as the Air Force's first-line fighter. With Gross's concurrence, Kelly Johnson submitted a proposal to the Air Force in late 1952 to develop a Mach 2 fighter.[24] This led promptly to a contract for the F-104 Starfighter, which provided consistent sales for the next twenty years.[25]

In January 1951 Gross accepted an Air Force contract for Lockheed to re-open a government-owned plant in Marietta, Georgia, and refurbish moth-balled Boeing B-29 bombers.[26] Lockheed Georgia soon became the second-source manufacturer of Boeing B-47 jet bombers. This initiative used existing designs and manufacturing facilities, required minimum capital, and returned a good profit. Gross initiated this geographical expansion and, after air transport problems in the Korean War, decided in 1954 that a new Lockheed plane designed in Burbank, the C-130 transport, would also be manufactured in Georgia. This far-reaching decision marked the start of a centrifugal trend for Lockheed, shifting operations out of Southern California into other regions. Lockheed Georgia expanded into a full-capability aircraft company, including a formidable design organization, resulting in a major duplication of Lockheed's California capabilities. The Georgia plant, however, focused on large military transport aircraft, for example winning a major contract in 1962 for the jet-powered C-141 Starlifter.

Gross also sought business opportunities in international markets. Under Gross, Lockheed initiated, with U.S. government approval and support, the licensed production of Lockheed military aircraft in several countries. The selected programs generated significant profits, based on a large initial licensing fee and then a royalty payment for each aircraft produced. In 1954 Japan initiated, with U.S. government approval, a T-33 jet trainer program. The initial aircraft were built by Lockheed, followed by licensed production by Kawasaki Aircraft in Japan. Similarly, in 1959 West Germany issued a contract to Lockheed for sixty-six F-104 Starfighters and also negotiated licensed production rights. In 1960, the Netherlands, Belgium, and Italy joined the program under the NATO political umbrella, and later users included Norway, Denmark, Greece,

Turkey, Japan, Jordan, Spain, Taiwan, and Pakistan. Eventually over 2,500 F-104s were produced between 1954 and 1980, 741 by Lockheed and the rest under license with royalty payments to Lockheed. For decades Lockheed dominated the international market for maritime patrol and anti-submarine warfare aircraft, first with the P-2 Neptune and then the P-3 Orion. Other U.S. companies pursued international business but did not match Lockheed's activity.[27]

By 1954 Lockheed was the third-largest U.S. aircraft firm in terms of revenue, with its $733 million in sales trailing only Boeing and Douglas. It had 46,000 employees, three times as many as in 1947, and ranked thirty-fourth on the Fortune 500 list of largest American companies.[28] By 1956 revenues increased to $742.6 million and employment to 62,000. Other aircraft firms did not adapt to the postwar context so well. In 1951 Glenn Martin, with his company facing bankruptcy, was forced out as CEO. Northrop, too, fell on hard times, and in 1952 its president and founder John Northrop resigned over frustration with the Northrop board. Bell Aircraft was financially failing when its founder Lawrence Bell died in 1956, and Douglas weathered a series of down cycles before its Wall Street backers forced a merger with McDonnell in the 1970s.

These tales of corporate downturn demonstrate that, although the Cold War provided boom times for many aerospace firms, survival and success still required financial acumen. In choosing his successors, Gross ensured that finance, not engineering, would lead Lockheed. In 1956 he promoted Daniel Haughton and A. Carl Kotchian to senior positions; both were financial and marketing managers, not engineers, with strong commitments to planning, scheduling, budgeting, and cost accounting.[29]

Despite the rapid growth in military contracts from the Cold War and Korean War, Gross strove to stay in the commercial aircraft business. The airline industry was growing in the 1950s, with increasing leisure travel now expanding from domestic to international destinations. Gross struggled to decide what would succeed the Constellation for this market. In the early 1950s Boeing and Douglas committed to build four-engine jet airliners, the 707 and DC-8. In 1955 Gross announced instead that Lockheed would develop a four-engine turboprop called the Electra, in part thanks to interest in turboprops from American Airlines. The Electra entered service in 1958. In the next two years three Electras experienced catastrophic accidents in service, two of them from structural failures of the outer wing traced to the propulsion system, in what became called the "Electra whirl mode problem." Correcting it required major structural modifications, and Gross committed Lockheed to retrofit all

Electras at Lockheed's expense, absorbing the cost of $25 million. The Electra contributed to Lockheed taking a loss of $43 million in 1960, on revenues of $1.33 billion.

Despite his continuing efforts to develop commercial aircraft, Gross's leadership in the 1950s was dominated by the Cold War. Three major trends in military business in the 1950s aided Lockheed's success. The first centered on the Skunk Works, which developed remarkable new capabilities for U.S. intelligence agencies. The second was the rise of electronics and increasing emphasis on integrating avionics systems, which provided a new source of contracts and also brought new engineering disciplines to the forefront at Lockheed. The third was the space race, which marked the transition from the aircraft industry to aerospace.

The Skunk Works: Robert Gross and the "Black" World, 1954–1961

One of President Eisenhower's major initiatives after 1953 was to expand the intelligence-gathering capability of the CIA, using unique aircraft and, later, pioneering satellites. This was to have a major impact on Lockheed and its Skunk Works. From 1954 to 1961 Gross oversaw three covert (or "black") CIA programs of national importance. The first was the U-2 high-altitude "spy" aircraft. Lockheed involvement resulted primarily from the freewheeling initiative of Kelly Johnson, with Gross's support. Johnson's technical creativity won Lockheed a quick CIA contract in December 1954 to design, produce, and support a small fleet of U-2 aircraft.[30] The U-2 aimed to obtain high-resolution photographs over Soviet territory while flying at very high altitudes to minimize detection. This required an extremely unusual lightweight, low-drag aircraft, with jet engines capable of performing in low oxygen levels at extreme altitude.

The U-2 program permanently changed the Skunk Works. Previously a fluid organization, the Skunk Works evolved to provide the design, flight-testing, production, and logistical support of a small fleet of aircraft not disclosed within Lockheed or publicly. It also had its own business-management capability, including pricing, contracting, and financial performance management. This decision, dictated by the blackest of black security, was made at Gross's home on 21 November 1954, with only Gross, Johnson, and Hall Hibbard present. Thus Gross became the first of a series of Skunk Works "protectors" at the top of Lockheed. Starting in late 1954 Lockheed had, in effect, three full-capability aircraft companies, each with a distinct organizational culture. For security reasons, and because of Kelly Johnson's unique operating methods, the Skunk Works had virtually no interaction with the rest of Lockheed after the 1954 U-2 decision.[31] Lockheed Georgia developed its own culture, with a lot of Southern influence and a specialized leading capability in very large military transport aircraft. The branch with the broadest capability was the original home ranch in Burbank, which produced commercial aircraft, fighters, and maritime patrol aircraft. All three developed the belief that their way was the right way.

U-2 flights by the CIA commenced in 1956 with direct Skunk Works support at several international locations. Over the next four years, while personally overseen by Dwight Eisenhower, the program produced unprecedented intelligence.[32] U-2 operations over the Soviet Union came to a sensational end on 1 May 1960, when a Soviet missile shot down a U-2 piloted by Francis Gary Powers, but the U-2 would continue in service for decades.

Meanwhile, in April 1958 and with Gross's approval, Johnson quietly initiated the design of a high-altitude Mach 3 reconnaissance aircraft. He opened a new Lockheed engineering notebook and started the design of what he called the U-3. On page 1 he sketched out the requirements: a plane capable of flying at over 2,000 mph at altitudes up to 90,000 feet, beyond the reach of any known threat. The preliminary design evolved through twelve iterations, A-1 to A-12, and in August 1959 Lockheed beat out General Dynamics for a CIA contract. Lockheed built the A-12 in complete secrecy and overcame extremely demanding technical obstacles. The A-12 first flew in 1962 and soon became the first aircraft in history to fly at Mach 3, about 2,100 mph. It led rapidly to the Air Force's SR-71 "Blackbird" aircraft fleet, which operated high above the Earth until the end of the Cold War. The Blackbird remains the fastest aircraft ever built, hitting 2,193 mph.[33]

Rise of the Coneheads

Over the long term, the most important contribution of the commercially disappointing Electra was that it led to the P-3 Orion maritime patrol aircraft, one of Lockheed's most successful programs. In 1958 Lockheed won a Navy competition for an aircraft to replace the Lockheed P-2 Neptune. The design derived from the Electra, except for its shortened fuselage and advanced antisubmarine-warfare electronics. Subsequent modifications over the years incorporated ever-more-sophisticated digital avionics, including software. These avionics systems marked the impact of the digital electronic computer on the aircraft industry. Avionics systems required engineering expertise not in aerodynamics, propulsion, structures, or other familiar disciplines in the industry, but rather in electronics and computer-systems engineering. Traditional engineers mocked these new electronics and computer-systems engineers as "coneheads," but the coneheads had the last laugh on the tin-benders. Airframes began shrinking as a fraction of the total cost of the aircraft, and by the end of the century more than half an airplane's cost and much of its value came from avionics and software.

Lockheed and the Space Race

Lockheed's third covert-intelligence project came at a new Lockheed facility. In October 1957 the Soviet Union launched *Sputnik 1*, the world's first satellite, into orbit. The so-called space race had begun, and Lockheed would be a major participant in the U.S. space-and-missile effort for the remainder of the Cold War.

In 1954 Gross established a missile-systems division, which evolved into the Lockheed Missiles and Space Company (LMSC). The missile work evolved from early postwar projects under engineer Willis Hawkins. In 1947 Hawkins, at Gross's urging, had responded to an Air Force request for a pilotless vehicle for testing ramjet engines. The resulting X-7 program ran until 1960 and provided Lockheed's engineers experience not only with ramjets and solid rockets, but also structures and materials, supersonic aerodynamics, instrumentation, and telemetry. By 1954 a small number of key people and some of the basic technology needed for the new Lockheed division were in place.[34]

Designing and producing missiles and satellites required very different capabilities than making aircraft. With a few notable exceptions, the engineers and managers of the new division were new to Lockheed, engineers and scientists from many disciplines either recruited from other organizations or, at the junior level, newly graduated. The LMSC division's culture differed substantially from those of the established aircraft divisions. In 1954 aircraft design, manufacturing, and logistics support technologies were mature, while system design, manufacturing, and system-test technologies for missile and space systems were embryonic.

The missiles and space group initially worked from a Lockheed plant in Van Nuys, but there was soon a debate over where to locate the division permanently. Because a very large site was needed, Southern California was considered too costly. After some consideration of Asheville, North Carolina, Lockheed decided to locate the main plant in Sunnyvale, California, adjacent to the Navy's Moffett Field, and to locate its new research and development laboratories in the hills of Palo Alto, next to Stanford University. In 1955 Lockheed purchased 275 acres of farm-land in Sunnyvale and additional land in Palo Alto for the research and development facility.[35] Together with the Georgia plant for air transports, missiles and space continued the centrifugal trend spinning Lockheed units away from Southern California.

Two major programs secured Lockheed's new missiles and space business. The first was the Polaris missile. In 1955 the Navy had decided to develop a sea-based intermediate-range ballistic missile (IRBM) and chose Lockheed to build it, based on Lockheed's successful experimen-tal solid-rocket-propelled research vehicle projects. The Navy originally planned to use a derivative of the Army's Jupiter rocket, which was pro-pelled by liquid fuel and liquid oxygen, pumped into the missile just before launch. The Jupiter design was deemed unacceptable, to put it mildly, for a missile to be launched from a submarine. Polaris would re-quire propulsion by solid fuels. Over the next two years Lockheed, the Navy, and the other contractors integrated a wide range of new tech-nologies into the Polaris missile system: a unique two-stage solid-rocket engine, and a missile guidance system that used thrust vectoring, con-trolled by a lightweight digital computer. A new class of nuclear-powered submarines would carry Polaris missiles and launch them while sub-merged.[36]

From the beginning the Polaris program had very tight deadlines, and after *Sputnik 1*, Polaris was given higher national priority and the schedule was further compressed. This was in the golden days of defense-systems acquisition when concurrent design and manufacture was a virtue, not a sin. The program proceeded very rapidly, and on 15 No-vember 1960 the USS *George Washington*, with sixteen Lockheed Polaris missiles in its launch tubes, deployed in the Atlantic. Gross's decision to form the new division in 1954 had contributed enormously to Lockheed and to U.S. deterrent capabilities in the Cold War.

The second major project was a space system that built on Lock-heed's connections with U.S. intelligence agencies. In January 1958 Pres-ident Eisenhower initiated what became the Corona reconnaissance satellite program. Based on a pioneering design by a team led by James Plummer, Lockheed was selected as prime contractor, responsible to both the CIA and the Air Force. Corona was as "black" as black gets. The very small Lockheed team under Plummer in the space systems group in Sunnyvale, working under extremely tight security rules, designed and built the new satellites and performed system integration for this complex project. The first stage was a Thor liquid rocket booster, built by Douglas Aircraft. The second stage, which put the unique satellite in orbit, was the new Lockheed Agena spacecraft. After the satellite had orbited over the Soviet Union and taken photographs, a satellite recovery vehicle, built by General Electric, returned the satellite to a precise point over the Pacific Ocean, where a specially equipped aircraft snagged it by its parachute.[37]

This was not a low-risk program. Thirteen launches failed in 1959 and 1960, until Discoverer 14, as the program was called in public, launched in August 1960, returned to Earth after seventeen orbits and was successfully recovered. The developed film yielded a stunning amount of vital intelligence. A total of 145 Corona satellites were launched through May 1972. It was the most important United States strategic-intelligence system of the era but remained hidden in deep secrecy until 1995. Gross approved the large capital investments in plant and equipment to make the Sunnyvale plant a unique, world-class facility.

Polaris and Corona helped launch Lockheed's missiles and space technology business. In 1957 Lockheed sales revenue was $879 million. Missiles and space contributed only $73 million, about 8 percent. By 1961 Lockheed corporate sales were $1.45 billion, with missiles and space contributing $735 million, or 51 percent. Within four years, missiles and space had become the majority of Lockheed's business. This began the transformation of Lockheed from a Southern California aircraft company to an aerospace company, and many of Lockheed's future leaders would come from the missiles and space business instead of aircraft. Lockheed was not alone in this transition: Boeing, Douglas, Martin, North American, and Northrop all entered the missiles and space business, with some firms, like Hughes and Martin, abandoning airframes altogether. Lockheed's entry into space systems focused on military space; it did not have a significant role in NASA's manned space-flight programs, and instead its main customers were the Navy, Air Force, and CIA.

The success of the expansion into missiles and space, together with ups and downs in the aircraft business, encouraged Gross to continue looking beyond aircraft for business. Gross never lost the deep entrepreneurial urge that led him to leap into the aircraft business in 1928. In his last years as Lockheed CEO, he gave high priority to diversification through acquisitions, resulting in three new Lockheed divisions specializing in electronics, shipbuilding, and solid-rocket engines. Together with missiles and space, diversification diluted Lockheed's identification with airplanes, and eventually, in 1977, Lockheed Aircraft Corporation dropped the "Aircraft" and became Lockheed Corporation. It also continued the centrifugal trend, further diminishing its identification with Southern California.

Conclusion

Robert Gross died of pancreatic cancer on 1 September 1961, at the age of sixty-four. Successive CEOs, starting with his brother Courtlandt, continued the tradition of having a financial manager, not an engineer, at the helm. Robert Gross preached, "Look ahead where the horizons are absolutely unlimited," a philosophy enshrined in countless Lockheed documents for decades. To many engineers this had a technical meaning: higher, faster, better than any competitor. To Gross and his successors it also had an entrepreneurial meaning, fundamental to Lockheed business strategy for decades: success had to include financial profit and customer satisfaction. Not until 1989, when Dan Tellep became CEO, did an engineer run Lockheed.[38] Tellep, who admired Robert Gross, did not change the Lockheed culture created and nurtured by Gross and his successors.

In 1990 Tellep decided to close the sprawling, aged Burbank plant. Lockheed moved the Skunk Works to its Palmdale plant, originally built to produce L-1011 airliners, and in 1994 sold off the historic 300-acre Burbank site. Much of the revenue from the property sale was spent on extensive environmental remediation. In 1995 Lockheed merged with Martin Marietta Corporation, forming the Lockheed Martin Corporation, with Tellep as the first chairman and CEO.[39] The corporate headquarters moved from Calabasas, California, to the former Martin headquarters in Bethesda, Maryland.

The Lockheed that Robert Gross and his associates rescued from bankruptcy in 1932 survived, but its Southern California footprint has dwindled. The strategy of technological, product, and geographic diversification Gross implemented in the 1950s differed significantly from his competitors and had a lasting impact on Lockheed and the region. One unplanned result was the incremental departure of Lockheed from Southern California, completed in 1995. The only exception was the Skunk Works, which continued to flourish by serving the black world from Burbank, where its F-117 Stealth fighter (fig. 2) was the last aircraft built, and then in Palmdale.[40]

The initial investment and subsequent expansion of Lockheed Missiles and Space Company in Sunnyvale saved Lockheed from bankruptcy in the 1970s, when its profits and cash flow helped offset the red ink hemorrhaging from the firm's commercial aircraft business. Another unplanned benefit of the rapid growth of the missiles and space business

Figure 2. Lockheed's F-117 Stealth fighter. Courtesy of Lockheed Martin.

was the extensive recruitment of new talent in engineering and finance. The last three CEOs of Lockheed, from 1977 to the 1995 merger with Martin, joined the corporation at the LMSC plant in Sunnyvale in the 1950s: Roy Anderson, Larry Kitchen, and Dan Tellep. Similarly, Gross's decision in 1954 to manufacture the C-130 in Georgia instead of Burbank paid off in the long run. The Georgia division survived major financial problems with the giant C-5A Galaxy military transport in the 1970s and continues to produce the C-130, still in wide use around the world as a military transport. Geographical diversification allowed Lockheed, despite its declining Southern California presence, to increase annual sales to $9.3 billion by the time of the merger with Martin Marietta in 1995.

As chief executive officer for twenty-nine years, Robert Gross helped transform Lockheed from a small, nearly defunct airplane builder to one of the largest businesses in the United States. He did this with unique entrepreneurial skills and financial experience, combined with a commitment to honesty and good personal relationships. He was respected by customers, attracted and nurtured a large, diverse group of engineers and managers, and created substantial wealth for shareholders.

Gross's legacy was not flawless. Several planes failed commercially, and none of his 1950s acquisitions in shipbuilding, rocket propulsion, and electronics proved sustainable. He tolerated risk and occasional failure as the price of success. Years later his younger brother Courtlandt wrote that

Gross "gave birth to about 50 ideas a week, of which 49 were about as effective as a foul tip into the opposing team's dugout, but the 50th was a screaming home run from Harvard Square, Cambridge, Massachusetts to Turkey Crossing, Burbank, California. That is the way things were and no one I have ever talked to can figure out how Robert got that 50th hit."

Gross also never achieved his objective of leading a corporation with commercial aircraft as its primary business. Boeing's early push in commercial airliners gave it a lead it never surrendered. Like Convair and Douglas, Lockheed eventually left the field after decades of competition and deep financial problems. Lockheed's last gasp was the L-1011 Tristar, initiated in 1968 by Gross protégés Dan Haughton and Carl Kotchian. The Tristar was a technical success but a financial disaster, with losses exceeding $1 billion, and Lockheed finally canceled it in 1981.

Cyril Chappellet, his longtime friend and colleague, recalled Gross's commitment to commercial aircraft: "Bob had boundless enthusiasm for the future of aviation. He felt there was nothing that could stop it from continuing to grow almost forever, and that carrying people was the end of the business you ought to be in. So we never went after military business at all until World War II, and never had any ambitions to do so. We were always interested in passenger carrying airplanes." Instead, to Gross's regret, his life and career were enormously influenced by war: World War II and the Cold War, including the Korean conflict and the space race following Sputnik.[41] But he was also a tireless supporter of national security, and he led Lockheed's large, sustained contributions to the defense of the United States and its allies. Despite his failure to achieve his civilian aircraft objectives, Gross succeeded in making Lockheed one of the major aerospace companies in the world.

This essay is the work of an amateur historian, longtime student of World War II and the Cold War, and retired Lockheed executive. I was with Lockheed from 1959 to 1994. I never met Robert or Courtlandt Gross. I appreciate support from the following: Peter Westwick provided valuable critical comments and sustained encouragement; William Deverell initiated my involvement in the creation of the Huntington Library's aerospace archive and stimulated my thinking on Lockheed history; Ellen Bendell and Dianne Knippel cheerfully provided relevant information; and R. Richard Heppe, Lockheedian from 1947 to 1988, provided important information. The Pusey Library at Harvard University graciously provided a copy of their records on Robert Gross, and the Library of Congress Manuscript Division provided access to the Gross papers and a helpful work environment. I also benefited from a number of oral histories with senior Lockheed figures, conducted by William Perrault of Lockheed in the 1980s. My wife, Judia B. Mullin, provided more support than she ever realized. Except for informal assistance by a few individuals this work was not supported or reviewed by the Lockheed Martin Corporation, which does not maintain a corporate historical archive.

NOTES

1   Walter J. Boyne, *Beyond the Horizons: The Lockheed Story* (New York: St. Martin's Press, 1998).

2   Robert E. Gross Papers, Library of Congress Manuscript Division.

3   Robert E. Gross Records, Pusey Library, Harvard University.

4   Boyne, *Beyond the Horizons*, 1–51.

5   Ibid., 37–39.

6   Rene J. Francillon, *Lockheed Aircraft since 1913* (London: Putnam and Co., 1982).

7   Cyril Chappellet, interview by William D. Perreault, 12 February 1982, Lockheed Oral History Project, Sherman N. Mullin Collection, Huntington Library.

8   Harvey Christen, interview by William D. Perreault, 4 February 1982, Lockheed Oral History Project.

9   Gross Papers, Library of Congress.

10 Chappellet interview.

11 Francillon, *Lockheed Aircraft*, 118.

12 Clarence L. "Kelly" Johnson with Maggie Smith, *Kelly: More than My Share of It All* (Washington, D.C.: Smithsonian Institution Press, 1985), 42–46.

13 Boyne, *Beyond the Horizons*, 72.

14 Chappellet interview.

15 John "Jack" C. Duffendack, interview by Bill Deverell, Sherman Mullin, and Peter Westwick, 12 June 2008, Aerospace History Project, Huntington Library.

16 Francillon, *Lockheed Aircraft*, 50–51.

17 Ibid.

18 William R. Wilson, interview by William D. Perrault, 1 April 1982, Lockheed Oral History Project.

19 Jay Miller, *Lockheed's Skunk Works: The First Fifty Years* (Arlington, Texas: Aerofax, 1993).

20 Vernon A. Johnson, interview by William D. Perrault, 7 May 1982, Lockheed Oral History Project.

21 Francillon, *Lockheed Aircraft*, 51–52, 286–300.

22 Gross Papers, Library of Congress.

23 Francillon, *Lockheed Aircraft*, 48.

24 Miller, *Lockheed's Skunk Works*, 63–69.

25 Francillon, *Lockheed Aircraft*, 323–45.

26 Boyne, *Beyond the Horizons*, 227–28.

27 Francillon, *Lockheed Aircraft*, 258–76, 291, 327, 405–13.

28   Donald M. Pattillo, *Pushing the Envelope: The American Aircraft Industry* (Ann Arbor: University of Michigan Press, 1998).

29   Boyne, *Beyond the Horizons*, 225–28, 254–55.

30   Miller, *Lockheed's Skunk Works*, 75.

31   Johnson, *Kelly*; Miller, *Lockheed's Skunk Works*, 75.

32   Chris Pocock, *The U-2 Spyplane: Toward the Unknown, A New History of the Early Years* (Atglen, Pa.: Schiffer Publishing, 2000).

33   Miller, *Lockheed's Skunk Works*, 112–33, 142–51.

34   Willis M. Hawkins, interview by William D. Perrault, 1 February 1981, Lockheed Oral History Project.

35   Boyne, *Beyond the Horizons*, 274.

36   Ibid., 276–84.

37   Ibid., 295–305.

38   Ibid., 449–50.

39   Ibid., 453, 464–70.

40   Miller, *Lockheed's Skunk Works*, 186–87.

41   Gross Papers, Library of Congress. See also Boyne, *Beyond the Horizons*, x–xi.

Los Angeles Aircraft Workers and the Consolidation of Cold War Politics

O n 5 June 1941, thousands of workers walked off their jobs at the North American Aviation plant in Inglewood, California, in the largest strike mobilization that Southern California had ever seen. Four days later, amid denunciations of the strike as a Communist conspiracy to sabotage defense production, the Roosevelt administration sent 2,500 troops to break the picket lines. While the radical credentials of the United Auto Workers (UAW) organizers and leaders at the North American factory were indisputable, the goals of the strike—to increase the minimum wage at the aircraft factory and more generally improve workers' pay and benefits—were in line with the basic demands of unions everywhere. What set this strike apart was that it stopped defense production in a region and industry with little tradition of labor militancy at a time of growing international tension. The negative public portrayals of the strike and its disavowal by national UAW officials equated militant action with Communist subversion and ignored demands for improvement of poor working conditions. The characterization of the strike as a political act of sabotage cleared the way for the use of state violence. The rhetoric surrounding the strike, the cooperation between high-level union officials and Democratic leaders, and the Roosevelt administration's shift to intervening against labor in a high-profile dispute, clearly foreshadowed the obstacles Southern California aircraft workers would face in the postwar period.

This essay examines Los Angeles–area aircraft workers and their unions during that time, from the years immediately following World War II through the Korean War. These workers were doubly disadvantaged, first by a hostile political climate that undermined the labor movement as a whole, and second by structures of production and bargaining peculiar to the aircraft industry that posed additional barriers to exercising labor rights. A great deal has been written on the first point.[1] In the

late 1940s, anti-Communism and growing corporate power marginal-
ized voices of dissent against a national security state and circumscribed
union power by declaring illegitimate both militant union action and
unions' embrace of public-policy issues that went beyond collective
bargaining on wages and benefits.[2] But these trends were exacerbated
among Los Angeles–area aircraft industry unions by long-standing political hostility to working-class movements in Southern California and
the particularities of aircraft manufacturing. Sharp fluctuations in production due to the disparity between wartime military orders and peacetime commercial demand, along with the failure of diversification efforts,
made organizing at aircraft manufacturers more difficult than other comparable industries. State intervention, both directly during aircraft strikes
and indirectly through wage controls, impeded workers' ability to press
their case in wartime, when they had the strongest bargaining position.
While scholars have examined national anti-Communist and anti-labor
sentiment, the influences specific to the Southern California air business
have received much less attention. This study aims to explore the distinctive obstacles to organizing in this industry during the Cold War.

I focus on International Association of Machinists (IAM) Lodge 727
at Lockheed Aircraft and United Auto Workers (UAW) Local 887 at North
American Aviation to illustrate these difficulties.[3] I have chosen these two
companies because of their size and importance to the industry and because their management styles and attitudes toward unions were at opposite ends of the spectrum at the outset of the period under discussion.[4]
Lockheed was the only airframe manufacturer in Southern California to
voluntarily extend union recognition, and its management was more open
to dialogue with the union than were their counterparts at other companies. Believing unionization to be inevitable, and fearing the industrial
unionism of the UAW, Lockheed management opened the door to the
IAM in 1937.[5] North American Aviation was at the other end of the spectrum. President James H. Kindelberger's attitudes toward unions closely
followed those of his mentor Donald Douglas, who defeated numerous attempts to organize his factories through the late 1930s and early 1940s.
North American management bitterly fought the establishment of the
union in the prewar period and continued its intransigence in bargaining
and other negotiations into the 1950s.

The two unions involved also had contrasting political and organizing
traditions. The IAM was a conservative craft union, and Lodge 727 was
held up by labor experts in the 1940s as an exemplar of reasonable, peaceful collective bargaining.[6] The UAW's aircraft organizing, on the other

hand, reflected the union's origins in the wave of industrial unionism that swept the Midwest in the 1930s. UAW leaders and organizers in Southern California were more aggressive in their rhetoric than their counterparts in the IAM and established an early reputation for militancy with a series of high-profile strikes. The Communist Party membership of early local leaders also sparked controversy. But in spite of the stark differences between these two cases before World War II, bargaining in both companies came to follow remarkably similar lines by the early 1950s. Lodge 727 belied its initial characterization as a company union, and came to struggle with management over wages, benefits, and decision making no less than its UAW counterparts; meanwhile the anti-union climate in Southern California and the fallout from ongoing factional splits within the UAW hampered the North American local's ability to maintain its militancy and social vision.

The discussion below is divided into three parts. In the first, I explore the fallout from the 1941 North American strike and the ways that it was used in anti-Communist attacks against both aircraft workers and those in other industries in the postwar period. In the second, I examine the ways in which anti-Communist attacks helped narrow the agendas of Lodge 727 and Local 887 in other ways, including their positions on foreign policy and racial justice. The last section looks at the effects of the peculiar dynamics of the aircraft industry on these unions' attempts to build power.

The 1941 North American Aviation Strike

The UAW and the IAM both began organizing Southern California aircraft workers in the late 1930s. Low-skilled workers in the industry were very poorly paid, with wages on a par with those of southern textile workers.[7] Union organizers had to contend with the notoriously anti-union political climate in Southern California. The same civic boosters who courted early aircraft pioneers had fought to establish and maintain a region-wide open shop. The ongoing influx of migrants to Southern California provided a large and renewable source of cheap labor. Initial organizing attempts were often rebuffed or delayed by anti-union employers until they had run out of momentum.[8] Furthermore, the UAW in particular faced the challenge of unfortunate timing, launching its major mobilizations to establish aircraft industry unions just as the Roosevelt administration's push for increased aircraft production sharply decreased its tolerance for militant union action.

The UAW began representing workers at North American after striking to win a one-year contract in 1937. Efforts to renew the contract stalled through a combination of management intransigence and a fight over jurisdiction between the two major union federations, the American Federation of Labor (AFL) and the Congress of Industrial Organizations (CIO).[9] The UAW finally re-entered negotiations with North American Aviation in April 1941, after a narrow election victory over the IAM. Buoyed by a recent organizing success and wage gains at Vultee Aircraft, UAW organizers sought to overturn the prevailing wage structure in Southern California aircraft work by demanding "75 and 10": a 50 percent increase in the minimum wage at the plant, bringing it to 75 cents, and an across-the-board hourly increase of 10 cents. Additional demands included paid holidays and vacation time, sick leave, union security provisions, and a nondiscrimination clause.[10] John Jouett, president of the Aeronautical Chamber of Commerce, denounced these "extravagant demands on one of the most vitally important airplane manufacturing plants in the nation." He warned that defense production would suffer even in the absence of an actual strike because of the "unrest and excitement occasioned by the threat of a strike."[11] After over four weeks of deadlocked negotiations, a strike vote put before six thousand workers at North American garnered almost unanimous support. The dispute was then referred to the National Defense Mediation Board, and union and company representatives traveled to Washington, D.C., for talks.

Impatient with delays and the company's intransigence and worried that their position would grow weaker as a flood of new workers was hired at the plant, the Local 683 negotiating committee, both those who had gone to the capitol and those in California, decided to go forward with the strike.[12] On 5 June, thousands of workers walked out and picket lines halted the assembly of B-25 bombers, Mustang fighters, and AT-6 trainers. Local labor organizations sent support for the strike even as national UAW and CIO leaders, under pressure from the Roosevelt administration, distanced themselves and urged strikers back to work. Richard Frankensteen, national director of the CIO's aircraft industry organizing campaign, gave a radio address on 7 June in which he declared the strike unsanctioned, denounced "vicious underhand maneuvering of the Communist party" in its instigation, and called for its immediate end.[13] On 9 June, Roosevelt signed an executive order turning the plant over to the War Department, and 2,500 troops with bayonets dispersed picket lines to restart production. Roosevelt's public statement accompanying the order justified his actions on national security grounds: "Continuous production in the Los Angeles plant of North American Aviation, Inc., is essential to national defense. It is engaged in the production of airplanes vital to our defense and much of the property in the plant is owned, directly or indirectly, by the United States."[14] Belying the characterization of the strike as the work of a few malcontents or a political project of a Communist minority, a military force had to remain at the plant for more than two weeks to compel workers to resume and maintain production. The Army also maintained patrols in southwest Los Angeles neighborhoods, where the majority of North American workers lived.[15]

Even before the strike began, Local 683 had been dogged by anti-Communist attacks. At the end of May, while union leaders were in Washington for mediation talks, the House Un-American Activities Committee, chaired by Martin Dies Jr., held hearings on radical influence at North American Aviation, and particularly into the alleged Communist Party membership of the Local 683 president, Elmer Freitag. The Communist Party membership of UAW Southern California aircraft industry organizer Wyndham Mortimer and regional director Lew Michener had become a source of controversy in a strike at Vultee in November 1940, and those charges were recycled in the North American conflict.[16] The Dies committee heard testimony from anti-Communist UAW members at West Coast automobile plants claiming that Communists and leaders of the German American Bund were collaborating within the UAW and could jointly wreck the U.S. defense effort.[17] Even after the War Department took over North American on 9 June, Dies urged continued vigilance and warned that "the same agents of Stalin, Hitler and Mussolini, if permitted to continue their work in the factory, will blow up North American Aviation and other plants which are key defense units."[18]

Attacks on alleged subversives in the union ranks came from within the labor movement as well. The IAM had made the Communist affiliation of UAW leaders and organizers a major theme of its campaign to take over representation of workers at North American. Their leaflets contrasted the IAM's "100 percent American" organizers with UAW representatives who would put North American workers at the mercy of "foreign dictators."[19] The day after the strike began, the AFL-affiliated secretary of the Los Angeles Central Labor Council declared that "strikes in key defense industries such as aviation manufacturing should be avoided wherever possible," charged that the strike had been called for political purposes, and threatened to send AFL-affiliated workers to cross picket lines and restart production at North American.[20] After the strike was broken, the Lodge 727 newspaper at Lockheed claimed that several

strike leaders had been expelled from the AFL as Communists, and reported on the military crackdown with approval. The paper denounced
strike leaders as "a radical and irresponsible minority" who "were afraid
that negotiations might get something for workers and the chance for a
strike would be lost."[21]

As part of its justification for intervening in the strike, the Roosevelt
administration reiterated the charges of Communist subversion.[22] Office of Production Management associate director and longtime labor
leader Sidney Hillman denounced the strike leaders as "a small band of
irresponsibles" and "subversives." Attorney general Robert H. Jackson declared that "the distinction between loyal labor leaders and those who
are following the Communist party line is easy to observe. Loyal labor
leaders fight for a settlement of labor grievances. Disloyal men who have
wormed their way into the labor movement do not want settlements;
they want strikes. That is the Communist party line." The administration
also issued an order to reconsider the draft deferments of strikers at
North American and elsewhere who "have ceased to perform jobs for
which they were deferred and who are by such failure impeding the national defense program."[23]

After the strike, the UAW fired Wyndham Mortimer and three other
organizers, suspended eight Local 683 officers, and reorganized the local.
Several dozen strikers were placed under military arrest and questioned
at a nearby Army base, and North American ultimately fired a number
of rank-and-file strike leaders.[24] Although the strike was broken with
overwhelming force and its leaders punished, a contract settlement in
July granted the union's primary demands, including a graduated starting wage that began at 60 cents but increased to 75 cents by the end of
three months on the job.

The strike had immediate national ramifications, as it made clear
the limits of the Roosevelt administration's support for labor and thereby
helped cement the commitment of labor leaders to a no-strike pledge for
the duration of the war. In the postwar period, the North American strike
appeared again and again in speeches by business leaders and anti-
Communist politicians, along with those at the Allis-Chalmers Manufacturing Company in Wisconsin, as illustrations of the potential threat
posed by Communist sabotage to U.S. defenses. These strikes were also
invoked to justify support for loyalty oaths and continued attacks on
labor and other progressive organizations. The U. S. Chamber of Commerce, in its 1947 pamphlet *Communists within the Labor Movement*,
cited the North American and Allis-Chalmers 1941 strikes as "purely

political strikes" that "were inspired by the then current Soviet policy of preventing aid to Hitler's enemies."[25] The Senate Committee on Un-American Activities in California reiterated allegations against North American strike leaders in 1949, warning that "the people of California and the United States should never forget that the defense efforts of our great Nation would have been ruthlessly sabotaged by what purported to be an American labor movement—had it not been for the need of a foreign dictatorship thousands of miles away."[26] This accusation echoed a common anti-Communist charge that the strike was the beginning of a Soviet-directed plan to sabotage American war industries that ended only because of the Nazi attack on the Soviet Union.

On a local level, the outcome of the strike and the national union leadership's denunciation and expulsion of strike leaders provided a clear warning to Southern California aircraft workers about the potential risks of militant action. Thousands of workers had faced down local police and eventually the military only to have their national leadership denounce their efforts. It was a decade before the next significant strike in a Los Angeles aircraft factory.[27]

It also provided local right-wing forces a basis for questioning the legitimacy of union struggles for better wages and benefits across a range of industries, by tarring them with charges of Communist subversion. Anti-Communism was well established in Southern California long before the Cold War, most visibly through the Los Angeles Police Department's "Red Squad," which targeted left-wing and labor activity in the 1920s and 1930s. If much of the form and content of anti-Communist attacks was in place well before the Cold War era, however, the consensus around them grew significantly in the late 1940s. Los Angeles was a center of anti-Communist activity, in part because of the high-profile investigations into Hollywood, and Los Angeles County was the first in the United States to require loyalty oaths of its employees, a requirement that was extended by the California legislature in the 1950 Levering Act to cover all public employees as well as those at nonprofit institutions.

Unions could occasionally marshal Cold War rhetoric to attack employers, as in a December 1946 letter from IAM president Harvey W. Brown to President Truman that asked the federal government to regulate prices and curb inflation. Brown appealed to Truman to "break through the iron curtain behind which business is strangling and bleeding the consumers." Lockheed's refusal in 1949 to allow a union shop election on its property provoked the Lodge 727 newspaper to compare its position to the "fascism of Hitler against which grows the totalitarian despotism of Joe Stalin."[28] However, far more common was the use of such rhetoric to attack progressive positions that had been rather mainstream just a year or two before. A typical September 1946 editorial in the Lockheed union paper warned that "the mob uprisings in Greece and elsewhere are examples of what we may expect in the United States if the ranks of Labor are going to permit themselves to be used in the mass demonstrations that the Communist fringe want to call on the slightest provocation."[29] Anti-union forces easily translated such sentiments into denunciation of labor militancy more generally. An April 1948 *Los Angeles Times* editorial separating responsible, acceptable unionists from radicals who purportedly sought strife for its own sake provides a typical example. Differentiating the "legitimate aims of unionism," to secure good wages and working conditions, from the Communist aim of disruption, the editorial argued that "Communist leaders would rather lose a strike than win one; the strike, not its results, is their objective. Hence they call as many as possible."[30]

The rewriting of the 1941 North American strike from a legitimate expression of workers' rights to a Communist-inspired plot to disrupt American defense robbed aircraft workers of what could have been an important achievement. The dominant narrative, adopted within the labor movement as well as outside it, ignored the impressive gains made through the strike, which effectively raised the wage floor throughout the industry in Southern California just at the moment that it was becoming a significant part of the economy. A moment that could have served as the West Coast equivalent of the 1937 Flint sit-down strikes, inspiring a wave of organization and mobilization, instead became a point of shame and division.[31]

The outcome of this strike also points to an inherent political obstacle facing aircraft workers in pressing their claims through direct action. Their strongest moments for bargaining, when their work was most needed, almost always coincided with times of national emergency, when it was all too easy to portray the interests of workers as antithetical to the needs of national security. It is not surprising that the strikes that sparked the most vociferous anti-union attacks and warnings of Communist attempts to take over the American labor movement were at defense factories. As a federal arbitration panel found in its 1952 award to North American workers: "these employees have been incapable, practically, of exerting their bargaining strength when the industry was prosperous, because at such times they have been restricted by law as well as by moral deterrents."[32] This position was echoed by Lodge 727 president John Snider, who noted in October 1953 that since 1940 his union had either "a hot war or a depressed economic condition in the industry to prevent us from securing economic justice."[33]

Anti-Communism and Postwar Union Politics

Nelson Lichtenstein and Jennifer Klein have written about the shift in labor politics, particularly in the CIO, from broad societal demands to a focus on employer-based bargaining.[34] For Southern California aircraft industry unions, this trend is evident in their abandonment of demands for full employment to focus more narrowly on advocacy to maintain jobs at their own companies, using national security rhetoric. In the final years of the war, both AFL- and CIO-affiliated unions pushed for guaranteed full employment, with shorter workweeks compensated by higher pay to avoid a postwar decrease in the standard of living. Lockheed union members advocated a thirty-hour workweek with a $1 minimum wage in late 1944 and, in mid-1945, circulated a petition demanding that wages hold steady after the decrease to a forty-hour workweek from the wartime standard of forty-eight hours.[35] An October 1945 CIO rally for full employment at Los Angeles City Hall drew over 5,000 workers.[36] However, aircraft unions quickly shifted to a narrower focus on ensuring the profitability of their own companies, a strategy that included pushing for continued military production. As early as October 1945, the IAM Aircraft Committee called for guaranteed ongoing military orders for the fifteen major airframe companies with an aim of "creating an air force to assist in maintaining peace."[37] The IAM also joined aircraft company heads in 1947 in testifying before the Congressional Aviation Policy Board, where they called for larger and more predictable government expenditures on aircraft.[38] While the CIO initially maintained a more critical position toward Cold War policies, including a November 1946 condemnation of U.S. stockpiling of atomic bombs and the associated arms race, consensus shifted by the end of 1948 to supporting U.S. foreign policy.[39] By 1950, workers at UAW automobile factories in Wisconsin and New Jersey were subject to union sanction and even physical attack for opposing the war in Korea and advocating disarmament.[40]

Aircraft industry unions had affirmative and negative reasons to embrace a militarized foreign policy. On the one hand, their inability to obtain job security or other provisions to blunt the boom-and-bust cycle of aircraft production militated in favor of a strategy of joining their employers to encourage continued military production. On the other, anti-Communist attacks quickly placed dissent from the foreign policies of the Truman administration outside the boundaries of acceptable political expression and called into question the legitimacy of labor organizations addressing foreign policy at all. This sentiment was expressed clearly in a September 1946 article in the Lodge 727 newspaper: "While we realize that we live in a complex society and are affected by what is done at the Paris Peace Conference or the disposition that is made of the Trieste matter we have often wondered if the basic reasons for our organizing, wages, hours and working conditions have not been neglected while Labor has pursued willow-the-wisps [sic] in the political and other fields."[41]

Another clear example of these unions' contracting vision comes from the fight for racial equality. The Los Angeles County CIO was significantly involved in the formation of the Negro Victory Committee in April 1941 to protest discrimination in the defense industries and in public transportation. African Americans seeking employment in the war industries at the time faced multiple barriers, from racism within management and unions, to the ineffectiveness of federal mechanisms to enforce nondiscrimination laws, to prohibitions against training in particular skill areas. In one of its most public and successful actions, the Negro Victory Committee organized a mass march on the United States Employment Service in July 1942, where hundreds of African American women demanded referrals to defense training classes.[42]

As a part of the CIO, and drawing on the UAW's activism around civil rights, Local 887 fought alongside black workers facing racist North American policies during the war. In March 1941, North American president James H. Kindelberger helped galvanize protests by civil rights organizations when he announced that North American Aviation would only hire black workers "as janitors and in other similar capacities" but "under no circumstances" would hire them as production workers, regardless of their training.[43] Kindelberger's rhetoric might have been unusually blunt, but it reflected the reality that there were only four black production workers in the Southern California aircraft industry at the time.[44] Although he backed away from that position following Roosevelt's Executive Order 8802 barring discrimination in defense industries, North American maintained discriminatory policies, including keeping black workers in segregated departments and barring them from high-skilled work. Local 887 filed a number of individual grievances challenging these practices; for example, they demanded and won the reinstatement with full back pay of janitor Horace Dickey, who was fired in March 1942 after he spoke with a white female employee.[45]

Although the IAM maintained racist practices and policies, Lodge 727 defied the national leadership to play an important role in the desegregation of the Lockheed plant during the war. Their position was supported by the Lockheed management, which took an unusually proactive stance toward desegregating its workforce following Executive Order 8802. In an August 1941 letter to employees, vice president Cyril Chappellet announced that "special effort will be made to comply with the request of the President," and called on managers to "lend their full interest" to the training and hiring of African American workers.[46]

Shortly thereafter, Lodge 727 began signing up black workers for membership in the union, disregarding a "whites only" restriction in the IAM initiation ritual. A committee including both black and white workers, which came to be known as the "Yea Vote Committee," continued throughout the war to push for a change in IAM national policies and to advocate for full membership for black workers on a local level. In January 1943, the lodge initiated a petition asking for a national referendum on the membership restriction in the IAM constitution.[47] This initiative quickly foundered, overshadowed in national IAM politics by debates about disaffiliation from the AFL. In August 1943, Herbert C. Ward, the chairman of the Yea Vote Committee, filed a complaint over the discriminatory language with the Fair Employment Practice Committee. Although the FEPC ultimately failed to act on the complaint, the work of the committee and its community allies pushed Lodge 727 to continue admitting black workers as members, although they were not able to obtain full voting rights. By the fall of 1944, the number of black members in Lodge 727 had grown to four hundred, up from less than two hundred the year before. This growth is more significant when set against the contraction of the working population at Lockheed, which cut the number of black workers by two-thirds.[48] While Lodge 727's support for the rights of black workers was inconsistent and incomplete, it stood in stark contrast to the policies of other local AFL craft unions like the International Brotherhood of Boilermakers.[49]

By 1946, Lodge 727 had backed away from its commitment to equal rights. The lodge failed to intervene when several white members of the "Yea Vote Committee" were fired as Communists before the end of 1945.[50] In at least one case, Lockheed received government back-up for these actions: in August 1944, the War Manpower Commission upheld the firing of a Lockheed worker because "the weight of the evidence indicates that the employer was justified in questioning the worker's loyalty to the American form of Government."[51] Resolutions introduced within Lodge 727 condemning Ku Klux Klan attacks in the summer of 1946 were amended to include a condemnation of Communist activities as well.[52]

While Lodge 727 initially gathered signatures for a ballot initiative to set up a state Fair Employment Practices Commission, by the time of the election in November 1946 it had backed away from its support for the issue. It took no official position on the ballot initiative (Proposition 11), and its newspaper, *American Aeronaut*, reflected the strong opposition to the measure of the national IAM, arguing that "the measure from its inception has been the stepchild of the extreme left portion of society and the board Proposition 11 could create, could not be more absolute and dictatorial if it came out of the Kremlin itself."[53]

Coming out of the war, black employment in the aircraft industry fell precipitously and the fight for racial equality was increasingly seen as synonymous with Communist leanings or at least sympathies. This became a self-fulfilling prophecy: as struggles for racial equality became more controversial, the Communist Party and other affiliated organizations were the only ones willing to take on racist hiring practices, police brutality, or Klan violence.[54] This, in turn, made many labor and community organizations more wary of joining these fights for fear of appearing to be influenced by Communists. The result was a less inclusive labor movement and less racially diverse workforce than might have been achievable in the Southern California aircraft industry.

If anti-Communism had remained the purview of the right wing alone, it would not have had such a profound effect on the labor movement. But, either because they sought to fend off right-wing attacks or because they were looking for expedient ways to silence critics, labor leaders also engaged in anti-Communist politics. Conservative factions within the UAW and the CIO made deft use of anti-Communism to discredit their opponents. In the last years of the war, Lodge 727 officers were under pressure from members of the union who were angry about their frozen wages and impatient with the wartime no-strike pledge. The Lodge 727 leadership received cooperation from Lockheed management to remove some of these critics within the union. As a contemporary study puts it: "The company helped purge the 'left-wing' and sustained moderates. It fired about a dozen leading 'left-wingers.' Union officers refused to process their grievances. When discharged workers took cases to court, Lockheed made an out-of-court financial settlement."[55] Many Communists certainly did much to harm their cause, from nurturing a culture of secrecy and factionalism, to embracing wartime policies that undermined labor power in the service of an all-out production ideology, to flip-flopping in response to changes in Soviet policy. But anti-Communist attacks also resulted in the loss of many talented and visionary organizers and leaders from the labor movement in the 1940s, a loss that affects labor to this day.[56]

Impediments to Postwar Aircraft Industry Organizing

The situation for workers in Los Angeles coming out of World War II was complicated. On the one hand, workers and their unions were more powerful than they had been before the war. A demographic cross-section had found greater economic rights through geographic mobility and labor shortages in the exploding war industries. Government support for organizing ended the open shop that had prevailed in Southern California for decades. A New Deal culture that stressed popular power, combined with the relative prosperity and purposefulness of wartime life, raised workers' expectations. Wages in California had, on average, doubled since 1939, and the growth was even greater in the manufacturing sector.[57] On the other hand, labor also faced increasingly confident business leaders who were intransigent in their protection of profits, less interested in compromises around social welfare, and eager to re-establish management prerogatives that had been worn away by government mediation of labor disputes during the war.[58] Even before the end of the war, business groups in Los Angeles began to attack what they saw as the alarming power of labor, for example by proposing in 1944 an amendment to the California constitution that would have mandated an open shop.[59]

Adding to workers' anxieties were concerns about the capacity of the economy to absorb returning veterans and fear that the withdrawal of government war contracts would spark a renewed depression. April 1945 estimates by the California State Reconstruction and Reemployment Commission found that, in order to accommodate wartime migrants and returning veterans, full employment in the postwar period would require 1 to 1.5 million more jobs than had existed in 1940.[60] A July 1945 statement by the California CIO Council warned that "the days of the early 30's would look like prosperity, compared to what is liable to happen." To avoid this, "the market that has been created in California by some 19 billion dollars worth of Federal contracts must be replaced by increased domestic consumption of both civilian goods and services, and supplemented to a much greater extent than ever before by foreign trade."[61]

Los Angeles aircraft workers found themselves in a weaker position than their counterparts in other industries. Their recently established unions had relied unusually heavily on government support and intervention to reach agreements with reluctant employers and had little history of operating outside of the highly regulated wartime context.[62] More importantly, they faced a postwar collapse in their industry. By the end of 1943, airframe manufacturers had begun anticipating a postwar downturn in production and exploring diversification. However, these plans were in little more than experimental form by the end of the war, and production fell sharply in 1945. With production cuts came mass layoffs, and reductions in work hours and overtime meant a decline in real income in the postwar period, even for those workers who retained their jobs.[63] Aircraft industry employment in Southern California fell by 50 percent in the second half of 1945, and in some cases thousands of workers were laid off within days.[64]

On 20 August 1945, North American president James Kindelberger sent a "Notice to Employees," informing them that the Army had canceled three-quarters of planned production at the Inglewood plant and that North American would therefore be cutting staff by 50 percent in the coming days.[65] By January 1946, employment had dropped to 5,000. Many of those remaining were high-level employees, including those returning from North American's shuttered factories in Kansas City and Dallas.[66] At Lockheed, the Army Air Force and Navy canceled over half of their outstanding orders, more than $1 billion worth, in 1945. Although Lockheed came into the postwar period in a stronger position than its competitors, primarily because of large outstanding orders for its Constellation passenger aircraft, this advantage was soon erased by a combination of high-profile mechanical problems and a weaker-than-anticipated market for commercial air travel. The company's layoffs were therefore more gradual, but ultimately no smaller in magnitude, as employment shrunk from a wartime high of 94,000 to 17,000 at the end of 1946.[67]

Lockheed workers, by mobilizing in the last year of the war, achieved in November 1945 the last significant increase in aircraft workers' standards until the Korean War. Their wage gains were also made possible by Lockheed's anomalous position of expecting steady commercial production. Workers voted down a proposed contract in the summer of 1944 and petitioned the National Labor Relations Board for a strike vote in April 1945, complaining of wages that were considerably lower than those of workers at outside subcontractors doing the same work. Over 20,000 Lockheed workers voted to strike in May in spite of language on the strike ballot, mandated by the 1943 Smith-Connally Act, reading, "DO YOU WISH TO PERMIT AN INTERRUPTION OF WAR PRODUCTION IN WAR TIME AS A RESULT OF THIS DISPUTE?"[68] The company and the union finally obtained approval to negotiate outside the Southern California Aircraft Industry

Committee wage standards and reached agreement on a 15 percent wage increase in November 1945, which was subsequently adopted by other Los Angeles–area airframe manufacturers. The UAW, following the national postwar CIO position, demanded a 30 percent wage increase at all of its aircraft plants, but was unable to improve upon the 15 percent won at Lockheed.[69] This period also saw a struggle at Lockheed over the ultimately unsuccessful attempt by foremen to join the IAM. In spite of its reputation for enlightened coexistence with its unions, Lockheed management ran a campaign for over a year to discourage supervisory employees from joining the union, culminating in a personal appeal by president Robert Gross on the eve of the October 1946 vote.[70]

Southern California aircraft unions almost entirely sat out the postwar strike wave that swept other industries, although workers at both Lockheed and North American took strike votes repeatedly during contract negotiations from 1945 to 1949. The postwar contraction of the industry, combined with generous government tax refunds to offset companies' losses, created an unfavorable context for pressing workers' case for higher wages and benefits.

Steep inflation in 1946 and 1947 quickly wiped out the postwar Lockheed-initiated raise, and aircraft workers were unable to achieve wage and benefits improvements on a par with those in other industries over the next several years. The end of wartime rent controls led to increases in housing costs of up to 400 percent in the Los Angeles area in 1946.[71] By September 1947, food prices had reached an all-time high.[72] Yet, in spite of strong strike votes in May and June of 1947, Lockheed and North American workers both settled for 5-cent raises in 1947, a year in which wage increases in the manufacturing sector averaged 11 cents.[73] Lockheed workers took another 5-cent increase in 1948, putting their compensation below the prevailing wages in the Southern California aircraft industry for the first time, while North American workers received 10 cents. By contrast, the General Motors contract of the same year not only granted an 11-cent across-the-board increase, but also pioneered a cost-of-living adjustment and an additional 2 percent "annual improvement factor" increase. The arbitration panel appointed by Harry Truman to settle a 1952 wage dispute at North American found that aircraft workers' postwar wages had consistently lagged behind those in the automobile industry, with the gap steadily increasing from 6.6 cents in 1946 to almost 22 cents in June 1952.[74]

By 1949, both Lockheed and North American had large backlogs of military orders, as advocates of air power had prevailed in debates about

U.S. national security. But neither the IAM nor the UAW was able to make gains commensurate with the change in their companies' financial position. After protracted negotiations and a strike vote, Lockheed workers obtained an average raise of 10 cents, bringing them back up to the industry standard, as well as improved contract language on seniority privileges and union security. In August 1949, North American workers took a strike vote in support of contract demands that included flat wage rates with automatic increases, a 10 percent cost-of-living adjustment, and the establishment of pensions. Of these demands, their only significant victory was on the automatic wage progression.[75]

The long-standing bitter competition between the UAW and the IAM also hampered aircraft workers' push for better conditions during this period. Inter-union raiding at Convair and Ryan consumed considerable resources from both unions between 1946 and 1948 and provided these companies with an excuse not to bargain or follow the wage increases that were prevalent in the rest of the industry.[76] Contemporary observers made much of the effect of the rivalry between the UAW and IAM, which they supposed created pressure on union leadership to make contract improvements. But the unions' inability to work together on an industry-wide strategy against aircraft employers, who were cooperating among themselves to limit worker gains, clearly undermined both unions' bargaining positions. In early 1950, the two unions signed a no-raiding agreement and began coordinating their negotiations, but full cooperation did not begin until the mid-1950s.

In general, the UAW won greater increases in wages and benefits from 1946 to 1950 at North American than the IAM did at Lockheed, reversing the pattern that had existed for almost a decade. This likely resulted from spillover into the aircraft industry from the union's national gains in its automobile contracts. For example, the 1950 North American contract borrowed provisions for cost-of-living wage increases and a modified union shop directly from the recently settled General Motors contract.[77] The contract also granted significant wage increases and improved healthcare benefits.[78]

The outbreak of the Korean War consolidated political support for ongoing high levels of defense spending and for expanded aircraft production, resulting in a boom for Southern California aircraft manufacturers. The number of employees in the aircraft and parts industries in the Los Angeles area increased from around 65,000 in 1949 to over 150,000 in 1952.[79] Southern California aircraft workers took unprecedented action in an attempt to secure wage and benefits demands that had been building over the postwar years. The period between 1951 and 1953 saw major strikes at Douglas (twice), Lockheed, and North American.

But even in a time of high production, the gains of these strikes were limited and the costs to the unions and workers high. Government-imposed wartime wage controls, aimed at fighting inflation, added additional hurdles to unions' fight for higher pay. In addition, the federal government, as the primary customer for aircraft, was not the impartial mediator in aircraft labor disputes that it might have been in other industries. Even the more union-friendly administrations had an interest in containing labor costs at aircraft manufacturers because of the impact of wages on the price of military aircraft.[80] This factor was particularly important in Southern California, where unions were unusually dependent on government regulation to offset local political hostility. In addition, aircraft workers and their unions faced particular difficulties in striking an industry with a guaranteed government market. Unlike in industries producing for a commercial or consumer market, where production stoppages resulted in sales losses and potentially in market share, government demand for defense production was quite inelastic. Defense contractors were unlikely to lose contracts because of a strike and were often able to pass along any additional costs incurred during a strike to military purchasers.

These structural factors played a role in both the Lockheed strike in September 1952 and the North American strike in October through December of 1953. In both cases, contract negotiations began with the companies offering small or no wage increases, in spite of the defense boom. The unions, in contrast, sought both significant increases in wages and qualitative improvements in benefits and union security and representation provisions.[81] Both Lockheed and North American made improved contract offers on the eve of strike deadlines, but still fell far short of union demands. Neither Lodge 727 nor Local 887, in spite of strong strike participation, was able to win further concessions from the companies by striking. In fact, both strikes were widely considered to have resulted in management victories. In both cases, the contracts signed were similar to management's last pre-strike offer, and in both cases, the unions had to agree to weakened union security provisions. In both cases, management was able to rely on the sympathy of the local press and courts. The Los Angeles Superior Court produced injunctions that limited the effectiveness of union pickets, while the Los Angeles Times, in particular, wrote stories that uncritically quoted management positions and covered extensively the alleged lawlessness of picketers. The cost of the unions' failure to fully cooperate with one another is also evident in both strikes. In 1952, the UAW agreed to arbitration, leaving Lockheed workers to strike on their own. Lockheed management's final offer matched the wage increases granted in the North American arbitration agreement and repeatedly referenced that as a fair benchmark. In 1953, the IAM continued to negotiate with Lockheed throughout the Local 887 strike.

In the 1952 round of negotiations, the IAM sought a 10.5 percent wage increase with cost-of-living adjustments, a union shop, and improvements in vacation and health benefits. The company countered with a 2-cent wage increase and did not move from this position until the night before the strike. Although they participated in talks facilitated by the Federal Mediation and Conciliation Service, neither the company nor the union was willing to submit the contract to arbitration. On 10 August, at the Hollywood American Legion Stadium, 99 percent of the 7,000 workers present voted to strike.[82] On 8 September, 25,000 workers walked out on strike, paralyzing production of twelve aircraft models. On 10 September, in response to a Lockheed complaint alleging violence and illegal harassment against employees crossing the picket line, a Los Angeles Superior Court restraining order against picketers forced them to move across the street from the factory entrance.[83] The following week, Lockheed workers were joined on strike by 15,000 workers at the Douglas El Segundo plant. On 27 September, President Truman called for an end to the strike in the interest of national defense, and the IAM agreed to a recess for both strikes. In November, Lodge 727 members approved a contract with 9-cent raises with annual 1-cent cost-of-living increases, full healthcare coverage, and increases in wage minimums. However, the company was able to re-insert an escape clause into the maintenance-of-membership language, which allowed workers a set period of time during which to leave the union (and stop paying their dues) during the contract.

At North American, negotiations over wages in the spring of 1952 broke down, as the UAW asked for an increase of 24 cents in order to bring aircraft workers up to the pay level of autoworkers. This long-standing UAW demand gathered additional strength from the resumption of subcontracting of aircraft work to automobile factories during the Korean War. A strike was averted in late June only after a last-minute appeal from a federal mediator based on the fact that North American plants were responsible for half of jet fighter production for the Korean front, and the company and union agreed to submit to arbitration.[84] The arbitration decision, issued in September in the middle of the Lockheed strike, was very favorable to the union, resulting in a 22-cent wage increase, and although it did not endorse the union's claim that aircraft workers' pay should equal that of automobile workers, it did find that automobile workers' wages should be taken into account as a relevant factor in setting aircraft workers' wages. The contrast between the UAW's significant gains through the federal arbitration panel and the terms that the IAM was able to garner through direct action again underlines the unique difficulties facing Southern California aircraft workers in pressing for gains through rank-and-file militancy.

The UAW continued to push the comparison with automobile workers in its 1953 negotiations at North American. The union's opening demands included a 23.4-cent wage increase, cost-of-living and annual productivity increases, an elimination of the lowest-paid job classifications, improved health benefits, increases in paid time off, and the establishment of severance pay and pensions. The company's starting offer, in contrast, included no wage increases, weakened union security provisions, and decreased disability and pregnancy benefits. Union leaders were also frustrated by management's disrespectful attitude toward the union and its hard-line approach to negotiations and handling grievances. In early October, a strike vote by workers at the Inglewood factory passed overwhelmingly, with 95 percent in favor. Separate votes were held in the North American factory in Columbus, Ohio, and its smaller modification facility in Fresno.[85]

As in the Lockheed strike the previous year, a superior court restraining order went into effect within the first week of the strike, requiring picketers to remain twenty feet apart, in single file. In response, strikers formed "The World's Longest Picket Line." The union initiated a daily fifteen-minute radio broadcast with strike updates and produced a half-hour television documentary in the middle of the strike.[86] The company, for its part, ran an aggressive back-to-work campaign, publicizing wage losses for each striker, the numbers returning to work, and numbers of aircraft assembled and delivered in full-page newspaper advertisements throughout the strike. The *Los Angeles Times* echoed these themes in its news stories about the strike. The fact that support for the strike was strongest among the skilled workers meant that production was disproportionately affected even when thousands of lower-skilled workers began returning to work after the first few weeks.[87] Nevertheless, by the beginning of December, the union's position was clearly deteriorating, and they resorted to (unsuccessful) calls for government intervention to settle the contract. As at Lockheed the year before, the union had to settle for a package that the company had offered on the eve of the strike. Also as at Lockheed, the union was unable to stop the company's assault on union security provisions. The modified union shop was replaced with a maintenance-of-membership policy, which meant that workers had to remain members only for the duration of the contract. Wage increases were 4 percent, less than half what the union had asked, and benefits increased only marginally.

Two important factors placed North American workers at an additional disadvantage relative to strikers at Lockheed the year before. First was the new Republican administration, which was even less sympathetic to labor claims. Second, the end of the Korean War decreased the urgent need for aircraft production, and therefore the potential for government pressure on North American management to meet union demands to end the strike. However, when viewed in the slightly longer term, the tenacity of Local 887 workers in the fifty-four-day strike did pay off in the 1954 contract negotiations, when North American management took an unprecedentedly cooperative attitude and agreed to the first company-paid pension plan in the industry.[88]

Aircraft and the Creation of Postwar Los Angeles

Los Angeles aircraft unions profoundly affected the shape of the Southern California working class in the postwar period, and by extension the physical and political landscape of the region. Aircraft and aerospace accounted for nearly one-half of manufacturing jobs in the Los Angeles area during much of the postwar period, and defense spending was the primary driver of industrial development throughout Southern California.[89] The cultural significance of the industry may have superseded this economic impact, for example in its role in driving suburbanization and the development of planned communities with housing affordable enough for aircraft workers to purchase.[90] Yet, even as public representations of aircraft workers' affluence—suburban subdivisions with neat yards, cars, and modern appliances—became increasingly commonplace in the postwar period, the struggle and mobilizations that made them possible fell further and further from view.

The contradiction between the material well-being supported by aircraft jobs in boom times and the profound economic insecurity faced by aircraft workers does much to explain the economic and political landscape that developed in Southern California through the Cold War and the creation of what Joan Didion has called an "artificial ownership class." On the one hand, a generation of struggle combined with baseline federal support for union rights had cracked through the open shop to establish aircraft jobs as good jobs that could support the dream of consumer plenty. A flood of military spending into Southern California created an archipelago of suburbs and "managed to increase the proletariat and simultaneously, by calling it middle class, to co-opt it."[91] Defense build-up continued supporting good manufacturing jobs for the Los Angeles working class long after similar jobs began to disappear in eastern and midwestern industrial centers. At the same time, the very real political and economic constraints faced by aircraft workers prevented them from pushing for real job security and middle-class stability. Even as the unions owed their existence to federal intervention, they quickly discovered the limits of that support, exacerbated by the government's role as a consumer, rather than simply a regulator, in their industry. The boom-and-bust cycle of aircraft manufacture meant frequent lay-offs and high turnover in the workforce. As a UAW pamphlet put it: "Aircraft workers earn less, thrive on overtime, live in shadowy fear of a 'bust' in defense industry orders."[92] For example, a majority of workers at North American Aviation at the time of the 1953 strike had been hired within the previous two years.[93] Aircraft workers failed to achieve anything like the enhanced unemployment benefits that helped mitigate the impact of arrhythmic work cycles in the automobile industry.[94]

Aircraft unions' growing conservatism, both on the shop floor and on questions of national and international politics, and their support for expanded military production in particular, thus must be seen not just as part of larger postwar cultural and political trends but also in the context of their struggle with employers for economic security. Their difficult bargaining position spurred decisions within these unions to concentrate more narrowly on contractual issues, with significant long-term costs to workers. After anti-Communist purges removed from the ranks of leaders those who were best placed to provide an ambitious alternative social vision for prosperity, workers' remaining option to protect their interests lay in backing the growth of the national security state.

Notes

1   See, for example, George Lipsitz, *Rainbow at Midnight: Labor and Culture in the 1940s* (Urbana and Chicago: University of Illinois Press, 1994); *Labor's Cold War: Local Politics in a Global Context*, ed. Sheldon Stromquist (Urbana and Chicago: University of Illinois Press, 2008); and *American Labor and the Cold War*, ed. Robert W. Cherny, William Issel, and Kieran Walsh Taylor (New Brunswick, N.J.: Rutgers University Press, 2004).

2   Steven K. Ashby, "Shattered Dreams: The American Working Class and the Origins of the Cold War" (PhD diss., University of Chicago, 1993); Nelson Lichtenstein, "From Corporatism to Collective Bargaining: Organized Labor and the Eclipse of Social Democracy in the Postwar Era," in *The Rise and Fall of the New Deal Order, 1930–1980*, ed. Gary Gerstle and Steve Fraser (Princeton, N.J.: Princeton University Press, 1989), 122–52; and Ellen Schrecker, "Labor and the Cold War: The Legacy of McCarthyism," in *American Labor and the Cold War*, ed. Issel and Taylor, 7–24.

3   Prior to a reorganization following the 1941 strike, workers at North American were represented by UAW Local 683.

4   Union politics at Douglas Aircraft, the other major Los Angeles–area aircraft company, were complicated by split representation. The IAM represented the Douglas plant at Santa Monica, while the UAW represented the Long Beach and El Segundo plants.

5   Unlike those running other Southern California airframe concerns during and after the war, Lockheed President Robert Gross was a financier rather than an engineer, and this may have influenced his approach.

6   Clark Kerr and George Halverson, *Lockheed Aircraft Corporation and the International Association of Machinists: A Case Study* (Washington, D.C.: National Planning Association, 1949); Lockheed Aircraft Corporation, *Eighteenth Annual Report*, 21 March 1950. Lodge 727 actually exemplified the evolution of the union away from its craft-based roots, which led it to take some unorthodox positions within the organization, such as questioning its whites-only membership policy, discussed below.

7   Nelson Lichtenstein, *Labor's War at Home: The CIO in World War II* (Cambridge and New York: Cambridge University Press, 1982), 56.

8   Carey McWilliams, *Southern California Country: An Island on the Land* (New York: Duell, Sloan & Pearce, 1946), 273–94; Arthur P. Allen and Betty V. H. Schneider, *Industrial Relations in the California Aircraft Industry* (Berkeley, Calif.: University of California Institute of Industrial Relations, 1956), 7–17.

9   At a local level, this fight pitted the IAM (affiliated with the AFL) against the UAW (part of the CIO).

10   Lichtenstein, *Labor's War at Home*, 59; *Los Angeles Times*, 17 April 1941.

11   *Los Angeles Times*, 7 May 1941.

12   Accounts of this strike, and particularly the relative role of rank-and-file militants and Communist-affiliated organizers, vary wildly. The most comprehensive treatments are: James R. Prickett, "Communist Conspiracy or Wage Dispute? The 1941 Strike at North American Aviation," *Pacific Historical Review* 50 (1981): 215–33; Lichtenstein, *Labor's War at Home*, 56–66; Wyndham Mortimer, *Organize! My Life As a Union Man* (Boston: Beacon Press, 1971), 174–87; and Wyndham Mortimer, interview by Elizabeth L. Dixon, 1967, Oral History Program, University of California, Los Angeles. *Dear Brother: A Letter to You from a North American Aircraft Worker* (Los Angeles: Local 683 United Auto Workers—CIO, 1941) provides a day-by-day account of the strike from

the point of view of its organizers and defenders. I agree with Prickett's case that the strike was an expression of workers' desires for better wages and benefits and that Communist organizers were faithfully supporting those desires. I have found no evidence to support the common assertion that the conflict was instigated by these organizers to stop the flow of aircraft to Britain. Existing evidence of Soviet espionage in the California aircraft industry demonstrates an effort to obtain technical and design secrets, not to engage in sabotage.

13   The full text of Frankensteen's speech was reprinted in the *Los Angeles Times*, 8 June 1941.

14   *New York Times*, 10 June 1941.

15   *Los Angeles Times*, 10 June 1941.

16   *Los Angeles Times*, 24 and 26 November 1940; Prickett, "Communist Conspiracy," 222; Senate Committee on Un-American Activities in California, "Report from Joint Fact-Finding Committee on Un-American Activities in California to the California Legislature," 1949, Dorothy Healey Collection, California State University, Long Beach.

17   *Washington Post*, 30 May 1941.

18   *Los Angeles Times*, 10 June 1941.

19   Prickett, "Communist Conspiracy," 219; Mortimer, *Organize!*, 174–76.

20   *Los Angeles Times*, 6 June 1941.

21   *American Aeronaut*, 13 June 1941.

22   For the Roosevelt administration's concern about the potential for Communist-organized strikes to paralyze defense and its growing willingness to take action on anti-Communist allegations, see Ellen Schrecker, *Many Are the Crimes: McCarthyism in America* (Boston: Little, Brown, 1998), 98–102.

23   *New York Times*, 10 June 1941.

24   Mortimer, *Organize!*, 212; *Los Angeles Times*, 11 June 1941.

25   Chamber of Commerce of the United States of America, *Communists within the Labor Movement: A Handbook on the Facts and Counter-Measures* (Washington, D.C.: Chamber of Commerce, [1947]), 8.

26   Senate Committee on Un-American Activities in California, "Report."

27   John Olszowka argues that the strike altered the UAW's approach to organizing aircraft workers, with consequences that extended to aircraft companies on the East Coast as well. See "The UAW and the Struggle to Organize Aircraft, 1937–1942," *Labor History* 49 (2008): 297–317.

28   *American Aeronaut*, 20 December 1946.

29   Ibid., 6 September 1946.

30   *Los Angeles Times*, 15 April 1948.

31   Wyndham Mortimer made this argument in a letter to CIO head Philip Murray, 18 June 1941; reprinted in Mortimer, *Organize!*, 208–14.

32   David L. Cole, Benjamin Aaron, and W. Willard Wirtz, "In the Matter of North American Aviation, Inc. and International Union, United Automobile,

Aircraft & Agricultural Implement Workers of American and ITS Units, Locals 887 and 927," 13 September 1952, 9–10, UAW Local 887 Records Collection, box 13, folder 2, Walter P. Reuther Library, Wayne State University.

33   *American Aeronaut*, 27 October 1953.

34   Lichtenstein, "From Corporatism to Collective Bargaining"; Klein, *For All These Rights: Business, Labor, and the Shaping of American's Public–Private Welfare State* (Princeton, N.J.: Princeton University Press, 2003).

35   *American Aeronaut*, 3 November 1944 and 20 July 1945. Similar demands were made by workers in manufacturing industries across the country; see Lipsitz, *Rainbow at Midnight*, chap. 4.

36   *Los Angeles Times*, 4 October 1945.

37   *American Aeronaut*, 1 February and 15 February 1946.

38   Ibid., 30 January 1948.

39   See Ashby, "Shattered Dreams."

40   Seth Wigderson, "The Wages of Anticommunism: U.S. Labor and the Korean War," in *Labor's Cold War*, ed. Stromquist, 231–32.

41   *American Aeronaut*, 20 September 1946.

42   *California Eagle*, 16 July 1942. Reverend Clayton Russell, interview by Sherna Berger Gluck with Jan Fischer, 7 November 1979, Rosie the Riveter Revisited Oral History Project, California State University, Long Beach. For more on African Americans in Los Angeles during this period, see Josh Sides, *L.A. City Limits: African American Los Angeles from the Great Depression to the Present* (Berkeley and Los Angeles: University of California Press, 2003), esp. chap. 3. On the aircraft industry in particular, see James R. Wilburn, "Social and Economic Aspects of the Aircraft Industry in Metropolitan Los Angeles During World War II" (PhD diss., University of California, Los Angeles, 1971), chap. 5.

43   *Chicago Defender*, 29 March 1946.

44   Wilburn, "Social and Economic Aspects," 165.

45   *California Eagle*, 17 February 1943.

46   Quoted in Wilburn, "Social and Economic Aspects," 175–76.

47   *California Eagle*, 10 February 1943.

48   Harry L. Kingman, regional director FEPC Region XII, to Will Maslow, director of field operations, "Final Disposition Report," 29 December 1944. Ward remained an active member in Lodge 727 into the 1960s, eventually holding a number of elected positions. *American Aeronaut*, 4 November 1959 and 21 June 1961.

49   Sides, *L.A. City Limits*, chap. 3; *California Eagle*, 10 February 1943.

50   *New York Amsterdam News*, 10 November 1945.

51   Stanley V. White, WMC Regional Appeals, to Katz, Gallagher & Margolis, 12 August 1944, Charles Bratt Papers, folder 11, Southern California Library for Social Studies and Research.

52   *American Aeronaut*, 7 June and 5 July 1946.

53   Ibid., 1 November 1946.

54   Sides, *L.A. City Limits*, 145–47.

55   Kerr and Halverson, *Lockheed Aircraft Corporation*, 58.

56   For a larger view of the impact of anti-Communism on the labor movement, see Schrecker, "Labor and the Cold War."

57   California CIO Council, "The Impact of the War on California," July 1945, Special Collections, California State University, Long Beach.

58   Lichtenstein, "From Corporatism to Collective Bargaining."

59   *American Aeronaut*, 16 June and 14 July 1944.

60   "Summary of Statement on Wartime Expansion and Postwar Shifts in Employment in California," prepared by California State Reconstruction and Reemployment Commission for Distribution at So. California Manpower Commission Conference on Utilization of Minority Group Workers, 20 April 1945, Charles Bratt Papers, Southern California Library for Social Studies and Research.

61   California CIO Council, "The Impact of the War on California."

62   Allen and Schneider, *Industrial Relations*, 24.

63   *Los Angeles Times*, 19 August 1941.

64   California Department of Labor Statistics and Research, "California Aircraft Employment, 1940–52," February 1953, Special Collections, California State University, Long Beach. The Douglas Long Beach plant, for example, laid off 15,000 workers in one week; Allen and Schneider, *Industrial Relations*, 34.

65   A copy of this notice is in the David L. Clark collection, folder 21, University of California, Los Angeles Archives.

66   North American Aviation, *Annual Report*, 1946. The true magnitude of the cut is only apparent when one considers not only the Inglewood plant (with wartime employment of 25,000) but the size of North American's workforce as a whole, including the Texas and Kansas plants, which reached 100,000 employees at its height. J. Leland Atwood, interview by Dr. Albert Hibbs, 30 November 1987 (videotape), California Institute of Technology Archives.

67   Walter J. Boyne, *Beyond the Horizons: The Lockheed Story* (New York: St. Martin's, 1998), 130–45; Lockheed, *Annual Report*, 1943–48. Employment was already down to 54,000 by the end of 1944 and decreased steadily for the following two years. Employment did not begin to increase again until mid-1948.

68   *American Aeronaut*, 6 April, 11 May, and 25 May 1945.

69   *Los Angeles Times*, 25 November 1945.

70   Kerr and Halverson, *Lockheed Aircraft Corporation*, 24–26, 50.

71   Tom Sitton, *Los Angeles Transformed: Fletcher Bowron's Urban Reform Revival, 1938–1953* (Albuquerque: University of New Mexico Press, 2005), 115; *American Aeronaut*, 2 August 1946.

72   *American Aeronaut*, 19 September 1947.

73   In December 1946, Lodge 727 president Michael Carroll argued that Lockheed workers should get a 22.5-cent raise to offset inflation; *American Aeronaut*, 6 December 1946.

74   Cole, Aaron, and Wirtz, "In the Matter of North American Aviation, Inc.," 7.

75   *Los Angeles Times*, 26 August 1949 and 22 October 1949; Allen and Schneider, *Industrial Relations*, 38.

76   Allen and Schneider, *Industrial Relations*, 39–41.

77   Ibid., 44–45.

78   *Los Angeles Times*, 12 October 1950.

79   California Department of Labor Statistics and Research, "California Aircraft Employment, 1940–1952."

80   Paul Schrade, interview by Thomas J. Connors, 1989–90, "UAW Workplace and Community Action Oral History Transcript, 1989–1990: Paul Schrade," transcript, Oral History Collection, University of California, Los Angeles.

81   Union security language was a particularly contentious issue. The government had imposed maintenance-of-membership clauses on the industry during the Second World War. Following the war, local unions sought unsuccessfully to establish full union shops, while management sought to weaken the existing union-security language. By 1950, both Lodge 727 and Local 887 had achieved significant improvements in union-security language that stopped just shy of requiring union membership for employment.

82   *Los Angeles Times*, 11 August 1952; *American Aeronaut*, 19 August 1952.

83   *Los Angeles Times*, 9 and 11 September 1952.

84   Ibid., 26 June 1952.

85   The strike ultimately involved 19,000 workers in Inglewood, 13,000 in Columbus, and 1,000 in Fresno.

86   *Strike Home: A Report on the 54-Day Strike of 33,000 North American Workers* (Los Angeles: Local 887 UAW-CIO, 1953).

87   Schrade interview; *Los Angeles Times*, 23 October 1953.

88   Schrade interview.

89   Los Angeles Community Analysis Bureau, *The Economic Development of Southern California, 1920–1976*, 2 vols. to date (Los Angeles: Community Analysis Bureau, 1976–), vol. 1.

90   Greg Hise, "Home Building and Industrial Decentralization in Los Angeles: The Roots of the Postwar Urban Region," *Journal of Urban History* 19 (1993): 95–125, and *Magnetic Los Angeles: Planning the Twentieth-Century Metropolis* (Baltimore and London: Johns Hopkins University Press, 1997).

91   Joan Didion, *Where I Was From* (New York: Alfred A. Knopf, 2003), 113–15.

92   *Strike Home*, 9.

93   Ibid., 9–10.

94   Schrade interview.

M I H I R   P A N D Y A

THE VANISHING ACT: STEALTH AIRPLANES AND COLD WAR SOUTHERN CALIFORNIA

D uring the Cold War, American military contractors built weapons systems alongside civilian industries, rather than in isolated environments. Part of an effort to regulate the circulation of sensitive information, classification procedures intentionally obscured some of these projects from public view. The scale of classification during the Cold War was extensive.[1] The practice of secrecy in various guises, including classification, fostered omissions from the public record.[2] One consequence of these absences is a fragmented Cold War archive. Our ability to access the past has thus been compromised by a process that made classified practices translucent in the moment and over time.[3] While there have been noteworthy efforts to show how the military-industrial economy shaped places like Southern California,[4] none of these studies accounts for the defense industry's relative absence from the national imaginary. This amnesia, I suggest, is partly induced by the norms of secrecy that governed military-industrial production.[5]

In what follows, I map some of the features of the aerospace economy in Cold War Los Angeles. This outline of the scale and scope of the industry leads to the following question: Why does aerospace, an influential social and technological formation in Southern California and an important part of the larger Cold War infrastructure, seem to flicker in the national imaginary? I explore answers to this question through a close study of a set of classified projects to develop Stealth airplanes, military planes with small radar signatures.[6] I show that secrecy practices were neither stable nor consistent, but were collectively effective in limiting what was known about Stealth technology.[7] I also suggest that one broader social effect of the tight regulation of sensitive knowledge was the liminality of aerospace in the public sphere.[8]

An Emergent System

Los Angeles was the preeminent site for the postwar joint venture between the military and the defense industry. While the history of the airplane in Los Angeles reaches back to the early twentieth century,[9] the county's defense infrastructure was very much a child of the Second World War. The increase in airplane manufacturing prior to and during the war built the sites that would house much of Cold War defense production in the Los Angeles Basin, including the Lockheed facilities in Burbank, the Douglas Aircraft facility in Santa Monica, and North American's facilities in Hawthorne.[10] During the Cold War, 20 percent of the U.S. Department of Defense budget, on average, found its way to California.[11] Southern California sprouted airfields, testing ranges, Army and Air Force bases, Navy shipyards, assembly plants, and thousands of small businesses that served as contractors and suppliers for this economy.

The influx of federal dollars funded a growing web of support institutions; instead of manufacturing assistance, these provided research support, oversight, education, and training. Along with the RAND Corporation, which gave extensive strategic advice and analysis for military agencies, the less well-known Aerospace Corporation provided technical oversight for the Air Force and the space program.[12] Schools like the College of Engineering at the University of California, Los Angeles; California State University, Long Beach; and the California Institute of Technology in Pasadena offered a range of courses in aerospace engineering and programs in the management of defense projects. Smaller private businesses and corporate firms provided training and certification programs. Throughout the Cold War, small organizations, large manufacturing sites, and training and testing centers formed a constellation of interdependent defense businesses in Southern California.

As the institutional architecture of the aerospace industry coalesced, defense technology went through a series of evolutions. These shifts were generated not only by increasing federal funding but also due to the hothouse atmosphere within and between regional defense networks,[13] and perhaps more importantly, the external pressures of the Cold War. The growing importance of analog and digital computing, for example, transformed the manufacturing process and the types of commodities produced. Then, in the wake of Sputnik, the aircraft business also expanded vertically, from air to space.[14] Consequently, new aerospace instruments and products were added to Southern California's industrial base, including missiles, satellites, and space vehicles.[15]

The California defense economy remained formidable despite the cyclicality of federal aerospace funding, evident after the Korean War and in the wake of Vietnam, in part because of the logic of federal allocations. After a congressional outlay of funds, the allocation first went to governmental defense agencies (the Department of Defense or the Central Intelligence Agency, for example) that had their own, usually distinct, systems of managing procurement and disbursing allocations. After winning a contract, defense firms usually had to produce something before getting a "progress payment" for their efforts. These progress payments could continue to come in long after the initial awarding of production contracts. As a result, even when the winds shifted in Washington and a new political mood led to a reduction in the defense budget, federal dollars continued to flow into California's military-industrial economy. Defense spending in California was therefore not only dependent on annual defense allotments, but also tied to specific projects (such as airplanes or weapons systems) that could stretch over many years. A combination of projects constituted a company's portfolio, and the large number of aerospace companies around Los Angeles allowed a network of people, companies, and support institutions to sediment regionally.

The density of regional aerospace firms powered large and volatile labor markets. Some who joined companies like Lockheed during World War II continued to work at the same company for their whole careers. Aerospace workers, especially those in the upper echelons, speak with understated pride about their experiences and about the ethic of elite enclaves like Lockheed's Skunk Works and Northrop's Advanced Projects Division. Other aerospace workers recall that things started to change as the Cold War progressed and companies became less distinct and more transactional in feel, inducing worker mobility. For some, employment had always occurred on a project-by-project basis. When one job ended, another position could be found with a different company on another project.

Periodic uncertainty forced workers to rely on their own skill sets rather than on any single employer. One aerospace mechanic with whom I spoke began at North American in 1960. Over a forty-year career in aerospace, he worked for Beechcraft West, Rocketdyne, twice more for North American, and three times for Lockheed. While public advertisements and corporate recruitment occasionally induced workers to change employers, usually it was informal links connecting friends and colleagues that led people to new positions. The trade associations, unions, training centers, and work sites that dotted the Los Angeles region also served as nodes of information about available jobs. The near-underground quality of defense networks were enhanced by structures of classification and secrecy. These procedures made personal bonds more sacrosanct and amplified the meanings of trust within these more bounded social communities. As we shall see later, these networks served not only to broadcast open positions, but also as opportunities for friendship, gossip, rumor, and other modes of safe sociability.

A Snapshot of the California Defense Industry, 1970s and 1980s

In the late 1970s, appropriations by a Republican Congress and the Carter White House drove a large surge in defense aircraft manufacturing. These investments responded to a growing bipartisan concern that there had been a substantial loss of military capability in the wake of Vietnam. When Ronald Reagan became president, he continued the majority of existing defense programs and launched a series of new projects. For example, he fulfilled a campaign promise to revive the B-1 bomber program by quickly issuing a contract to a California company, Rockwell International, to produce one hundred aircraft in forty-eight months. This was no small feat, considering the complexity of aerospace manufacturing by the early 1980s. At the peak of production, nearly one B-1 a week rolled out of the newly constructed facility in Palmdale, in the Antelope Valley. The project employed over 50,000 workers, most of them in Southern California.

Ronald Reagan also signed off on the B-2, or Stealth bomber (discussed in the next section). While Rockwell was producing the last of the B-1s in Southern California in 1988, Northrop began developing the technology for the B-2. The B-2 was also a massive financial and technological undertaking. It was one of the first airplanes of its size built using primarily computer-aided design and manufacturing technologies. Again, tens of thousands of workers were involved, with subcontractors in the region and in almost every state in the country.

In the 1980s, no single defense firm dominated; three or four players competed in each segment of the market. Plants that employed thousands dotted the Southland and produced airplanes for a global market. Along with its B-2 research and development in El Segundo, Northrop produced the fuselage of the F-18 for the U.S. Air Force as well as the F-5 fighter for such markets as Mexico, Norway, Ethiopia, Taiwan, Singapore, and Brazil. Meanwhile, in Burbank, along with the classified projects undertaken by the Skunk Works, Lockheed built the P-3 Orion, an aircraft specifically designed to hunt Soviet submarines, and marketed it internationally as a maritime patrol and reconnaissance airplane. In Long Beach, McDonnell Douglas began developing the C-17 transport plane. The economic depth of the aerospace infrastructure in Southern California meshed military production with a large commercial aviation industry: Northrop built the 747 fuselage in Southern California; McDonnell Douglas built large segments of three commercial planes locally—the MD-80, the DC-10, and the MD-11; and, until 1984, Lockheed built the L-1011 in Burbank and Palmdale.

By the later stages of the Cold War, several aerospace programs—intercontinental missiles, tactical weapons systems, and commercial and military satellites—had found homes in Los Angeles. One close observer of the industry recalled the scope of the industry at that time with some amazement: "There were five other major companies around there; Loral was producing defense electronics, Western Gear was also a big producer. Litton Industries was the biggest navy contractor, and they did all the guidance [systems] for the Navy."[16] Other corporate actors not commonly associated with the defense industry also sought military projects during the Cold War. In its large Pomona Division, General Dynamics produced four different tactical missiles. Ford Aerospace produced the ill-fated M247 Sergeant York antiaircraft weapon in Orange County. Xerox, Goodyear, Unisys, Honeywell, General Motors, and General Electric all competed for defense contracts.

The concentration of electronics and computing businesses also brought defense-related computing, communications, and electronics projects to the region. For example, Northrop built the intricate guidance system for the MX missile. Hughes Aircraft, based initially in Culver City and later in El Segundo, built antitank and antiaircraft missiles and, along with Westinghouse, produced most of the radar systems for U.S. military jet fighters. Meanwhile, many companies in the region, including Hughes, TRW in Redondo Beach, and Lockheed's Missiles and Space division in Sunnyvale (in the Bay Area) specialized in both commercial and military satellites.[17]

As prime contractors began depending increasingly on subcontractors for whole subsystem assemblies and for smaller parts, aerospace companies blossomed in the South Bay. Companies like Teledyne and Lear Siegler focused mainly on components, such as small jet engines for cruise missiles or control sticks for jet fighters. At the same time, thousands of subsystem houses supplied a wide range of airplane manufacturing services: machine and paint shops, heat treatment plants, and casting, forging, and plating companies.[18] In the 1980s, one could drive through working-class communities like Paramount or the City of Industry and see the footprint of thriving aerospace manufacturing networks. Such businesses sprouted across Los Angeles County, as well as on its periphery in towns like North Hollywood in the San Fernando Valley. As one observer explained, these subsystem houses clustered together, creating self-supporting circuits of commerce:

> If you're going to cast a piece of aluminum, you are going to heat treat it here, then you're going to send it to a plater, the plater is going to finish plating it, then it's going to have to be tested to make sure there are no voids or defects. It turns out there is a non-destructive testing place down the street. . . . So there [were] all these little enclaves where you [could] see all these little separate companies operating like this."[19]

With the noteworthy exception of jet engines, an encyclopedic array of aerospace parts and expertise were locally available. In the 1980s, the Los Angeles Basin was one of the few places in the world where a regional supply chain could support a nearly complete aircraft system.

At this economy's peak in the mid-1980s, there were close to 470,000 military-related jobs in Los Angeles, many of them in large plants employing more than a thousand people. The majority of these positions were in private industry (370,000), and the rest in the military (57,000) or in civilian jobs in military sites (42,000).[20] The job listings in the Sunday *Los Angeles Times* arrived each week with foldouts for each major aerospace manufacturer listing hundreds of vacancies. Some listings targeted aerospace engineers, but others were for the often-forgotten support staff that propped up the industry: accountants, human resource personnel, kitchen workers, managers, and secretaries.

The tens of thousands of aerospace workers also powered segments of the regional economy not directly related to defense. Area home prices, for instance, doubled in the 1980s.[21] In Orange, San Bernardino, and Riverside Counties, new communities sprang up seemingly overnight. A reporter who covered the industry recounted that the Moreno Valley in Riverside County had been a small community in the 1970s, but by the 1980s, the city's population exploded with thousands "trying to commute on clogged freeways to their aerospace jobs."[22] Engineers and other skilled workers across the nation had flocked to California's well-paying defense jobs. Migrants from Mexico and Central America soon filled the low-skilled service positions that supported those who worked in and around aerospace. Ironically, some migrants who had fled the use of American power in their homelands—in Guatemala and El Salvador, for instance—found employment supporting the manufacture of American power (aerospace and weapons systems) when they arrived across the border.

How Classification and Secrecy Worked

When one thinks of postwar Los Angeles, airplanes are usually not the first things that come to mind. The media industries, the beach, highways, and suburbs all represent the city in the national imagination, while defense remains largely absent. Considering the military economy's dimensions during the postwar period, how could this industrial formation hide in plain sight? One reason for the absence of military production from public discourse is the practice of classification. Governments classify information they deem sensitive. While there is disagreement about the effects of classification—whether the risks averted by classifying information overwhelm the knowledge gained by having open access—the scale of classification efforts in the United States is noteworthy. According to Peter Galison, "some suspect as many as a trillion pages are classified. . . . [meaning that] the classified universe is. . . . on the order of five to ten times larger than the open literature that finds its way to our libraries."[23]

In the United States, formal military efforts to provide security through secrecy trace their roots to the Manhattan Project, the iconic effort to build the atomic bomb. The subsequent 1946 Atomic Energy Act and the National Security Act of 1947 created the National Security Council and the Central Intelligence Agency and hid a growing security apparatus from public view.[24] With the expanding sense of threat during the Cold War, concerns about all aspects of the military's readiness increased, and classification spread as culture and practice.[25]

In order to appreciate how classification practices and informal cultures of secrecy worked, I now turn to a set of classified Stealth airplane projects built in the Los Angeles Basin and the Antelope Valley from the early 1970s through the early 1990s.[26] Stealth aircraft were designed late in the Cold War under the twin specters of increasingly effective radar systems (equipped with surface-to-air missiles) and a three-to-one Soviet advantage in conventional weapons and ground forces. Stealth airplanes could potentially give U.S. military planners an advantage; hence, their development programs were classified. Studying some of the classification practices surrounding Stealth programs gives us a sense of how secrecy shaped life in defense-saturated cities like Los Angeles, where the aerospace economy was large, complex, and civilian dependent.

In classified sites, where technologies like Stealth originated, the conventions of secrecy were not only linked to the content of the secret but also dependent on context. This meant that in practice, secrecy was often defined differently by different actors, creating variable distinctions between public and secret information. This was true even when classification regulations were consistent and compliance was sincere. For example, in the 1970s, Northrop built the Stealth reconnaissance test plane Tacit Blue, which was nicknamed "the whale." According to one report, pictures of real whales soon populated the California headquarters of Northrop's Advanced Projects Division. Whale paintings graced the lobby, whale drawings appeared on letterhead, and whale logos were inscribed on company equipment. Visitors' inquiries about the décor were politely, if knowingly, rebuffed. "It was something you couldn't talk about," remembered a Northrop engineer.[27]

The story of the whale shows the complex and public ways in which objects and their representations delineated the borders of secrecy in everyday interactions. The images of whales were not technically classified, yet the teasing way in which they were displayed signaled the secret in public. The whale became publicly visible as a known unknown. The secret—in this case embodied in the emblem—was projected into new contexts (the lobby, the factory floor, and so on) and, in the process, it redefined each new physical location as a site that housed a secret, known to some and unknown to others. It was an inside joke that provided opportunities to reinscribe belonging. But these repositionings also created public spaces inside secret ones, secret spaces inside public ones.[28]

Such secret spaces could be momentary (like the refusal to share a secret with those who asked) or more permanent (and enforceable through legal measures if what was officially marked secret had been shared). The story of the whale also implies some of the ways in which people could access the secret (by acquiring a security clearance to work on black projects)[29] and how those rituals of access were institutionalized (through secrecy procedures, and cultures of reticence within a company). The boundaries between the secret and the public might have seemed fixed from the outside, but in use, those boundaries were often permeable. This is not to suggest that classification was not effective. Rather, what emerged in the case of Stealth was a quasi-public secret, where the existence of a secret is known among select populations, but not its content.[30]

Historically speaking then, secrets like Stealth existed in the gray world—between absolute secrecy and official publicity—for much longer than anyone cares to admit.

Family, Secrets

Classified work generated many of the same stresses as any other form of employment. For instance, secret projects fostered environments in which long hours and intense pressure were the norm. Building Stealth airplanes sometimes involved extended travel to bases, factories, and offices all over California and the nation. The effects were predictable. Some marriages did not last, and those that did often experienced redistributions of authority and decision-making. As one spouse described it, because she stayed behind, she learned "to take care of things."[31] If workers were gone for long periods of time, they had to adjust to changing household dynamics, especially with regard to children. One couple recounted how, until the age of three, their daughter did not quite understand "who the stranger in the house was" on weekends. The segregation of work experiences from family life came naturally to many couples. Some found it quite natural to talk only about their children, friends, money, and other everyday routines and rituals. Other Stealth workers had spouses who worked as military officers, aerospace workers, and mental health professionals. These spouses therefore also had limits about how *they* could discuss their work lives.

Aside from these commonalities with corporate or other working environments, there were specific ways in which secrecy in the defense industry shaped the domestic sphere. In particular, secrecy mediated the relationship between what was considered public and private. When the topic of work was broached, for example, what couples would *not* talk about varied. People working in the Stealth-related programs made decisions largely on their own, in separate contexts and in real time, about what constituted transmittable or "safe" information. The wife of an aerospace engineer insisted that it was necessary to talk about work in some fashion: "While Bob couldn't tell me about the plane, he could tell me about personalities, and what the dynamics were in making the plane. So we could talk about that. It gave me a connection to him: frustrations, the funny things that happened.... otherwise you feel pretty lonely." Office politics, bureaucratic routines, and personal histories might be officially secret, but for participants these spaces were safe enough to explore within the family while still complying with the formal norms of classification. For many, office gossip was used to articulate the shareable "public" experience of working within classified environments with one's intimates.

Even as couples found ways of conversing with each other about Stealth, workers and their families feared revealing secrets to outsiders. The watchful eye of the state or the company was not just a theoretical threat; it occasionally came calling, making family life part of a public narrative. Here secret work came into the domestic sphere for employees and their families, while the domestic space came under the "public" purview of security personnel. Working on a secret program was in many ways public in nature because it was federally funded and open to bureaucratic pressures, public since it was service to the nation, and all-too-public, from the perspective of the family, in its constraints on domestic life.

Secrecy within Communities

Many communities in California came to know something about Stealth during the manufacturing process, but what constituted knowledge in these groups depended on the context. In local communities, glimmers of information flowed through informal networks to family, friends, and acquaintances. For example, crowds quietly gathered at the gates in Burbank (and later in Palmdale in the Antelope Valley) when Stealth airplanes were first moved outside their hangars. A Palmdale resident described how these gatherings took place: "someone would say 'I can't tell you what, but be on Sierra Highway [in front of Lockheed's Skunk Works] at seven.'" Cars and trucks lined up promptly in the lot across the street when these calls were made. The secret broke through the surface in these communal gatherings, becoming temporarily public before disappearing again. Therefore the existence of a secret was broadcast, but the precise content of the secret remained hidden from view.

In these communities the absence of communicable information fostered new ways of talking through and around missing segments of information. In Palmdale, significant proportions of the population worked in aerospace through the mid-1990s. As a longtime resident told me, "It wasn't uncommon at that time to be having a conversation with someone and you asked them what they did, and they said, 'Oh, I work at Lockheed'; and I said, 'Oh ... and what do you do there?' and they say 'Oh! I can't tell you!'"[32] In Palmdale both parties knew that if one worked in the Skunk Works, you were not allowed to talk about any aspect of your work in public. So, some information was communicated in this exchange: that the person was employed by Lockheed (stated plainly) and worked at the Skunk Works (unsaid but assumed by the addressee). There is still a gap—what exactly the person did at the Skunk Works— but some information was transferred nonetheless.

In a curious reversal of how secrets are assumed to operate in places like Palmdale, Stealth came to be "seen" everywhere in town, even where it was not present. Rather than visual sightings, these were rumors and assumptions about the activities of workers. A local reporter recounted how he and his wife assumed that his father-in-law worked on the B-2 Stealth because all he would tell them was that he worked for Northrop. The reporter learned years later that his father-in-law had been reverse-engineering Russian airplane parts and had had nothing to do with the Stealth program.[33] Like Lockheed became code for the Skunk Works and classified work, here, Northrop became code for Stealth. So even though people talked, knowledge was assumed and often inaccurate.

Stealth information also circulated virtually in a semi-public market-place. Government agencies and associated professionals like lawyers, consultants, and bankers all served as information brokers.[34] News re-porters sometimes served as nodes in the circulation of information for industry insiders. A news story could provide useful information about a competitor, and a reporter's story could become an effective way of reg-istering a grievance. Once again, the logic of secrecy repeated itself: there were false secrets, which were useful if made public (reports portraying the airplanes and their capacities in a positive light to a domestic con-stituency and, simultaneously, as dangerous threats to foreign interests), and real secrets (which might endanger national security if released), which were truly "private." In other words, through a simple news story, a variety of "truths" could become public, while others remained secret.[35] These semi-official routes also supported the larger circulation of the secret without actually compromising it.

Secrecy at Work

Black sites—the physical locations where secret projects were designed, produced, assembled, and tested—usually did not announce their pres-ence. They either operated quietly in the open or were sequestered be-hind the gates of secured military installations. While a black site might look like any other office or factory from the outside, the buildings' re-stricted access shaped the internal circulation of commodities, docu-ments, and populations. Secret sites were sometimes situated within already-secure locations in commercial and military buildings: certain floors, corridors, and rooms of buildings were accessible only to select personnel. This Russian doll–like quality of nesting structures of secrecy was common within the industry. Classified meetings were held in sealed rooms, and each night most engineers and managers (those working on classified projects) were required to place all of their documents in safes, creating secret spaces inside secret spaces. It should also be noted that sites that housed many secret projects also contained public spaces. The Skunk Works complex outside of Palmdale has a gift shop and a credit union, for example. In this way, secret projects "nested" in public spaces as well as in secret spaces.

Within these sites efforts were made to create "public" working environments that mirrored commercial environments, with varying degrees of success. One of the major production facilities for the B-2 bomber, which at that time was acknowledged but still highly classified, was a windowless former Ford factory in Pico Rivera, a working-class community in Los Angeles's South Bay. In the mid-1980s, 12,000 workers manned the shop floor. Access was limited to specified areas, implying that some spaces were more secret than others. Employees were assigned badges that opened doors accessible to their classifications. They were forbidden from bringing in radios, tape recorders, cameras, or devices that could potentially capture or transmit information outside the facility. Yet, within the largely secret space of the factory, a quasi-public sphere existed. The *Los Angeles Times* reported that the circulation of information within the plant was supported by the plant newspaper, an underground newspaper, rumor mills, and the networks formed on the shop floor and in the formal and informal social gatherings of employees. The *Times* details some of the stories covered in the official circular, including stories about the company golf tournament, the company credit union, and awards for cafeteria workers. However, the company newspaper never mentioned—indeed was not allowed to mention—the bomber that the factory was designed to build.[36] The secret was plain to see all over the factory but could not be officially spoken by name. The airplane served as an absence around which the life of the factory was narrated, a pattern that can also be seen in family lives of Stealth workers, or in the communal life of aerospace towns like Palmdale.

Secrecy at the Collective Register

For those involved in the varied Stealth projects, the overarching logic of secrecy was that, in order to make something unknowable to the outside world, one needed to make it unknowable inside the nation. Competing strains of secrecy—corporate concerns over proprietary knowledge, military secrecy, and deeply encoded cultures of secrecy within military industrial communities—also placed limits on what could, and can even now, be made public. But people talked, and most attempted to make personal judgments about what was *really* secret, in families and in their communities. These individual efforts were met with complex and at times conflicting efforts by the state to keep some aspects of Stealth secret and strategically reveal others. Secrets were made public in a variety of ways, through revealing the technology or its related processes, and through coded icons for both. While secrecy as a method of controlling information was uneven in everyday interactions, when viewed through the long lens of history, military industrial secrecy worked. Secrecy practices hid a sizable and sophisticated defense economy in plain sight and, as far as we know, kept essential technical knowledge from the Soviet Union. I would argue that secrecy also served (perhaps unintentionally) another purpose: it helped mask the collective memory of the period. The practice of secrecy severely limited what could be said about classified projects. Consequently, a range of experiences of living and working in Cold War Southern California were muted in public memory.[37]

At end of the Cold War, aerospace communities began to wither. By 1996, there were 200,000 fewer defense jobs in California than there were in 1988. Four-fifths of the job losses were in Southern California, with two-thirds occurring in Los Angeles County.[38] This trauma may have been the moment in Los Angeles's history when aerospace was most visible; commissions were created to look into retooling the industry, newspapers published stories about existing and impending plagues of job losses, and aerospace businesses tried to reinvent themselves by making everything from car parts to hot tubs. Eventually, interest in these news stories faded, and aerospace slowly loosened its grip on the regional economy and its already tenuous footing in the regional imaginary.[39]

Memorializing a Secret History

There are currently efforts underway to memorialize Stealth and what it represented. For example, an F-117 Stealth fighter has recently been added to the Blackbird Airpark on the outskirts of Palmdale. This open-air museum is visited by tourists, airplane enthusiasts, and former Stealth workers. For the disparate communities of the Antelope Valley, the park is a proximate historical attraction. For devotees, Palmdale is a site of pilgrimage, where these elusive objects can now finally be seen. And for former workers, this kind of public display is an evocative prop with which to narrate their hidden careers to friends and family after the fact.[40]

What is truly remarkable is how limited these public efforts are and how little public interest there is, considering the scale and consequence of military projects like Stealth and their role in the Cold War.[41] While regional displays of Stealth aircraft and the inclusion of Stealth airplanes in the museum of the United States Air Force in Dayton, Ohio, are serious efforts at memorialization, I would argue that overall the act of remembering Stealth—and, for that matter, the Cold War—has not found purchase in the American imagination. Public remembrances are usually local and, according to officials in places like Antelope Valley, they are shrinking in popularity. Some suggest that the absence of the Cold War from public memory stems from its very "unfinishedness."[42] The "war" was never won; and now modulated versions of Marxism linger in parts of Asia and in Latin America. I would only add that part of the answer for the curious absence of this large enterprise from public memory is the secret nature of much of the Cold War economy.

Conclusion: Stealth and Place

Stealth—by definition, an invisible presence—serves as a useful icon of the Cold War aerospace industry in Los Angeles, which seemed absent and present at the same time. In Los Angeles, defense sites, landscapes, and populations operated in public but were concealed from public view. As a metaphor and as an example, Stealth then captures this essential feature of life in Southern California during the Cold War—a life which, for many, was governed by shifting designations of what was known and unknown, said and unsaid, about an economy operating above and underneath the public surface of the region.

Secrecy fostered two cities laminated to each other, one seen and the other unseen. The resulting alignments and misalignments—places where the secret operated quietly, and others where it became public—shaped the feel of the city. One of the ways in which this double consciousness is most routinely captured is in the ways Los Angeles plays itself. Los Angeles as a cultural imaginary reveals its fractured character in its films and its fictions: of power hidden underneath the surface, of violence coupled with fine weather. This union of purity and danger, which so regularly reappears in and as Los Angeles, was also a central trope that helped mask one of the largest knowledge production and manufacturing efforts during the Cold War.

NOTES

1   For a detailed discussion of the size and meaning of classification practices, see Peter Galison, "Removing Knowledge," *Critical Inquiry* 31 (2004), 229–43.

2   On Cold War secrecy, see Daniel Patrick Moynihan, *Secrecy: The American Experience* (New Haven, Conn.: Yale University Press, 1998); and Edward A. Shills, *The Torments of Secrecy: The Costs and Consequences of American Security Policies* (Glencoe, Ill.: Free Press, 1956). On the structure of classification, see Steve Aftergood, "Government Secrecy and Knowledge Production: A Survey of Some General Issues," in *Secrecy and Knowledge Production,* ed. Judith Reppy, Cornell University Peace Studies Program Occasional Papers 23 (Ithaca, N.Y.: Cornell University, Peace Studies Program, 1999), 17–29. On the cultures of secrecy within secure sites, see Hugh Gusterson, *Nuclear Rites: A Weapons Laboratory at the End of the Cold War* (Berkeley: University of California Press, 1996). On the implications of secrecy as state practice, see Joseph Masco, *Nuclear Borderlands: The Manhattan Project in Post–Cold War New Mexico* (Princeton, N.J.: Princeton University Press, 2006).

3   A series of historical contingencies may also help account for this phenomenon, including the changing nature of military service for most Americans in the wake of Vietnam, the diffuse nature and scope of a "cold" war fought on foreign ground, and the technological complexities of military industrial production, among many others. I suggest here that secrecy and classification practices helped promote this historical absence at an accelerated rate.

4   See Mike Davis, *City of Quartz: Excavating the Future in Los Angeles* (New York: Vintage, 1992); Jennifer Light, *From Warfare to Welfare: Defense Intellectuals and the Urban Problems in Cold War America* (Baltimore: John Hopkins University Press, 2003); Robert W. Lotchin, *Fortress California 1910–1960: From Warfare to Welfare* (New York: Oxford University Press, 1992); Allen J. Scott, *Technopolis: High-Technology Industry and Regional Development in Southern California* (Berkeley: University of California Press, 1993); and Edward Soja, *Postmodern Geographies: The Reassertion of Space in Critical Social Theory* (London: Verso, 1989).

5   There are, of course, other contributing factors; for example, much of the work that happens in these military industrial sites happens quietly. It is partly the nature of the work; defense commodities like satellites and airplanes are intricate instruments that require the combined efforts of many actors, often at a variety of sites. Segmentation reduces the field of vision of a company or a worker from the general to the particular, to the part of a part on which they work. Over time, layers of complexity produce both specialization and a degree of myopia. I explore these aspects of defense work and their consequences in much more detail in my dissertation, "The Stealth Effect: Aerospace and Cold War Southern California" (University of Chicago, forthcoming 2012). Here I am exploring only the ways in which military secrecy can also help account for what might be termed the social production of absence.

6   The term *Stealth* represents a series of innovations in the manufacturing of coatings and materials and a set of insights about the shaping of the exterior shell of an airframe. When combined, these efforts minimize a plane's radar cross section, or its footprint on a radar screen. The term began as a description of a desire: that an airplane be stealthy or difficult to track on radar. Officially these airplanes were called low-observable aircraft. Over time the term *Stealth* became an informal moniker associated with a specific set of technologies and airplane projects (the Have Blue test airplane, the F-117 fighter, the Tacit Blue test airplane, and the B-2 bomber). I have therefore chosen to capitalize the term when used to refer to those technologies and projects.

7   While informed by history, historical concerns, and historical methods, the approach taken here—of examining the cultural and institutional relationships as well as exploring the feel of aerospace for the communities from within—is explicitly anthropological in orientation.

8   This essay relies on archival and secondary source materials, which are cited in the notes. As part of a larger ethnographic investigation, I also interviewed participants in the defense industry in the Los Angeles Basin. Efforts have been made to keep their contributions anonymous, as per the ethics guidelines required by academic institutions when working with human subjects. These restrictions (anonymity, no monetary inducements, and so forth) are in place to safeguard participants. The interviews were conducted over the summer and fall of 2005, and from 2007 through 2011.

9   Wayne Biddle, *Barons of the Sky: From Early Flight to Strategic Warfare, the Story of the American Aerospace Industry* (New York: Simon & Schuster, 1991); Lotchin, *Fortress California*; Donald M. Pattillo, *Pushing the Envelope: The American Aircraft Industry* (Ann Arbor: University of Michigan Press, 1998).

10   Defense production also spread south to Orange County and San Diego, east to Riverside and San Bernardino Counties, and northeast to the Antelope Valley.

11   California Legislative Analyst's Office, "Trends in the Southern California Economic Region," in *State and Regional Economic Developments in California: Part II*, September 1998, http://www.lao.ca.gov/1998/0998_regional_econ/0998_regional_economic_part2.html.

12   RAND is an acronym for "Research ANd Development." RAND produced basic and applied research, policy, and strategy recommendations for the U.S. Air Force, the U.S. Army, and many other governmental and nongovernmental clients during the Cold War.

13   See Scott, *Technopolis*.

14   Political urgency and public fascination are credited with creating a national fervor to fund science education and research in the wake of Sputnik. Intriguingly, the military-industrial component—employment, funding—is often mistakenly seen as the beneficiary, rather than the cause, of the institutionalization of science knowledge in the postwar period.

15   For example, the U.S. Air Force ran its satellite program from the Los Angeles Space and Missile Systems Center, and NASA's deep-space exploration program centered on the Jet Propulsion Laboratory in Pasadena.

16   Industry observer, interview with the author, 17 April 2007.

17   Military work in Los Angeles was not just related to the airplane. For example, the Reagan years also saw a large Navy build-up, most famously summed up by Reagan's call for a "600-ship U.S. Navy." While San Diego got most of this business, Los Angeles had its share. For example, in San Pedro, Todd Pacific Shipyards produced frigates for the U.S. Navy.

18   See Scott, *Technopolis*.

19   Industry observer, interview with the author, 15 September 2008.

20   California Legislative Analyst's Office, "Trends in the Southern California Economic Region."

21   Research Division of the National Association of Realtors, "Home Price Analysis for Los Angeles Region" (Washington, D. C., July 2006), http://www.beachpacificescrow.com/External/06CALos%20Angeles.pdf.

22   Interview with the author, 19 January 2009.

23   Galison, "Removing Knowledge," 230.

24   Joseph Masco, "'Sensitive but Unclassified': Secrecy and the Counterterrorist State," *Public Culture* 22, no. 3 (2010): 434.

25   This is not to suggest that there were no conflicts generated by military secrecy in rural locations, only that the specific logic of interaction between the classified and civilian worlds differed in defense-saturated urban spaces like postwar Southern California. For a thorough discussion of secrecy in rural spaces, and the emergence of a national security state, see Masco, *Nuclear Borderlands*.

26   The major players in the early Stealth projects were the Defense Advanced Research Projects Agency (DARPA) in the Department of Defense, the Pentagon, the Air Force, and the Lockheed and Northrop corporations, which had won the right to compete for contracts. The first round of the invited competition was won by Lockheed's premier design shop, the Skunk Works. Their effort produced the prototype Have Blue, which led to the first manufactured Stealth aircraft, the F-117 fighter. Northrop's Tacit Blue project soon followed and served as a testbed, proving that curved surfaces could be used to scatter radar waves; these were adopted in the iconic B-2 Stealth bomber.

27   Northrop was not alone in using circulating images of this kind. The Skunk Works also has a very recognizable and comparatively ubiquitous logo, which also circulated within and outside defense sites and the larger public sphere. Other examples include the badges that are collected by employees, which "tell" the viewer about a project (or part of the project) an employee may be affiliated with through coded images. These have become collectors' items and therefore also have semi-public lives. See Peter Grier, "The (Tacit) Blue Whale," *Airforce-Magazine.com* 79, no. 8 (August 1996), http://www.airforce-magazine.com/MagazineArchive/Pages/1996/August%201996/0896tacit.aspx. For a discussion of badges and their meanings, see Trevor Paglen's book on emblems from black programs, *I Could Tell You But Then You Would Have to Be Destroyed by Me: Emblems from the Pentagon's Black World* (Brooklyn: Melville House Publishing, 2008).

28   My formulations about the nesting qualities of secrecy have been influenced by Susan Gal's work on the public/private distinction. See "A Semiotics of the Public/Private Distinction," *Differences: A Journal of Feminist Cultural Studies* 13, no. 1 (Spring 2002): 77-95.

29   For an in-depth discussion of how clearance works in restricted facilities, see Gusterson, *Nuclear Rites*.

30   For the canonical discussion of secrecy, including how secrets can be both open and empty, see Georg Simmel, "The Sociology of Secrecy and of Secret Societies," *Journal of Sociology* 11 (1906): 441–98.

31   This and the other quotations in this subsection are drawn from a series of interviews with spouses of aerospace workers on 12 February 2008.

32   Palmdale resident, interview with the author, 12 February 2009.

33   Reporter, interview with the author, 12 February 2009.

34   Other actors could be listed here. For example, Stealth enthusiasts also congregated around places like Area 51 in Nevada. They played a role in negotiating the publicity of Stealth through their accounts of what could be seen and known about Stealth aircraft. See Phil Patton, *Dreamland: Travels Inside the Secret World of Roswell and Area 51* (New York: Random House, 1998); and Trevor Paglen, *Blank Spots on the Map: The Dark Geography of the Pentagon's Secret World* (Boston: Dutton, 2009).

35   As intimated in these examples, rumor was also a major instrument for circulating information within these communities. For a discussion of how rumors work, see Max Gluckman, "Gossip and Scandal," *Current Anthropology* 4 (1963): 307–16.

36   Ralph Vartabedian, "Pico Rivera Plant: Stealth Job is Living up to its Name," *Los Angeles Times*, 26 May 1987.

37   One question remains unanswered: To what degree did these measures prevent the Soviets from acquiring Stealth technology? Some answers may surface as information from the Soviet archives becomes more available. But partly, answers depend on where one stands on the causes of the demise of the Soviet Union. Was it induced by internal contradictions within the Soviet system (economic, social, and others) or the pressures of the American military build-up—including and especially Stealth technology? Many of those associated with Stealth believe that American military pressures created the economic pressures that led to the collapse of the Soviet Union.

38   California Legislative Analyst's Office, "Trends in the Southern California Economic Region."

39   While diminished from its Cold War heights, aerospace remains a significant if silent presence. All of the major players—Northrop Grumman (the only one of the big contractors still headquartered in Los Angeles), Lockheed Martin, Boeing, and others—continue to have offices, design shops, and testing facilities in the Los Angeles Basin. The regional focus has shifted to research and design efforts from manufacturing airplanes. These public, semi-public, and private military-industrial concerns continue to constitute a portion of Los Angeles's hidden economic infrastructure.

40   It should be noted that while public memorialization remains elusive, private memorials flourish. The dens and the hallways of retired workers' homes catalog the personal emblems—photographs, patches, plaques, citations, cartoons, and artifacts—of a hidden economy. Histories of the Cold War are found not in public today, but in private venues. In other words, a secret history has become a private one, embodied in individuals and their archives.

41   There are some efforts underway organized by those involved with Stealth. Retiree groups like the Pioneers of Stealth and the Flight Test Foundation host social gatherings to honor those who belong to the hidden communities of the Cold War as well as to support efforts to memorialize their history. What I point to as remarkable is that there are no major efforts underway outside these communities to memorialize projects like Stealth.

42   Chalmers Johnson, *The Sorrows of Empire: Militarism, Secrecy, and the End of the Republic* (New York: Metropolitan Books, 2004).

SECTION III
CULTURE

The essays in this section shift our gaze outward to consider aerospace's aesthetic, technological, and ideological influences on broader Southern California culture. Stuart W. Leslie examines the legacy of architect William Pereira, whose designs for aerospace buildings merged California modernism with space-age visions. The futuristic dreams of such firms as Convair Astronautics, Ford Aeronutronic, General Atomic, and the Autonetics division of Rockwell—their names alone conveyed Jetsonian technological enthusiasm—were rendered by Pereira in glass, steel, and concrete. Addressing the issue of secrecy raised earlier by Mihir Pandya, Leslie asks why aerospace firms built architectural wonders only to hide them behind security gates. The answer, Leslie demonstrates: to recruit top engineering talent.

Peter Westwick's essay notes that most people associate Southern California with Hollywood, not aerospace. What did it mean to have these two major industries, entertainment and aerospace, rubbing shoulders in Southern California? The essay describes how the space program—specifically, the Jet Propulsion Laboratory—developed important early animation methods using computer-generated imagery (CGI) and then propagated these techniques into Hollywood. One of the first, fitting fruits of this interaction came in the earliest *Star Wars* movies, which drew on, and drove, public interest in space. Today's graphics-dominated movies and video games, and perhaps today's space program as well, derive in part from this connection between aerospace and Hollywood. The intersection continues in the present, although now the flow of influence—and computer talent—runs more from movie studios to aerospace firms. Like Leslie's aerospace architects, CGI programmers have helped define Southern California's aesthetic idioms, in this case through technological tools developed by aerospace.

Westwick's essay highlights the role of federal aerospace programs in generating new private commercial opportunities. By contrast, Patrick McCray's essay explores more negative views of federally funded aerospace, those of the so-called alt-space or NewSpace movement. From its early days in the space-colony plans of the L5 Society in the 1970s to the more recent X Prize flights in the Mojave desert, many alt-space enthusiasts have seen the federal government (specifically NASA) as a brake on innovation and instead celebrated the initiative of private entrepreneurs. McCray's description of the alt-space movement revisits the X Prizes described by M. G. Lord and situates them in the ideological and cultural context of California—in particular, the "California Ideology," which combines hippie counterculture with yuppie entrepreneurialism. This ideology tapped currents of Northern California culture, especially among Silicon Valley's personal-computer enthusiasts, but it may have found an even friendlier environment in Southern California, with its history of technological futurism and libertarian thought. Glenn Bugos's essay later in the volume further explores the technological cultures of Northern California and Southern California.

SPACES FOR THE SPACE AGE:
WILLIAM PEREIRA'S AEROSPACE MODERNISM

N o architect better captured the exhilarating spirit of Southern California's aerospace era than William Pereira. For such emerging aerospace giants as Convair, Northrop, Lockheed, Douglas, and North American, Pereira scaled up the residential version of California modernism perfected by Richard Neutra to industrial proportions.[1] His corporate campuses in steel and glass, with their strong horizontal lines, lavish landscaping, pools and fountains, and deliberate blurring of interior and exterior space, perfectly expressed the "blue sky" optimism and scientific fervor of a place that had set its sights on the stars (fig. 1).

As that vision slowly faded, so did the relevance of Pereira's massive complexes. Several of his best have already been demolished in Southern California's latest "boom-and-bust" economic episode, the hot pursuit of real estate. Kearny Mesa, in San Diego, once home to Convair Astronautics and its more than 7,500 scientists, engineers, designers, and production workers for the Atlas missile program, has been turned into a commonplace mixed-use office and retail development. Pereira's elegant campus for Ford's Aeronutronic division in Newport Beach has surrendered to upscale housing. In Rye Canyon, at the base of the San Gabriel mountains north of Los Angeles, Pereira's basic science laboratory for Lockheed presides over the Rye Canyon Business Park; its owners now hope to attract the next new things, biomedical companies and Hollywood production teams; the latter seems fitting, given Pereira's start as a Paramount art director. Pereira's last corporate complex, a modern ziggurat for Rockwell's Autonetics division in Laguna Niguel, midway between Los Angeles and San Diego, ended up being so immense that only the General Services Administration could find any adaptive re-use for it. Pereira's unique laboratory-in-the-round for General Atomic, adjoining the campus of the University of California, San Diego (UCSD), survives as an active scientific workplace, though its idealistic founding

Figure 1. William Pereira with the master plan for
Irvine, California, 1962. Photo by John Loengard/
Time Life Pictures/Getty Images.

mission focused on "atoms for peace" has long since been supplanted by
a more pragmatic business plan. Nowadays General Atomics makes its
money from the Predator drone and its offspring, the current cutting
edge of Southern California aerospace.

In their prime, though, Pereira's aerospace laboratories embodied
the secret side of the space-age zeitgeist, one the public could only catch
glimpses of in photographs, advertisements, and carefully staged open
houses. Everyone could appreciate Pereira's iconic Theme Building, the
symbolic centerpiece of his master plan for Los Angeles International
Airport, and the model for the "jet set" and "Jetson" modernism.[2] Only
those with a "need to know" and the right clearances and passes had an
opportunity to experience the spaces Pereira designed as the very nerve
center of the military-industrial complex.

Hiring a brand-name architect to design signature buildings des-
tined to be hidden behind fences and guardhouses and set far back from
the public gaze may seem extravagant. Pereira's laboratories, however,
served up archetypes of the California dream for a select audience of scientists, engineers, and military officers, live-action commercials for a
lifestyle intended to lure the best and brightest to Southern California.[3]
Convair Astronautics needed to hire thousands of talented engineers for
the Atlas program. General Atomic had to offer some enticement to convince hundreds of established physicists to leave national laboratories
and top universities to join a startup company in what was then the middle of nowhere. Ford somehow had to shed its reputation as an old-line
automotive company and reinvent itself for the space race. Ballistic missiles, avionics, nuclear power and weapons—the defining technologies
of the Cold War—demanded scarce new skills. To give themselves an

edge in hiring and retaining the right people, Southern California's aerospace companies had to project the right image. No wonder Pereira's architecture featured so prominently in aerospace advertising. Pereira gave what David Kaiser has called "the suburbanization of American physics" a distinctly California flair.[4] His architecture embraced bright sunshine, mild temperatures, and dramatic vistas. Its open-air corridors, broad courtyards, shallow reflecting pools, and Mediterranean gardens all promised "California living at its finest," as an Aeronutronic advertisement put it, and would have looked completely out of place virtually anywhere else.[5] Pereira actually did design a $15 million California-style laboratory for Boston-based Avco's Research and Advanced Development division, which Avco showcased in its corporate promotions, but somehow it has never looked entirely comfortable in a chilly old New England mill town.[6]

Photographer Julius Shulman immortalized Pereira's aerospace modernism, just as he did the residential architecture of Richard Neutra, Pierre Koenig, Rudolph Schindler, and other masters of California modernism.[7] People who might otherwise shrug at Atlas (the missile program) immediately recognized Shulman's famous photograph of a couple ascending to the stars on Pereira's spiral ramp in Convair Astronautics' lobby. Through Shulman's lens, Aeronutronic looked nearly identical to Pereira's CBS Television City, or to Pereira's private Hollywood residence, for that matter. Was it mere coincidence that Spacely Space Sprockets, Inc. combined the spiral ramp of Convair Astronautics with the circular design of General Atomic? Where else would aspiring George Jetsons want to work?

Convair Astronautics

Atlas put Convair into the space business and San Diego into the space race. What began in 1946 as a modest feasibility study ramped up in the mid-1950s into a program with the highest national priority. Convair became a prime contractor for America's first intercontinental ballistic missile (ICBM), with stakes, and costs, to match the Manhattan Project.[8] As the self-proclaimed "Air Capital of the West," San Diego had been a significant center for aircraft manufacturing since the 1920s, though always a distant second to greater Los Angeles.[9] Ryan Aeronautical first mass-produced monoplanes there, and custom-built the *Spirit of St. Louis* for Charles Lindbergh's historic flight at its San Diego factory. Consolidated Aircraft (later Convair) moved to San Diego from Buffalo in 1935. During the war it churned out B-24 bombers. Later, as a division of defense giant General Dynamics, it manufactured F-102 fighters at its Lindbergh Field factory.[10] An ICBM capable of delivering a nuclear warhead 5,000 miles with unprecedented accuracy presented an entirely new set of engineering challenges—in materials, structures, propulsion, and guidance and control. Convair, on the strength of its innovative design—gimbaled engines in place of vanes and fins, multi-stage engines, a separable nose cone, and a pressure-stabilized fuel tank (a "stainless steel balloon")— won the Air Force contract for the Atlas vehicle. Other firms would supply the rocket engines, the guidance systems, and the nose cones, but Convair had responsibility for final assembly and testing.[11]

Convair's job, then, would be turning its promising prototype into a reliable weapon under the most demanding of deadlines. That meant taking a handpicked initial platoon of a few dozen scientists and engineers led by structural engineer Karel Bossart and building it into a well-drilled army of 20,000-plus, able to manufacture and deploy a dozen missiles a month. At the head of that army would be James Dempsey, who left the fast track in the Air Force missile command to join Convair's fledgling missile program. Just a couple years later, though only in his mid-thirties, Dempsey found himself in charge of the entire Astronautics division. For the Air Force and its contractors alike, missiles would be a young man's game. As one early recruit recalled: "Astro was a heady place to work. And it offered great opportunity for entry-level engineers. You could be cramming for college finals in April and working on the nation's highest priority missile in June—under a supervisor who had yet to hit age 30."[12] For a company trying to hire 1,000 scientists and engineers a month, 85 percent of them from out of state, image could be everything.[13]

Convair sought a corporate personality to match its space-age ambitions. John Jay Hopkins, founding chairman of defense giant General Dynamics, added Convair in 1954 to his diversified portfolio of companies that would include Electric Boat (nuclear-powered submarines), Stromberg-Carlson (electronics and communication), Liquid Carbonic (rocket fuels), Canadair (fighter aircraft), and General Atomic (nuclear reactors), a one-stop shop for the armed services. As Hopkins explained, "We are groups which are moving swiftly in the fields of hydro-dynamics, aerodynamics and nuclear dynamics, as such might appropriately be called, as a corporate unit, 'Dynamics for Defense.'"[14] To provide a collective brand for such a wide-ranging set of companies, Hopkins hired graphic artist Erik Nitsche and put him in charge of a corporate advertising and identity campaign as comprehensive and bold as Eliot Noyes's contemporary program for Thomas Watson Jr. and IBM.[15] Nitsche famously designed a series of six posters in six different languages for the Atoms for Peace conference in Geneva in 1955, showcasing General Dynamics' contributions to science and engineering, though deliberately downplaying its defense contracts. Later dubbed "Atomic Style," Nitsche's posters, annual reports, and his magisterial corporate history, *Dynamic America*, are considered graphic-design classics.[16] The original posters now decorate the General Dynamics headquarters in Falls Church, Virginia.[17] Pereira would provide the architectural counterpoint to Nitsche's graphics, as complementary and exemplary models of total design.

With the Atlas construction contract in hand, Convair had to gear up to actually build it. Its engineers began designing the jigs and fixtures in its old aircraft plant near the San Diego airport. Simultaneously, the company began scouting out possible sites for the dedicated missile plant the Air Force insisted upon. With good reason, the leaders of the American missile program—such as Gen. Bernard Schriever, head of the Western Development Division—as well as their corporate counterparts believed that new weapons systems like the ICBM required independence from the older generation of "fly-boys" with a vested interest in conventional aircraft.[18] To that end, Lockheed relocated its Missiles and Space division from Southern California all the way north to Sunnyvale, in the heart of what would become Silicon Valley.[19] Convair, with a less centralized corporate culture, did not think it needed quite that much distance but did stake out a new site for a self-contained missile facility on 250 acres at Kearny Mesa, ten miles northeast of its airport plants, sufficiently isolated for security, and close to Air Force test sites in remote Sycamore Canyon.[20]

Pereira, of course, had no experience designing a missile laboratory. Who did? He had earned his degree in architecture from the University of Illinois and spent a decade learning his profession with the legendary Chicago firm of Holabird & Root. He moved to Hollywood during the war, working as an architect and art director for Paramount, and winning an Oscar for special effects. He then joined the USC faculty. In 1951, he invited former classmate Charles Luckman to join him in founding their own firm, Pereira & Luckman. Pereira brought to the partnership the architectural imagination while Luckman, a trained architect but a born salesman, brought in the clients.[21] Dubbed the "boy wonder" of American business for his advertising savvy by no less than *Time* magazine, Luckman had become president of Lever Brothers before he turned forty, only to lose his job in 1950 when he could not keep pace with arch-rival Proctor and Gamble. Like few other executives, Luckman understood architecture as advertising and image-making. After all, he had commissioned Lever House, the first modernist corporate headquarters in New York City, by Gordon Bunshaft.[22]

No one could custom-tailor a corporate suit like Pereira & Luckman. Their design for CBS Television City put them on the architectural A-list and anticipated the same challenges they would face at Convair Astronautics. Like Convair, CBS was seeking a distinct identity for a promising but unproven division, where new ideas could flourish without interference from executives who had come up through the ranks of the older movie industry. Luckman recognized an enormous emerging market in airport design, especially for the Air Force, and the firm subsequently won commissions for master plans for Edwards, Nellis, Patrick, and other Air Force bases. That experience, along with designing the Navy Electronics Laboratory in San Diego, undoubtedly gave Pereira & Luckman the inside track in the architectural competition for Convair Astronautics.[23]

Pereira's master plan for Convair included twin rectangular office blocks for administration and engineering, joined by a common reception and lobby area. A low-slung laboratory complex, dubbed "the waffle" for its interwoven geometry of courtyards and open-air passageways, stretched out behind the administrative buildings. Adjoining the laboratories on one side was the factory building, with its forty-five-foot-high bay for fabrication and assembly, and on the other a separate laboratory building for electronics, the nerve system of the ICBM design (fig. 2).[24] Pereira placed static-test stands and other auxiliary buildings at a safe distance from the main structures. The total cost for the Astronautics plant, including $10 million worth of special tool and test facilities paid for by the Air Force, would come to some $40 million.[25]

Pereira appreciated the importance of the dramatic statement and lavished attention on the office blocks and the central lobby. He borrowed the basic design for the six-story office blocks from a recently completed community-hospital project in nearby La Mesa. Accented with alternating horizontal bands of black-and-white spandrels, the structures still cut a striking figure from the street. The real star was the lobby, an artificial island set atop a reflecting pool (which doubled as an emergency water reservoir) on the crest of the mesa. Walking in from the immense parking lot, visitors crossed a gleaming causeway toward a blue-tiled façade emblazoned with the logos of each General Dynamics division. Turning right, they then entered the reception area with its stunning signature staircase rising out of the pool below. Suspended from the ceiling by stainless steel rods and anchored by spokes to a hub just above the

Figure 2. Aerial view of Convair Astronautics, with the administration buildings flanking the lobby, the engineering laboratory "waffle" directly behind it, and the assembly building, with the gray roof, to the left. Note the splendid isolation of Kearny Mesa in the late 1950s and the immensity of parking lots. Courtesy of the San Diego Air & Space Museum.

water's surface, the aluminum ramp made two-and-a-half turns before reaching the executive suite and conference room on the second floor (fig. 3). Assembling it turned out to be something of a Chinese puzzle for Convair's construction crew, who managed at the last minute to pull it together before dedication day. One of them remembered "standing in the lobby when the doors were opened—by the guards—and here was a crowd of people, all surging into the lobby, running, literally running, to be the first to go up on that ramp."[26]

Pereira spent the money where it had the most impact, up front, though the cost of that lobby nearly broke the budget. The ramp was for sheer theatrics, though none of the generals or defense contractors walking up to meet Dempsey and his top executives could have failed to be impressed by it. Many recalled that it had a slightly unnerving sway. Before ascending, visitors could wait in comfort on the ground floor, basking in an atrium worthy of the Romans, though with a model of the Atlas

Figure 3. Interior of the Convair Astronautics lobby, showcasing Pereira's signature suspended ramp. Missile making was clearly men's work. Courtesy of the San Diego Air & Space Museum.

on the wall to remind them of its modern aspirations to "Pax Atomica." An elegant oriental garden that might have seemed out of place at almost any other factory seemed right at home in Pereira's space-age palazzo (fig. 4). To give the place more of a university than an industrial feel, Pereira specified plenty of landscaping, though because of the rush to complete the facility on time, most of the plants were still in their pots on opening day. Not missing a trick, company photographers, with an eye on snow-belt recruiting, strategically placed the "tiny trees so that it would look like the classic Southern California scene of buildings amid palm trees."[27]

The laboratories and high-bay fabrication and assembly areas could not measure up to the lobby for pure panache, in part because they had to meet some of the most exacting standards ever demanded in American manufacturing. Kearny Mesa was as much laboratory as factory, as the relative space allotted to administration, engineering, and production suggests. Of the 1.2 million total square feet of space in the facility, about half (579,000 square feet) went for manufacturing, while labora-

Figure 4. The Convair Astronautics lobby, with its Japanese garden and reflecting pool. The serene setting belied the serious business of creating the "ultimate weapon." © J. Paul Getty Trust. Used with permission. Julius Shulman Photography Archive, Research Library at the Getty Research Institute (2004.R.10).

tories (292,000 square feet) and engineering (117,000) accounted for most of the rest (fig. 5).[28] Just 1,600 of the plant's 20,000 employees manned the production line, with the lion's share of the rest engaged in research, engineering, and testing.[29] Like most laboratories, Convair Astronautics' primary product turned out to be paper. As one executive astutely observed, "The product of this plant is not hardware, it's knowledge," the essential template for future progress.[30] Building 5, the manufacturing facility, included not only the precise jigs and welding machines needed to fabricate the sheer stainless-steel bodies for the Atlas, but also some of the first "ultra-clean rooms" ever built, to handle intricate rocket assembly, with production by workers dressed in surgical garb to prevent contamination. With their paper-thin skins, the Atlas bodies—ten feet in diameter and seventy-six feet long—required delicate handling during metal forming, welding (with 150,000 individual welds for each missile), and fitting out, until pressurizing the fuel tanks finally gave them strength.

Figure 5. Ordinary engineering offices at Convair Astronautics hardly matched the glamour of the lobby. The "waffle" can be glimpsed below and to the right, with the high-bay building just beyond. Courtesy of the San Diego Air & Space Museum.

Gus Grissom's laconic speech, "Do good work," delivered during a visit to see the Atlas missile that would carry the Mercury astronauts into space, resonated strongly in this place on the cutting edge of high tech.[31] That slogan, along with blue *R*s, for reliability, could be seen everywhere in the plant, as a reminder of Convair's all-consuming goal.

With its Astro cafeteria and its Missile Park, an employee recreation area that included a Little League baseball field and, as the centerpiece, an actual Atlas, Convair Astronautics epitomized space-age California. The U.S. Information Agency even shot its publicity film *Architects of Space* there, featuring the Astronautics plant, products, and people.[32] Hans Friedrich, one-time protégé of Wernher von Braun who had come to Convair Astronautics as head of its dynamics group, put it this way in his pitch to prospective scientists and engineers: "As a graduate engineer or scientist with an aptitude for creative thinking, your future is with CONVAIR ASTRONAUTICS. Here you will associate with the leaders in this advanced field—work in our new $40,000,000 facility. You will see and feel the kind of achievement that means personal progress. And you will

Figure 6. Frederic de Hoffmann (far right) and Edward
Creutz (center) check out an architectural model of
General Atomic. Courtesy of General Atomics.

enjoy living at its best in beautiful, smog-free San Diego. For your future's sake, write today."[33]

Many did. For a decade, Atlas carried the American space race on
its shoulders, until the Minuteman, a newer generation of missiles, replaced it. Convair Astronautics later manufactured Centaur (as an upper
stage for Atlas) and the Tomahawk cruise missile, but Atlas would be
its defining achievement. For Pereira, too, Convair Astronautics would
be a defining commission, as sleek as the missiles it manufactured, built
on a scale to match the mission. Martin Marietta (later Lockheed Martin) bought Convair Astronautics in the 1990s and moved what remained to its Titan plant in Colorado, giving Denver a strong claim as
"America's Rocket Factory." But nothing there evoked the age quite like
Pereira's complex.[34]

General Atomic

Pereira made an even bolder architectural statement with his master plan
for General Atomic (fig. 6). Having already designed a space-age laboratory for one division of General Dynamics, Pereira was the obvious
choice as the architect for another. General Dynamics chairman John Jay
Hopkins considered space and atomic energy the emerging markets of
the future, and backed his commitment with cash, earmarking $20 mil-
lion for Convair Astronautics and $10 million in start-up funds to make
General Atomic a world-class center for the study of nuclear power.[35]

On the personal advice of Edward Teller, Hopkins hired Frederic de Hoffmann to organize and staff General Atomic. De Hoffmann, along with so many of the brightest physicists of his generation, had spent the war at Los Alamos. After completing his doctorate at Harvard, he returned to Los Alamos as Teller's assistant on the hydrogen bomb project, responsible for some of the trickier numerical computations. But it was nuclear power—the quest "to bring the sun down to the earth," as he often put it—that truly captivated de Hoffmann.[36] With his inside contacts at Los Alamos and the Atomic Energy Commission, de Hoffmann already knew virtually everyone in the field worth knowing, and now he had the money to make them offers they could hardly refuse. Hoping to recapture some of the magic of Los Alamos, de Hoffmann recruited heavily among its veterans. He lined up an all-star team of advisers, including Hans Bethe, Richard Courant, Frederick Seitz, and Teller. For laboratory director he brought in Edward Creutz, a group leader at Los Alamos who had worked on nuclear fuel-element design and had gone on to head the physics department at the Carnegie Institute of Technology (now Carnegie Mellon University) and build its synchrocyclotron.[37] Together they would put together one of the biggest and best physics departments in the country, a worthy rival (and potential partner) for any university or government laboratory.

Casting about for where they should locate their new laboratory, de Hoffmann and Creutz agreed that it should have a campus flavor, evoking an ideal research university, the kind without students and without pressure to bring in outside grants. They also thought close connections with the faculty of an established university could complement the General Atomic staff. Given General Dynamics' heavy investment in Convair Astronautics, San Diego might have seemed an obvious choice, except that it lacked a university of distinction. De Hoffmann and Creutz seriously considered other sites, including one in Massachusetts, where access to MIT and Harvard would be an important draw. An alternative strategy, the one they ultimately chose, was to create their own university, or better yet, convince the University of California to do it for them.[38] The city of San Diego proved to be the perfect ally for General Dynamics in this quest. The city was bullish on defense economics and had the political will and resources to push hard for a new University of California campus.[39]

General Atomic, like Convair Astronautics, faced dual challenges, needing not only to hire enough good scientists and engineers, but also to provide them with the advanced training they required. John Jay Hopkins himself pointed out that "our Convair Division has been laboring for a number of years under the serious handicap in our recruitment of engineers because we could not offer our engineers that opportunity of furthering their education by taking graduate courses in their chosen fields."[40] As a stopgap measure, Convair set up extensive in-house classes for subjects of particular priority, and 650 employees enrolled even before the new plant was completed. Nearly as many Convair employees took courses through UCLA's local extension program, even though they could not generally earn advanced degrees that way. Internal surveys suggested that hundreds more would sign up for graduate courses if they were offered. With the proportion of Convair scientists and engineers holding advanced degrees already at 20 percent and rising, having a strong university nearby seemed essential.[41] General Atomic set its sights even higher, since it would have to hire, train, and retain so many PhDs, more than any firm of its size.

Roger Revelle, director at the Scripps Institution of Oceanography in La Jolla, had long nurtured ambitions for a prestigious university in San Diego. Scripps had for years been running a small graduate program. Given appropriate resources, Revelle believed he could expand that program into a "publicly supported Cal Tech," organized around research institutes rather than conventional departments and geared to the current and future economic demands of the San Diego region.[42] Caltech seemed the ideal model, a selective institution of relatively small size, unsurpassed academic reputation, and powerful economic clout. The city of San Diego likewise recognized what a campus comparable to the University of California campuses at Santa Barbara and Riverside, both recent additions to the system, could mean for the region. To bolster its case with the University of California system, the city sent reporters from the local newspaper to Pasadena and Palo Alto to interview university and corporate officials about the importance of Caltech and Stanford in high-tech regional development. Even a short visit turned up a long list of the right kind of companies, many more in Los Angeles than in Santa Clara County. This is surprising only in light of the subsequent growth of Silicon Valley. In 1955, the Stanford Industrial Park was only a few years old and silicon transistors just a laboratory curiosity, while the already-sprawling Southern California aerospace industry had been drawing on Caltech and other local universities for decades. Still, no one could later argue that Revelle's conclusion had been inaccurate: "I have no doubt that a careful study would show that the influence of the basic research and teaching in the sciences at Cal Tech and Stanford has had in many subtle ways a profound influence on numerous other industrial developments in the Los Angeles and San Francisco areas."[43]

San Diego learned a great deal from these areas' experiences. A blue-ribbon San Diego Citizen's Committee, including John Jay Hopkins, Edward Creutz, and the director of the Navy Electronics Laboratory, met with the University of California regents in Los Angeles to discuss the proposed university. When the University of California subsequently sent a faculty delegation, whose members included Nobel laureates E. O. Lawrence and Glenn Seaborg, for a site visit to San Diego, the chamber of commerce had top executives from San Diego's high-tech companies ready to meet and greet them at the El Cortez Hotel's Poolview Dining Room.[44] As a final incentive, Hopkins pledged $1 million in corporate funds to underwrite a proposed "Institute for Pure and Applied Physics" and "Institute of Mechanics," but only if the University of California actually got the new La Jolla campus up and running.[45] Chancellor Robert Sproul and the regents took the deal, sweetened even more by General Atomic's offer to provide selected staff as free, part-time faculty. Sproul told Revelle he considered the General Atomic offer "indispensable" to putting the new university on sound financial footing.[46] Beyond the purely financial incentives, General Atomic offered the university an instant credibility no amount of money could buy. Creutz and de Hoffmann had been recruiting heavily and successfully in all fields of the physical sciences. Potentially, "they are a gold mine of information about the people, their abilities, attitudes and availability, which we could exploit, particularly with respect to the appointment of the highly important pace-setting leaders," one of Revelle's lieutenants reported after a visit to de Hoffmann. "If means could be devised by which Creutz could represent us as well as General Atomic, he would be armed with a double-barreled appeal in his frequent approach to prospects."[47]

Never shy about promoting pet projects, de Hoffmann told San Diego's city manager that General Atomic needed at least one hundred acres of prime real estate with adequate utilities for nuclear research, and access to housing that was also "convenient to cultural and civic activities." The essential premise of General Atomic, as de Hoffmann explained it, was "to create a laboratory which will effectively enable these senior men to delve into basic science, give some of their time to defense problems, and also to train others. This will be accomplished by attempting to set up a research laboratory that will bridge the gap between the universities and traditional industrial laboratories." General Atomic would not only become an outstanding research center, de Hoffman assured the city, but a good neighbor. "It is important to the Corporation that the physical surroundings of such a laboratory be in the nature of a university-type campus, and certainly not of an industrial appearance," he wrote. "Therefore, the buildings, research and development facilities and landscaping on such a site will enhance the community."[48] The university and its industrial supporters understood just how significant location and impression could be in recruiting the highest caliber scientists and engineers in the face of stiff competition from other regions. The city had what General Atomic and the University of California both craved, the perfect parcel of real estate. San Diego's voters, with strong encouragement from their political leaders, overwhelmingly passed propositions donating 320 acres of land on Torrey Pines for the General Atomic laboratory[49] (the company paid for utility connections and site improvements) and an adjacent 500 acres to the south for the new university.[50] The two campuses now had the best public land San Diego had to offer, especially the wooded bluffs of Torrey Pines overlooking pristine beaches and the Pacific Ocean.

In planning General Atomic, Pereira had to breathe life into de Hoffmann and Creutz's vision of a corporate version of a national laboratory, with the look and feel of a university and the financial and engineering resources to turn ideas into practical products. What its namesake, General Electric (GE), had done for an earlier era, General Atomic would do for the nuclear age. Back in the 1930s, GE's research laboratory had been dubbed "The House of Magic." Its brashly confident successor aspired to nothing less. As much competitor as role model in the field of nuclear energy, GE had a ten-year head start on General Atomic, thanks to a government contract with its Knolls Atomic Power Laboratory. Voorhees Walker Foley & Smith, the architectural firm that had designed the world-famous Bell Laboratories in Murray Hill, New Jersey, in 1939, had completed a major addition to the "House of Magic" in 1952, essentially a miniature Bell Labs, a functional though hardly inspiring design of brick facades and endless corridors. To poach a number of key people from GE and Knolls, Creutz would entice them with a visionary future, and what better way to sell a vision than architecturally? The difference between the old-style eastern corporation and its upstart western rival could not have been any clearer than the contrast between GE's red-brick industrial "campus" and Pereira's space-age design for General Atomic.

Creutz dismissed Pereira's first draft as little more than conventional thinking with a nod to the San Diego climate. The concept drawing did look suspiciously like Convair Astronautics' waffle building set into a

Figure 7. A view of the General Atomic hub from the administration building. Note the spider-leg supports. The encircling laboratory ring had not yet been filled in. © J. Paul Getty Trust. Used with permission. Julius Shulman Photography Archive, Research Library at the Getty Research Institute (2004.R.10).

grove: low, lots of glass, outdoor patios and passageways, and to Creutz, entirely at odds with good laboratory design.[51] Based on his prior experience in universities and in national laboratories, Creutz firmly believed that "complicated new technologies must develop on an interdisciplinary basis." Traditional campuses, of the sort Pereira had in mind, only reinforced disciplinary isolation. Encouraging Pereira to think outside the box, Creutz proposed a "circular laboratory, with a central library, a health center . . . conference rooms, and a cafeteria. Then all the disciplines could be considered on an equal basis, so there would not be a physics building, a chemistry building, or engineering, or metallurgy, but a research and development laboratory."[52] Without fully realizing it, Creutz sought exactly the kind of laboratory that Voorhees Walker had designed for Bell Labs and GE—"a single building that retained most of the advantages of separate buildings but assured more intimate contact among departments and discouraged department 'ownership' of space"—only Creutz wanted it in avant-garde style.[53]

Back to the drawing board, Pereira produced a "hub and wheel laboratory ring" that looked more like a tethered space station than a corporate laboratory (fig. 7). At its center, rising on spider-leg supports from a circular plinth, was the hub, 135 feet in diameter, enclosing a marble-paved courtyard with a fountain, a touch of the Alhambra in modern San Diego. Its top floor housed the cafeteria and executive dining room, with an extensive technical library and document center on the main floor below.[54] No one's laboratory or office was ever more than a short walk away across the lawn from the library, an indispensable resource in those days. The main laboratory building nearly encircled the hub. On the inner perimeter, the offices would open onto the forecourt. The laboratories would be strung along the interior corridor of the ring, then drop off into a second, lower story on the outer perimeter, giving the scientists and engineers easy access to work spaces and to social spaces. Outside the hub and ring, Pereira placed separate buildings for administration and for engineering. With the same sky-blue spider-leg motif as the library and laboratories, these too looked like they had just touched down from the future. So that General Atomic could grow into its new space, Pereira initially constructed twin segments, which could later be built out to complete the three-quarters arc.

Pereira's guiding aesthetic for the General Atomic commission might be dubbed California country club. The laboratories themselves reflected Creutz's no-frills frugality: they were painted cinder block with plain tile floors. The landscaping and hardscaping, in contrast, especially around the detached administration building at the entrance to the ring, would have looked right at home at Torrey Pines Golf Course, which had opened in 1957 just west of the General Atomic campus. In place of Convair's classic reflecting pool, General Atomic got a meandering, tiled pond that ran the entire length of the administration building, with fieldstone walkways, lush plantings, and ring-shaped fountains (fig. 8). De Hoffmann appreciated eastern expectations about the California climate. Even before he had hired an architect, he brought in a dozen full-size potted olive trees to decorate General Atomic's temporary headquarters in a converted San Diego schoolhouse, later transplanting them to the General Atomic campus.[55] Decades before in-house recreational facilities became de rigueur at high-tech companies, General Atomic had its own tennis courts and outdoor swimming pool, though a noontime splash in an unheated pool would have been a bracing experience in the winter, even in sunny San Diego.

General Atomic's civilian projects got the press, but its defense contracts made the money. The TRIGA (Training, Research, Isotopes, General Atomic) reactor, designed by Los Alamos veteran Ted Taylor and consultant Freeman Dyson, found a large market as a small, "safe

Figure 8. Lavish landscaping gave General Atomic the country club look de Hoff-mann thought essential to recruiting the best scientists and engineers to San Diego. © J. Paul Getty Trust. Used with permission. Julius Shulman Photography Archive, Research Library at the Getty Research Institute (2004.R.10).

reactor" for universities and hospitals. With funding from a utilities con-sortium, General Atomic developed the HTGR (High Temperature Gas-Cooled Reactor), though it never could work out all the bugs before nuclear power plant orders collapsed. A group of Texas utility compa-nies put up $10 million for research on fusion reactors, but nothing com-mercial came out of that effort either. For pure audacity, it would be hard to match Project Orion, the hydrogen-bomb-powered spacecraft envisioned by Taylor and Dyson for a mission to Mars. As fascinating as these projects may have sounded, George Dyson points out that only Air Force and Advanced Research Projects Agency funding for ballistic-missile defense and other weapons studies kept General Atomic in the "black," financially and otherwise. To house the classified research, Gen-eral Atomic added the secure "H-building" at the rear of the complex (fig. 9).[56]

By all accounts, Pereira's design accomplished its objective, a one-of-a-kind laboratory for a one-of-a-kind company. Though small com-pared with Convair Astronautics—less than 600 total employees in its early years, growing to 1,350 by 1962—the reputation General Atomic earned as a think-tank was out of all proportion to its size. From the be-

Figure 9. Aerial view of General Atomic looking toward the Pacific, with the hub and ring clearly visible. The H-building for classified research is in the foreground, with the recreational facilities to its right. Courtesy of General Atomics.

ginning it had the highest percentage of PhD physicists of any corporate laboratory. In such fields as plasma and reactor physics, General Atomic ranked with the best departments of any size in the world. General Atomic never entirely made good on its $1 million pledge for the new university, but it did help the fledgling school attract some world-class recruits. Keith Brueckner, the founding head of the university physics department, and Harold Urey, its first Nobel laureate, had both been participants in early General Atomic summer-study programs, and a number of General Atomic's scientific staff accepted joint appointments with university departments.[57]

For those involved in planning UCSD, General Atomic stood out as a model of practical aesthetics.[58] Site visits to other campuses, including Yale, Brandeis, Berkeley, and UCLA, showed how easy it was to confine scientists and engineers in architectural "strait jackets."[59] The General Atomic campus, by contrast, combined admirable functionality with high style. Having seen some preliminary designs for the university labs, one geophysicist on the planning committee, speaking from experience, took the unorthodox view that "a steel factory building is cheap and convenient for a laboratory," with the right combination of light, ventilation, and flexibility. "General Atomics laboratories are derived from this pattern," he noted. "Its circular shape is distinctive and prevents the building from

Figure 10. Ford Aeronutronic in Newport Beach. The breezeway connects the lobby and reception building on the left, afloat on its own "island," with the computer and electronics laboratories to the right. © J. Paul Getty Trust. Used with permission. Julius Shulman Photography Archive, Research Library at the Getty Research Institute (2004.R.10).

stretching out ad infinitum. Even though it is a one-story building, I would like to propose that the inclusion of one such building in the master plan would relieve the architectural monotony of the one that is being considered."[60] Unfortunately, Pereira never got the chance to do a laboratory for UCSD, though he did design its central library, as exuberant an expression of "jet set modernism" as General Atomic itself.[61] Still, he had set a high standard for laboratory architecture in San Diego, a standard against which such later icons as the Salk Institute by Louis Kahn and the Neurosciences Institute by Tod Williams and Billie Tsien, just short walks from the General Atomic campus, would measure themselves.[62]

Aeronutronic and Autonetics

For Aeronutronic Systems, Pereira envisioned a corporate campus worthy of Mies van der Rohe, while giving the visual vocabulary Mies had perfected for his landmark Illinois Institute of Technology campus in Chicago in the late 1940s a distinctly Southern California accent (fig. 10).[63] Aeronutronic was actually a spin-off from Lockheed's missiles-and-space division, which Lockheed set up in 1954 to demonstrate to the military the company's commitment to aerospace. The division's general manager, retired Air Force general E. P. Quesada, believed the best way for Lockheed to reinvent itself for the space age would be to hire scientists, especially physicists, and set them free in an academic atmosphere. Quesada promised to run his division "more like a university than a hardheaded business," on the theory that "scientists function best when they know they can work without dictation and develop theories irrespective of military contracts. We hope that through our ability to be original we will be able to translate a military requirement into a military weapon." He recruited scientists and engineers who shared his conviction that modern military and industrial laboratories should be modeled on universities, and told them he would "encourage them to soak up academic atmosphere by letting them teach part-time at three nearby universities: Cal Tech, U.C.L.A. and U.S.C."[64] To give the new missile division some autonomy from Lockheed's powerful and largely antagonistic aircraft designers, including the legendary Clarence "Kelly" Johnson and his Skunk Works, Quesada insisted on a separate campus in Van Nuys. Nonetheless, Quesada's university-in-exile almost immediately found itself at odds with the rest of Lockheed's more traditional corporate culture. Quesada resigned under pressure in November 1955, followed a month later by fifteen of his top scientists, who formed their own company, initially Systems Research Group and subsequently Aeronutronic Systems.[65]

Ford acquired Aeronutronic in 1956 as its entrée into the increasingly lucrative aerospace market. Ford's place in history as prime mover of the second industrial revolution was unchallenged, but convincing young scientists and engineers that it was ready to lead the aerospace revolution would require a more futuristic identity. In 1958, Ford Aeronutronic leased a two-hundred-acre site for its Engineering and Research Center on a mesa overlooking Balboa Bay in Newport, then a sleepy resort town south of Los Angeles. It would be the first industrial lease granted on the sprawling Irvine Ranch. There Aeronutronic set up a research and development complex for its missiles-and-space business, beginning with a design study of missile nose-cone reentry for the Air Force. Aeronutronic chose Pereira as the architect for the site's master plan, which would include laboratories, a pilot plant, test facilities, a technical library, cafeteria, and administrative offices. What Aeronutronic had in mind was similar to Convair Astronautics, a self-contained, dedicated facility expected to cost about $20 million and ultimately employ some 4,000 scientists and engineers.[66] Pereira himself designed the computer and electronics building to house an Army contract for mobile electronic command centers.[67]

Aeronutronic's very name suggested something entirely new in aeronautics and electronics. And if its slogan—"where men set ideas in motion"—was not particularly inspiring, its architecture surely was. Pereira crafted a strikingly theatrical entrance, as he had done for Convair Astronautics. He set the lobby onto a rectangular concrete slab surrounded by a shallow moat. On one side, a concrete causeway connected the lobby to the parking lot, while on the other a handsome breezeway, partially enclosed with translucent glass panels, joined the lobby to the main computer and electronics building, sheathed in metal and glass, directly behind it. The lobby itself had the severity of Mies van der Rohe's best work, simply a glass box topped with a flat steel roof supported by rectangular steel columns along the outer edge of the concrete slab. By day, the lobby offered breathtaking views of the bay and beach below. At night, floodlights under the overhang gave the building a luminescent quality, as if it were floating on a still pool. Back home in Dearborn, Michigan, Ford's engineering research laboratory, designed by Albert Kahn back in the 1920s, had the kind of factory aesthetic that so captivated the early Bauhaus.[68] In stark contrast, Aeronutronic's architecture signaled a new and very different corporate culture.

Aeronutronic aimed literally for the Moon and the stars. It designed and built the Far Side sounding rocket, launched from high-altitude balloons and equipped to carry small scientific instruments into the exosphere to gather data on cosmic rays, electromagnetic radiation, and particle densities, and other essential information for future space flights. It developed robust, lightweight transmitters to send data back to Earth-based antennas. And it studied the propulsion, guidance, communication, and flight trajectories needed to put a satellite in lunar orbit.[69] The complex rapidly expanded to include additional laboratories, environmental test facilities, and a prototype manufacturing building—about one million square feet of space in all—to accommodate Aeronutronic's growing defense contracts for space and weapons systems, electronics and computers, and aerodynamics and propulsion. Scientists and engineers working in classified laboratories did not always get much of a view. For both security and safety, earthen embankments had to be placed around the rocket propellant laboratory.[70] Though Pereira himself designed only the electronics and computer building, his former associate Nicholas Boratynski joined Aeronutronic as director of planning. Boratynski laid out the rest of the research center, including a creative design for the weapons-system laboratory that wrapped the offices like a "skin" around the laboratory "spine," a linear variation on the General Atomic scheme intended "to emphasize [the] close relationship between experimental development and pure research."[71] In the heady days of the early space program, when the Moon seemed positively close and the near planets not so very far away, Aeronutronic even won a contract for designing a Manned Mars Excursion Module, with an optimistic anticipated launch date of 1975.[72]

Despite its early promise, Aeronutronic never fit all that comfortably into the Ford family. Struggling in the 1980s to stay competitive in its core car business, and justifiably wary of the boom-and-bust cycles of the aerospace industry, Ford finally sold Aeronutronic in 1990 to Loral, a defense electronics company. Significantly, the sale did not include the land in Newport Beach.[73] Loral relocated the remaining employees to its other plants, and Ford cashed in by demolishing Pereira's campus and redeveloping the property for five hundred single-family luxury homes, in a deal worth an estimated one hundred million dollars.[74]

Pereira too found Orange County real estate to be more profitable than aerospace. Shortly after completing the Aeronutronic commission, Pereira prepared a master plan for what would become the University of California, Irvine (UCI). At the heart of the largest undeveloped property in Southern California, nearly 100,000 acres, Pereira envisioned a "city of intellect" anchored by UCI but integrated with a planned community of high-tech industry, commercial and residential development, public schools, parks, and recreational areas.[75] Unlike at UCSD, here Pereira got the opportunity to design as well as plan much of the new university, including its first eight buildings. Sufficiently "California brutalist" in style to stand in for a future totalitarian state in the film *Conquest of the Planet of the Apes*, Pereira's buildings nonetheless formed the core of what would become, even given its relatively short history, a campus of unusual architectural distinction and diversity, with later contributions from Frank Gehry, Robert Venturi, and Robert Stern, among others.[76]

Pereira did not entirely abandon aerospace modernism after the early 1960s, but his later work could not match the best of his previous commissions. His Basic Science Laboratory for Lockheed's Rye Canyon Research and Development Center pretty much recycled what he had done for Avco and Aeronutronic years earlier. Still, the reflecting pools and open-air courts looked as lustrous as ever, the sightlines to the San Gabriel Mountains just as eye-catching. By placing the labs along a service spine, Pereira gave the design maximum flexibility. In a touch the scientists and engineers at Convair Astronautics would surely have appreciated, Pereira even provided individual air-conditioning and heating for the offices.[77] As at Aeronutronic, the Basic Science Laboratory became the signature building in a vast research and development complex, planned by Pereira and completed by lesser architects. Set on five hundred acres to allow for tight security, Rye Canyon provided facilities for the legendary Lockheed Skunk Works and was renamed in honor of its founder, Kelly Johnson, in 1983. Lockheed eventually sold the site to a real estate company planning to convert it into film-studio space, and moved the Skunk Works to Palmdale.[78] Buildings designed as anechoic chambers to foil electronic surveillance now serve as locations for fictional high tech espionage.[79] In a post–Cold War (and aging baby-boomer) world, Advanced Bionics, which manufactures cochlear implants, now seems a more promising tenant for the Rye Canyon Business Park than aerospace firms.

Ironically, but perhaps also somehow fittingly, Pereira's last, largest, and most visually arresting "aero" space—a million square feet within a single building—was obsolete before its owner could even take possession. Autonetics, a spin-off of North American Aviation specializing in missile guidance-and-control systems, commissioned the structure in the late 1960s in anticipation of landing a major defense contract. Here, on ninety-two acres in Laguna Niguel, in southern Orange County, Pereira abandoned the elegant glass boxes of high modernism for the pre-cast, textured concrete of neo-Babylonian brutalism. From the right angle, the seven-tiered stepped pyramid looked dignified if heavy-set. By recessing the windows beneath deep overhangs, Pereira broke the surface into alternate bands of light and shadow, and subdued the sun's glare (fig. 11).

Only from the parking lot did the sheer immensity of the building fully reveal itself. Whatever Pereira's intent, the design seemed the perfect metaphor for the Vietnam War–era bunker mentality of the military-industrial complex. The rock-lined dry moat reinforced the fortress motif, and concrete planters and benches did nothing to soften it. Pereira specified thousands of trees and scrubs in the original plan, though they looked like lonely sentinels in the vast parking lot, with its 6,200 spaces. Where General Atomic and Aeronutronic looked to open a window on a bright future, Autonetics hunkered down behind a façade as massive, forbidding, and unapproachable as the Maginot Line, and in the end, just as vulnerable. When the expected defense contract fell through, Autonetics found itself with the quintessential white elephant. The General Services Administration, undoubtedly under some political pressure, agreed to take the building, now owned by Rockwell International,

Figure 11. From the parking lot, the sheer scale of Autonetics in Laguna Niguel becomes apparent. Autonetics never got the chance to occupy its distinctive ziggurat, which its parent company traded to the General Services Administration. © J. Paul Getty Trust. Used with permission. Julius Shulman Photography Archive, Research Library at the Getty Research Institute (2004.R.10).

Autonetics' new parent company, in exchange for several government-held properties. Eventually the agency found the ideal tenants for such a structure, first the IRS and, later, Homeland Security.[80]

Pereira's Legacy

Critic Allan Temko once dismissed Pereira as "Hollywood's idea of an architect." Pereira's younger partner, Scott Johnson, considered that assessment an unintended tribute to just how convincingly Pereira had "tapped into the romanticized zeitgeist of his time."[81] Pereira's buildings certainly helped put some Hollywood-style glamour into the aerospace epoch. Perhaps only an architect with Pereira's passion for science fiction could have envisioned laboratories so perfectly attuned to their place and purpose. His "dream factories" gave Southern California aerospace an identity, both distinctive and memorable. Elsewhere—at Grumman on Long Island, Boeing in Seattle, McDonnell in St. Louis—aerospace never entirely transcended the blue-collar factory aesthetic inherited from the Second World War. Only in Southern California did the space-age style really come into its own as a unique expression of Cold War culture. To compare McDonnell's Engineering Campus—designed by St. Louis architect Harris Armstrong in 1955 in a high-modernist style of unfinished concrete, glass, and aluminum—with Pereira's best work from the same era is to appreciate Mies van der Rohe's epigram, "God is in the details."[82]

Aerospace executives of the 1950s, drawing on the lessons of "the physicists' war," saw the campus as the ideal model for research and development. They sought spaces alluring to scientists and engineers accustomed to academic life or national laboratories, spaces with literal and organizational distance from the distractions of corporate deadlines and bottom lines. Like their counterparts in so many other high-technology industries, they believed in basic science as the key to future innovation and hired unprecedented numbers of scientists, especially physicists, to staff their new laboratories. Whether in suburban New York or suburban Los Angeles, the corporate campus became a key feature of the postwar scientific landscape. Eero Saarinen designed the best in the East, for IBM and Bell Labs. Pereira designed the best in the West.[83]

Paradoxically, while high-tech industries were reinventing themselves on an academic model, universities were becoming increasingly corporate in both look and outlook. Charles Draper's Instrumentation Laboratory at MIT did much of its best work in inertial guidance out of a converted shoe-polish factory adjoining the main campus. MIT's Lincoln Laboratory, which designed the SAGE air-defense system, can only be described as industrial-strength architecture.[84] Even MIT, flush as it was with defense contracts, could not afford Saarinen except for a chapel and auditorium. No one at the time seemed to think high style had much to contribute to high tech, anyway. Pereira was a member of the USC architecture faculty for many years, developed its 1960 campus master plan, and designed a number of its new science buildings. All of them, in brick and pre-cast concrete, look far more corporate than any of his work at Aeronutronic or General Atomic.[85] UCI could hardly be distinguished from the clusters of corporate office parks surrounding it. Perhaps Pereira's attempt to integrate town and gown succeeded a little too well.

Aerospace modernism appealed as much to the military as to its defense contractors. Air Force officers, like their corporate counterparts (often former colonels and generals themselves), embraced modernist design as a sign of forward thinking. To distinguish itself as an independent, and progressive, branch of the armed services, the Air Force chose Skidmore, Owings & Merrill to design the Air Force Academy in Colorado Springs. (Pereira and Luckman made the shortlist in the architectural competition.) There, during the same years that Pereira was designing his corporate classics, Walter Netsch and his colleagues laid out a high-modernist campus that spoke for the Cold War era as expressively as West Point and Annapolis had done for older traditions of military education. Though they had been enlarged and extensively redesigned at the turn of the century, West Point, in its neo-gothic citadel, and Annapolis, in its Beaux-Arts bravura, took history as their inspiration. The Air Force Academy, by contrast, kept its focus firmly on the future in its space-age campus of steel, aluminum, and glass. Netsch's stunning chapel, dubbed "Air Age Gothic" for its soaring aluminum-clad tetrahedron frames, seemed all but poised for takeoff into the wild blue yonder. In place of the statues and memorials to past victories featured so prominently at the other service academies, the Air Force highlighted the present by showcasing a ballistic missile and supersonic jet fighter.[86] The Air Force Academy became, like Pereira's laboratories, the public face of an otherwise invisible empire.

Do Pereira's space-age classics have a future? A decade ago, Yale's School of Architecture organized a symposium, Saving Corporate Modernism, to draw attention to such endangered landmarks as Gordon Bunshaft's headquarters buildings for Connecticut General Life Insurance Company and the nearby Emhart Manufacturing Company. Cigna did reconsider its decision to demolish Connecticut General, although whatever heightened public awareness was created by the symposium was not enough to save Emhart from the wrecking ball. Pereira's unique Transamerica Pyramid alone would stand as an architectural legacy of distinction. Still, doesn't General Atomic, lone survivor of a masterful vision for an age and still standing at the half-century mark, deserve a place on the National Register of Historic Places? In a provocative essay on the challenges of preserving and interpreting the industrial heritage of Los Angeles, Matthew Roth asked, "Who Will Love the Alameda Corridor?"[87] What makes a place worth saving, he suggests, is not how good it looks but why it mattered. Pereira's space-age spaces certainly mattered, and how good they looked in all their functional glory was a bonus, then and now. They remind us how an industry, a region, and an era were defined by the science and engineering of seemingly limitless possibilities. They also remind us that nothing stays modern forever.

notes overleaf

NOTES

1   Thomas S. Hines, *Richard Neutra and the Search for Modern Architecture* (New York: Oxford University Press, 1982), is the standard biography. Ehrhard Bahr, *Weimar on the Pacific: German Exile Culture in Los Angeles and the Crisis of Modernism* (Berkeley: University of California Press, 2007), explains how Neutra adopted the modernist ideals of his native Austria to the distinctive culture of interwar and postwar Los Angeles.

2   *William Pereira*, ed. James Steele (Los Angeles: USC Guild Press, 2002), the only scholarly appraisal of Pereira, includes detailed studies of his projects for CBS Television City, the University of California, Irvine, and Los Angeles International Airport, among others. It credits the Theme Building to James Langenheim of the Pereira & Luckman office (205).

3   Megan Prelinger, *Another Science Fiction: Advertising the Space Race, 1957–1962* (New York: Blast Books, 2010), looks at the print advertisements designed for the same purpose and includes a reproduction of a Convair advertisement featuring the Kearny Mesa plant orbiting the Earth (158).

4   David Kaiser, "The Postwar Suburbanization of American Physics," *American Quarterly* 56 (2004): 851–88.

5   *Aviation Week* 69 (1 December 1958): 98.

6   Ibid., 66 (3 June 1957): 370.

7   Joseph Rosa, Julius Shulman, and Esther McCoy, *A Constructed View: The Architectural Photography of Julius Shulman* (New York: Rizzoli, 2008); and Michael Stern and Alan Hess, *Julius Shulman: Palm Springs* (New York: Rizzoli, 2009).

8   Chuck Walker, *Atlas: The Ultimate Weapon* (Burlington, Ont.: Apogee Books, 2005), details the program from beginning to end, drawing on extensive interviews of fellow participants. See also Bill Yenne, *Into the Sunset: The Convair Story* (Lyme, Conn.: Greenwich Publishing Group, 1995).

9   Mary L. Scott, *San Diego: Air Capital of the West* (Belmont, Calif.: Wadsworth Publishing, 2005).

10   Roger W. Lotchin, *Fortress California: From Warfare to Welfare* (New York: Oxford University Press, 1992), includes an excellent chapter on San Diego's military boosterism (297–318).

11   Richard Martin, "A Brief History of the Atlas Rocket Vehicle: The First Fifty Years" (January 2007), offers a first-hand account by one of the key structural engineers.

12   Tom Leech, "When Aerospace Was King," *San Diego Magazine*, December 1997, 98.

13   R. H. Biron to T. C. Holy, 21 February 1956, RSS 0003, box 1, folder 3, The Register of Office of the Chancellor, Campus Expansion Files, 1951–1964, University of California, San Diego [hereafter UCSD] Special Collections.

14   Quoted in Yenne, *Into the Sunset*, 53.

15   Gordon Bruce, *Eliot Noyes: A Pioneer of Design and Architecture in the Age of American Modernism* (New York: Phaidon Press, 2007), details the contributions of Noyes and his collaborators to IBM's corporate makeover.

16   *Dynamic America: A History of General Dynamics and its Predecessor Companies*, ed. John Niven, Courtlandt Candy, and Vernon Welsh (New York: Doubleday, 1960).

17   Steven Heller, "Erik Nitsche: The Reluctant Modernist," 2004, Typotheque website, http://www.typotheque.com/articles/erik_nitsche_the_reluctant_modernist.

18   Neil Sheehan, *A Fiery Peace in a Cold War: Bernard Schriever and the Ultimate Weapon* (Random House: New York, 2009), provides an excellent political history of the Atlas.

19   Erica Schoenberger, *The Cultural Crisis of the Firm* (Cambridge, Mass.: Blackwell Publishers, 1997), devotes a "case study" to Lockheed's struggle to fit the Missiles and Space division into its larger corporate structure (155–82).

20   Walker, *Atlas*, 84–85.

21   *William Pereira*, ed. Steele, concisely covers Pereira's early career.

22   Charles Luckman, in *Twice in a Lifetime: From Soap to Skyscrapers* (New York: Norton, 1988), offers his perspective.

23   Ibid., 289–303. Pereira and Luckman were partners from 1951 until 1958, when Pereira left to found his own firm.

24   "Plans for New Plant Include Spacious Factory Area and Office Buildings," *Convariety*, 11 July 1956, 1.

25   "Astronautics Plant Gears to Space Role," *Aviation Week* 69 (28 July 1958): 47.

26   Walker, *Atlas*, 85.

27   Leech, "When Aerospace Was King," 99.

28   "Astronautics Plant Gears to Space Role," 51.

29   Robert de Roos, *Perspective '64* (San Diego: General Dynamics, Astronautics, 1964), 10.

30   Yenne, *Into the Sunset*, 71.

31   Leech, "When Aerospace Was King," 100.

32   USIA distributed the film worldwide in five languages; "Convair's Astronautics Plant Stars in 'Architects of Space,'" *Convariety*, 15 October 1959, 8.

33   *Aviation Week* 66 (10 June 1957): 8.

34   Rebecca Cantwell and Joseph Verrengia, "Colorado: America's Rocket Factory," *Rocky Mountain News*, 26 May 1996, R1–R32.

35   Robert Sheehan, "General Dynamics vs. the USSR," *Fortune*, February 1959, 87ff., provides a good history of the company, with particular attention to its San Diego divisions.

36   George Dyson, *Project Orion: The True Story of the Atomic Spaceship* (New York: Henry Holt, 2002), 32–35. Though Dyson's focus is on Project Orion,

in which his father played a key role, he offers the best account of General Atomic's early history.

37 Douglas Fouquet, "A Report on General Atomic Division of General Dynamics" (internal publication), March 1962, 61.

38 Nancy Anderson, *An Improbable Venture: A History of the University of California, San Diego* (San Diego: UCSD Press, 1993), 37–65, details the often-convoluted political maneuvering behind the university's founding.

39 Lotchin, *Fortress California*, 314–15.

40 John Jay Hopkins to San Diego Chamber of Commerce, 29 September 1955, RSS 0003, box 1, folder 3, UCSD Special Collections.

41 R. H. Biron to T. C. Holy, 21 February 1956, ibid.

42 Ronald Rainger, "Constructing a Landscape for Postwar Science: Roger Revelle, the Scripps Institution, and the University of California, San Diego," *Minerva* 39 (2001): 327–52; Roger Revelle to T. C. Holy, 5 August 1955, RSS 0003, box 1, folder 3, UCSD Special Collections.

43 Arnold Klaus to T. C. Holy, 3 April 1956, RSS 0003, box 1, folder 4, and Roger Revelle to T. C. Holy, 5 April 1956, RSS 0003, box 1, folder 1, both UCSD Special Collections.

44 "List of Those Receiving Invitations to the Luncheon at the Poolview Dining Room at the El Cortez Hotel," RSS 0003, box 1, folder 4, UCSD Special Collections.

45 John Jay Hopkins to Robert G. Sproul, 1 March 1956, RSS 0003, box 1, folder 3, UCSD Special Collections.

46 Robert Sproul to Roger Revelle, 5 September 1956, RSS 0003, box 1, folder 1, UCSD Special Collections.

47 Charles Wheeler to Roger Revelle, 29 May 1957, ibid.

48 Frederic de Hoffmann to O. W. Campbell, 26 January 1956, RSS 0003, box 1, folder 3, UCSD Special Collections.

49 Dyson, *Project Orion*, 33.

50 "University of California, La Jolla Campus Expansion: History of Events to the Present," 10 July 1957, RSS 0003, box 1, folder 10, UCSD Special Collections.

51 *Convariety*, 3 May 1956, has an artist's conception of the General Atomic laboratory.

52 Edward Creutz, "The Origins and Some Accomplishments of General Atomic," 12 February 1997, 9 (unpublished, provided to the author by Creutz).

53 Oliver E. Buckley, "Reminiscences," 26, AT&T Archives 55–10–01–16, Warren, N.J.

54 Dyson, *Project Orion*, 99–103.

55 James Britton, "Corporation with Soul: General Dynamics and Its Offspring, General Atomic," *San Diego and Point Magazine*, June 1956, 23.

56 Dyson, *Project Orion*.

57 Anderson, *An Improbable Venture*, 70–71.

58   Patricia Aguilar, *The UCSD Master Plan and Its Antecedents: A History of Physical Planning at the University of California, San Diego* (San Diego: Regents of the University of California, 1995), provides the background on the original campus plan and its successors; available at the Digital Archives of UCSD Special Collections, http://libraries.ucsd.edu/speccoll/DigitalArchives/ucsdmasterplan/.

59   Charles Wheelock to Victor Vacquier, 13 November 1959, RSS 0003, box 2, folder 4, UCSD Special Collections.

60   Victor Vacquier to Charles Wheelock, 23 November 1959, ibid.

61   Jacob Schoenly, "The Geisel Library: Concrete Expressionism," JetSet Modern.com website, http://www.jetsetmodern.com/geisel.htm.

62   Nathaniel Coleman, *Utopias and Architecture* (New York: Routledge, 2005), instructively compares the Salk Institute and the Neurosciences Institute as architectural programs.

63   Werner Blaser, *Mies van der Rohe: IIT Campus, Illinois Institute of Technology* (Basel: Birkhauser, 2002).

64   Quoted in *Time*, 23 August 1954, 67.

65   Schoenberger, *The Cultural Crisis of the Firm*, details the "rebellion of the scientists" and its consequences for Lockheed (162–69).

66   "Master Plan Slated for Scientific Center," *Los Angeles Times*, 16 March 1958, 5F; "Missile Research Lab Completed at Newport," ibid., 15 June 1958, F16.

67   "Big New Computer and Electronics Unit Begun," ibid., 31 August 1959, E1.

68   Frederico Bucci, *Albert Kahn: Architect of Ford* (Princeton, N.J.: Princeton University Press, 1993).

69   Irving Stone, "Ford Subsidiary Speeds Space Study," *Aviation Week* 68 (6 January 1958): 51–56.

70   "Additional Projects for $20 Million Plant Slated," *Los Angeles Times*, 19 April 1959, F1; "Missile Research Lab Completed at Newport," F16.

71   Stone, "Ford Subsidiary Speeds Space Study," 56.

72   Harold Watkins, "Vehicle Study for Extended Mars Mission," *Aviation Week and Space Technology* 80 (20 April 1964): 54–69.

73   "Ford Sells Aerospace Division to Loral: Keeps Newport Land," *Orange County Business Journal*, 30 July 1990.

74   John O'Dell, "Ford Plans Homes at Newport Plant Site," *Los Angeles Times*, 13 August 1993.

75   Ray Watson, "Irvine Ranch Master Plan," in *William Pereira*, ed. Steele, 108–39, covers the UCI history from a participant's perspective.

76   Rachel Sandoval, with Anne Mar and Spencer C. Olin, "Under Construction Indefinitely: Forty Years of Designing UCI," in *Designing UCI: A Symposium and Exhibit Celebrating Forty Years of Innovation*, ed. Jackie M. Dooley, UC Irvine Libraries Exhibition Catalog 19 (Irvine: The UC Irvine Libraries, 2005), catalog of an exhibit at UC Irvine Langson Library, November 2005– April 2006, curated by Rachel Sandoval. "William Pereira," Anteater Chronicles:

The UC Irvine Story, 2005, UCI Libraries website, http://www.lib.uci.edu/ucihistory/index.php?page=architecture&function=pereira.

77   "Science on a Central Court," *Architectural Record* 136 (July 1964): 173.

78   Dave McNary, "Lockheed Site May Become Studio," *Daily News*, 17 February 1998, B11.

79   "Rye Canyon Office Park," Land Use Database, The Center for Land Use Interpretation website, http://ludb.clui.org/ex/i/CA6082.

80   GSA provides a careful history of one of its signature buildings, now named in honor of California Congressman Chet Holifield: "Chet Holifield Federal Building, Laguna Niguel, CA," Historic Buildings Database, U.S. General Services Administration website, http://www.gsa.gov/portal/ext/html/site/hb/method/post/category/25431.

81   Scott Johnson, "William Pereira," *Los Angeles Forum for Architecture and Urban Design* 7 (7 January 2010), http://www.laforum.org/content/online-articles/william-pereira-by-scott-johnson.

82   "Engineering Campus by Harris Armstrong, Architect, for McDonnell Aircraft Corporation," *Arts and Architecture* 76 (March 1959): 18–19.

83   Stuart W. Leslie and Scott G. Knowles, "'Industrial Versailles': Eero Saarinen's Corporate Campuses for GM, IBM, and AT&T," *Isis* 92 (2001): 1–33.

84   Thomas P. Hughes, *Rescuing Prometheus* (New York: Random House, 1998), includes a chapter on Lincoln Laboratory and SAGE, and a photograph of the laboratory complex from the 1950s.

85   *William Pereira*, ed. Steele, 90–107.

86   *Modernism at Mid-Century: The Architecture of the United States Air Force Academy*, ed. Robert Bruegmann (Chicago: University of Chicago Press, 1994), and Robert Allen Nauman, *On the Wings of Modernism: The United States Air Force Academy* (Urbana: University of Illinois Press, 2004), comprehensively describe its conception, construction, and self-conscious symbolism.

87   Matthew W. Roth, "IA and the 20th Century City: Who Will Love the Alameda Corridor?" *IA: The Journal of the Society for Industrial Archaeology* 26 (2000): 71–84.

PETER J. WESTWICK

AEROSPACE AND HOLLYWOOD: HOW COMPUTER
ANIMATION WENT FROM SPACE TO CINEPLEX

W hat do people think about when they think of Southern California? Hollywood is probably high on the list, with beaches
and freeways close on its heels. Aerospace may not top the
list, but it should. Aerospace was the dominant industry in Southern California for much of the twentieth century; only after the end of the Cold
War did Hollywood pass aerospace as the main employer in the region.
What did it mean to have these two major industries, aerospace and entertainment, in such proximity? At first glance they seem to have little in
common: one appears technological, the other creative; one the child of
government demand, the other of commercial appeal. But the two share
an intertwined history, one that shaped Southern California—and the
rest of our world—in surprising ways.

Movie-making and aerospace grew up together in Los Angeles starting in the 1910s, and both industries reached national and even global
dominance by midcentury. The contact between these two global industries in and around the area produced sparks from the beginning. Flying
fascinated early Hollywood filmmakers, who went on to make many
movies about brash young pilots; Marilyn Monroe got her start working
in an aircraft factory; and Howard Hughes embodied a still more obvious overlap between aviation and Hollywood.[1] The connections extended
beyond the industries' abstract parallels—as "dream factories" devoted
to realizing whatever could be imagined, populated with technophiles,
futurists, and entrepreneurs—to the specific technologies that brought
those dreams to life. The connection between the technologies of motion
pictures and those of aircraft- and spacecraft-building may not seem obvious, but their little-known interaction in the field of computer animation turned out to be vastly influential. One cannot set foot in a cineplex
these days without experiencing CGI, or computer-generated images.
Most moviegoers or gamers are unaware that many CGI techniques were

invented by makers of spacecraft, not movies. Though Hollywood takes the lead today on high-tech CGI developments, the initial inspiration flowed in the other direction, from aerospace to entertainment.

JPL and Hollywood

The Jet Propulsion Laboratory in Pasadena is an offshoot of Caltech supported by NASA. JPL is not an aerospace corporation, but it is certainly part of Southern California's space enterprise. It emerged out of Caltech—which had developed as a center for aeronautical engineering in the 1920s, with close ties to local aircraft firms—and it was formally incorporated during World War II for work on jet-assisted takeoff for airplanes and, later, rocket engines and spacecraft. In addition to its connections to aviation and space, JPL had links to show business from its earliest days. Two of the lab's founders, Frank Malina and Jack Parsons, tried to sell a script about their rocket group to MGM to raise money for research, and Parsons later lost his life in an explosion while working on pyrotechnic special effects for Hollywood.[2] It took a while, but JPL would find better ways to provide special effects for the film industry.

Hollywood has a periodic fascination with space exploration, often inspired by recent developments in aerospace. One such vogue dates to the late 1970s, when the first *Star Trek* movie featured a mysterious, nearly sentient object known as V'Ger—a knowing nod to the Voyager spacecraft built by JPL. In the late 1990s, the discovery of a Martian meteorite with possible life forms, the impact of the Shoemaker-Levy 9 comet on Jupiter, and the landing of *Mars Pathfinder* were followed by such blockbusters as *Deep Impact* and *Armageddon*, which featured meteors on a collision course with Earth, and *Mission to Mars* and *Red Planet*, in which humans encounter mysterious life forms on Mars, not to mention several installments of the *Star Wars* saga. This "merging of entertainment and realities," as JPL's executive council called it, at times even obscured the origin of some ideas. A proposal to fire a 500-kilogram projectile into comet Tempel 1 and observe the resultant crater was dubbed Deep Impact, and JPL's project manager had to explain that the mission's name had been selected prior to the release of the movie.[3]

The Origins of Animation

More substantial connections between JPL and the movie business developed through the lab's technical program. In the late 1970s, a few JPL programmers were working on simple wireframe animations to simulate spacecraft trajectories. The lab's Bob Holzman then created a computer-

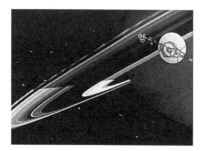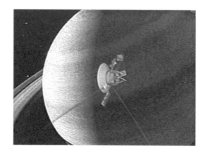

Screenshots from James Blinn's animations simulating the Voyager spacecraft flights past Saturn. Courtesy NASA/JPL-Caltech.

graphics group and invested in a powerful computer system to run graphics programs. At the time, the Voyager spacecraft were on their way to the outer planets, and Charley Kohlhase, a Voyager mission designer, was looking for more complex renderings. He heard about a young programmer from the University of Utah named James Blinn, who had just come to Caltech to work with computer guru Ivan Sutherland, himself recently relocated from Utah. The Utah graphics program had flourished after receiving funding from the Defense Advanced Research Projects Agency (DARPA) to design flight simulators. Blinn had finished his PhD in computer science in 1978 and was making a name as an up-and-comer in computer graphics. JPL hired him into the computer-graphics group, and he went to work generating three-dimensional animations to simulate the Voyager flights past Jupiter and Saturn, using data from Kohlhase and the mission design team. The results surpassed expectations. The clips took the viewer on a ride behind the Voyager craft, swooping past the planets and their rings and moons against the backdrop of interstellar space. Television news editors and viewers loved them, and the clips became a staple of the celebratory news coverage of the Voyager flights.[4]

Audiences today, jaded by years of CGI wizardry in movies and video games, may not appreciate the technical advance that Blinn's animation represented. For example, he pioneered a technique called bump mapping for adding craters and other surface features digitally to the smooth spheres of planets and moons. His method adjusted those features' appearance from frame to frame as the viewing perspective changed, allowed them to rotate with the planet or moon at the correct speed, and also showed the terminator—the line of shadow—gradually moving across the sphere. Though the spacecraft itself was a simpler collection of polygons, modeling its movements—such as the rotation of the camera on its extended arm—required another complex algorithm called hierarchical forward kinematics articulation.[5]

Blinn was a stickler for detail, to the point of calculating the correct location of the planets and the six thousand brightest stars in the background of each frame. And he did all this from scratch; he could not turn to off-the-shelf software packages for algorithms, so he coded it himself. Blinn's colleagues regarded him with something bordering on awe. Sutherland, himself no slouch, said at the time, "There are only a dozen great people in computer graphics, and Jim Blinn is six of them."[6]

There is a reason why these developments in computer animation happened at JPL instead of Hollywood. The Blinn sequences required mind-boggling computations, first in plain celestial mechanics to get the objects and light in the right place, then in the algorithms to render the objects as three-dimensional, textured color images. A three-minute clip had over four thousand frames, each one needing all of these calculations. At the time, the main places with the computing power to run such programs were government labs and universities. Blinn made the Voyager movies on JPL's PDP-11/55 computer, at the time probably the highest performing of the PDP-11 line from Digital Equipment Corporation (DEC) and also what he had used at Utah.[7] Blinn said of this hardware, "Someday artists and graphic designers may be able to own a system like this, but right now the $300,000 price tag is a bit high."[8] In addition to getting their numbers through the processing bottleneck, programmers had to wait for many minutes for their screens to refresh with each new image, even with the most advanced frame buffers. In order to create a moving picture, they then had to take a picture of the screen with a camera and string the images together on film. Because of these hardware requirements, Blinn did not think his programs would be widely useful; only a couple other places in the world had the hardware needed to run them.[9]

Blinn showed what was possible, and this inspired commercial firms to invest in computers to pursue these techniques themselves. Even so, some graphics houses hesitated to take the hardware plunge. For example, the firm Digital Productions raised eyebrows throughout the industry when it splurged on a Cray supercomputer in the early 1980s, and the expense did indeed drive the company out of business.[10] The computing bottlenecks began easing a few years later. The emergence of affordable graphics workstations and then the increasing power of personal computers, the development of faster monitors, and the incorporation of video cards into motherboards—all allowed smaller graphics firms to run their programs in-house.[11]

Blinn soon found an even broader audience for his techniques. In between the Voyager encounters in 1979 and 1981, he made contact with Carl Sagan, who was beginning work on his *Cosmos* television series for PBS. Sagan, who had many connections at JPL, heard about Blinn, and PBS hired him to provide special graphics sequences. One sequence showed a single-celled organism evolving into a fish, then a frog, through a dinosaur to a mammal and, finally, a woman—an early example of morphing techniques later used in the film *Terminator 2* (1991) and the music video for Michael Jackson's "Black and White" (1992). Another sequence simulated a DNA double helix twisting and turning as it replicated. The complex DNA sequences required an hour of computer calculations per frame, and since the filmmakers lacked access to computing power on that scale, JPL let Blinn use the lab's computers to crunch the numbers.[12]

Cosmos aired in 1980 and reached—not quite "billions and billions"— but about half a billion viewers worldwide. Together with the Voyager animations, it brought Blinn's techniques to a wide audience. Hollywood took note. JPL's proximity came in handy, since people from the movie business could just drop by the lab to see Blinn's codes in action. Soon he was giving a steady stream of demonstrations to high-end producers, lower-level animators, and special-effects people—from *Star Trek*'s Gene Roddenberry to Ward Kimball, one of Disney's "Nine Old Men." Blinn himself started getting attention from the movie business, and in 1980 he accepted an offer to help George Lucas establish a special-effects studio for the first *Star Wars* sequels. At the Lucas studio, Blinn joined forces with Ed Catmull, another Utah grad, and Alvy Ray Smith—or rather, rejoined them, since Catmull and Smith had stopped off at JPL on their way to Skywalker Ranch and worked briefly with Blinn on the *Cosmos* sequences. Blinn worked part time at Lucasfilm for about a year, spending two days a week at JPL, but he missed the real space business and returned to JPL full time to produce the Voyager Saturn sequences; he especially wanted a chance to show Voyager crossing Saturn's rings.[13]

Blinn continued to influence work at Lucasfilm despite his departure. Smith's team soon developed a video clip that persuaded George Lucas of the potential of computer graphics. The so-called Genesis shot for *Star Trek II: The Wrath of Khan* showed the view from a spacecraft flying past a dead, moon-like planet that is then transformed by a fiery cataclysm into an Earth-like environment. The shot has had a substantial effect on the graphics community and is viewed as a landmark in the business. In creating it, Smith declared, he "was still under the influence of Blinn's *Voyager* flybys of the planets at the Jet Propulsion Laboratory." Blinn, after all, had just finished working with the group, and his planetary flyby sequences had accustomed viewers to the perspective from a spacecraft.[14] Catmull and Smith went on to cofound Pixar, where their efforts on *Toy Story* and other computer-animated features would win them Academy Awards and further popularize computer graphics in film; today Catmull is the president of Pixar Animation Studios and Walt Disney Animation Studios.

Blinn's influence was thus inspirational as well as direct and technical. He did not cash in himself by setting up his own business or licensing software. Instead, he published his techniques in a series of seminal articles covering bump mapping, light reflection, the rendering of clouds and dusty surfaces, and blobby modeling (also known as "Blinn's blobs," a technique he developed for the *Cosmos* DNA sequence that enabled later effects like the dinosaurs in *Jurassic Park*). His disinterest in commercial possibilities reflected his own priorities, especially his commitment to working for the space program, and also his sense, at least at the outset, that few places could afford the sophisticated hardware needed to run his programs.[15]

Blinn's free dissemination of his algorithms and ideas was also characteristic of the computing community of the 1970s, which heaped scorn on a twenty-year-old Bill Gates for criticizing the free sharing of software; the computer counterculture itself reflected a characteristic California influence.[16] SIGGRAPH, the computer graphics society, manifested this communal, countercultural ethos, one reinforced by the academic background of many its members. Blinn was a star attraction at the annual SIGGRAPH meetings: his talks would have been popular even without the ingenuity of his ideas or his generosity in sharing them, since he delivered them with a lively, comic wit, and had a striking physical presence, with his six-foot-five frame, long beard, and ponytail.[17]

The communal SIGGRAPH ethic that Blinn exemplified changed in the 1980s, as graphics firms sprang up to serve Hollywood's growing interest, and a more proprietary attitude emerged in the graphics community. Commercial firms began happily packaging Blinn's techniques in software sold to movie studios, as their managers freely admit.[18] Several of these firms, not surprisingly, sprang up in Southern California, including Wavefront Technologies, Information International, Inc., and Digital Productions, whose founders, Gary Demos and John Whitney, were from Caltech. Graphics programmers today recognize Blinn's influence every time they use the "Blinn" button in Maya, the popular software for three-dimensional animation behind most CGI-driven feature films.

Blinn taught not only at Caltech, which he and Alan Barr and Jim Kajiya had made into a hotbed for new techniques, but also at Art Center College of Design, where his courses included an intensive introduction to computer graphics for a contingent from Disney's animation studios. SIGGRAPH members continued to look forward to learning about Blinn's latest techniques, which he developed in the 1980s for two popular series of educational videos, *The Mechanical Universe* and *Project Mathematics!* Blinn left JPL around 1987, staying at Caltech for a few years but eventually joining Microsoft (and hence rejoining Alvy Ray Smith) as a graphics fellow.[19]

A parallel but separate path for the influence of aerospace on Hollywood emerged in JPL's Image Processing Laboratory during roughly the same period. In the early 1960s, JPL engineers had pioneered the use of digital image processing, first to clean up pictures returned from the Ranger missions to the Moon and, later, to adjust other planetary spacecraft images. The first techniques corrected distortion and removed signal noise, such as a particular frequency superimposed on an image by vibration of the camera, and they grew to encompass algorithms for contrast enhancement, cartographic projection, motion compensation, and so on—in short, many of the techniques now available through such photo-editing programs as Adobe Photoshop.[20] By the mid-1970s, JPL had perhaps the most advanced image-processing capability in the country.

Although Blinn was not part of the Image Processing group, his computer animations for Voyager and *Cosmos* used similar techniques, such as reconstructing viewing geometries and surface reflectance. Like Blinn, the image processing effort depended on the advanced computing capabilities at JPL.[21] It had also produced its own motion pictures by combining still photos, such as those from the Ranger and Mariner spacecraft. Around the time of Blinn's work on Voyager, Kevin Hussey was doing some crude three-dimensional animation for atmospheric scientists, including a model of smog distribution in the Los Angeles Basin. Hussey heard about Blinn's work and approached him for help, but had no money to hire him. So Hussey used in-house code written by Michael Kobrick in the Image Processing Laboratory and tweaked by a young programmer named Bob Mortensen. The result, in 1987, was *L.A. the Movie*, which used topographic data from the Landsat satellite program to simulate a three-dimensional view from an aircraft swooping through the Los Angeles Basin.[22]

By that time, Hussey's group had grown from two to fourteen and had formally organized as the Digital Image Animation Laboratory (DIAL), alongside and overlapping the original Image Processing Laboratory. DIAL intersected Hollywood through its work on digital color correction, starting with a CBS program on the *Mona Lisa* and then working on old *Star Trek* backgrounds. The group helped William Shatner with a shot that zoomed from the galaxy down to Yosemite Valley for *Star Trek V: The Final Frontier* (1989), and it digitally erased telephone wires from the Egyptian skyline for *Raiders of the Lost Ark* (1981). It also did some work morphing images for Whitney/Demos Productions, a commercial graphics firm created by the former heads of Digital Productions, using a technique created to produce a continuous animation of ocean circulation from satellite images taken twelve hours apart. Movie producers again beat a path to JPL for demonstrations of VICAR (Video Image Communication and Retrieval) and other JPL digital-processing software.[23] In the 1990s, Disney would hire away Hussey and several others from DIAL to help build its own digital animation studio.

By then, Hollywood was committing vastly greater resources to computer animation, and the increasing availability of computing power had nourished a proliferation of graphics firms. Trying to keep up, DIAL turned to funding outside NASA, and by the 1990s, IMAX was its biggest sponsor.[24] But Hollywood was already outstripping JPL's capabilities, and influence began to run mostly in the opposite direction, from Hollywood to JPL. It is not a coincidence that in 1995, the entertainment industry passed aerospace as the main employer in California. A *Business Week* cover story in 1994, "The Entertainment Economy," declared that "the entertainment industry is now the driving force for new technology, as defense used to be."[25] In the 1920s Douglas rented a vacant movie studio to build airplanes; now the movie studios were leasing abandoned aircraft factories.

For the last several years, programmers from Hollywood studios have been coming to JPL, bringing with them the latest techniques, including those from video games. JPL is applying these not only in its outreach efforts—for instance, to create online games for kids related to planetary exploration—but also to help mission managers visualize what their spacecraft are doing in space, by transforming raw telemetry into real-time animations.[26] This return flow from Hollywood to JPL has closed the loop connecting aerospace to show business, and popular interest to technical capability.

Conclusion

In 2007 the Entertainment Economy Institute published a study on Hollywood's benefits to other local industries; the report highlighted the flow of animation talent from movie studios to local businesses, including aerospace.[27] The study failed to note that thirty years earlier, the initial stream ran the other way, from aerospace to Hollywood. Blinn's work at JPL in particular inspired the flowering of CGI in movies in two ways: first, by showing *what* could be done, with images that inspired movie studios to try a new approach; and second, by showing *how* to do it, publishing the algorithms that could then be taken up by studio animators.

These developments invite an analogy to the creation of the Internet, which was created by DARPA long before the dot-com craze of the 1990s.[28] DARPA also funded Utah's graphics program for flight simulation, the very program that launched Jim Blinn's career. DARPA also underwrote the development of early ray-tracing techniques by a company called MAGI (Mathematical Applications Group, Inc.) to model nuclear radiation effects for the military. New York–based MAGI, along with Information International, Inc. in Culver City, later developed graphics for the pioneering movie *Tron*, which Hollywood has recently revisited in a sequel capitalizing on CGI. For both computer graphics and the Internet, the government created a new technology and demonstrated its possibilities, and then the private sector adopted it and ran with it. The government's early role is not surprising, given the substantial long-term investment in computing capability required and the uncertain returns.

This investment flowed disproportionately to Southern California, given the substantial defense economy there. Then geographical proximity aided the transfer of ideas, techniques, and people from one industrial sector to the other. The intersection of aerospace and Hollywood made Southern California a unique incubator for computer graphics. The regional aerospace presence may have dwindled (though it has not disappeared), but it has left a substantial legacy in the thriving field of CGI, which literally and figuratively animates so many of Hollywood's current products. If Hollywood is a dream factory, it was the talent and resources of the aerospace industry that supplied some of the parts.

NOTES

Citations to material from the JPL archives follow the form: (JPL collection number, box/folder). All interviews are by the author unless otherwise noted.

1   Shawna Kelly, *Aviators in Early Hollywood* (Charleston, S.C.: Arcadia Publishing, 2008); George J. Marrett, *Howard Hughes: Aviator* (Annapolis, Md.: Naval Institute Press, 2004).

2   George Pendle, *Strange Angel: The Otherworldly Life of Rocket Scientist John Whiteside Parsons* (New York: Harcourt, 2005); Mike Davis, *City of Quartz: Excavating the Future in Los Angeles* (New York: Verso, 1990), 54–62.

3   Gael Squibb, notes on JPL Executive Council retreat, 11 March 1999 (JPL 259, 64/758); James Graf quoted in Matthew Fordahl, "Deep Impact," AP newswire, 9 July 1999; Andrew Murr and Jeff Giles, "The Red Planet Takes a Bow," *Newsweek* (6 December 1999), 61.

4   Charley Kohlhase interview, 2 July 2002; James Blinn interview, 20 July 2007.

5   Kohlhase interview; Blinn interview; Zareh Gorjian interview, 28 June 2007.

6   Natalie Angier, "It Was Love at First Byte," *Discover*, March 1981.

7   James F. Blinn, "The Jupiter and Saturn Fly-By Animations," 1980, http://www2.jpl.nasa.gov/saturn/anim4.html. *Tron* (1982) was created on a PDP-10 known as the Super Foonly F-1, the fastest version of that computer, owned by Information International, Inc. (Triple-I) in Culver City. There is a connection here, too, to JPL: one *Tron* character was a Solar Sailor, and JPL at the time had a popular proposal known as the "Solar Sail" spacecraft; it was to visit Halley's comet, powered by solar radiation pressure.

8   Angier, "First Byte."

9   Blinn interview.

10   John Grower interview, 17 July 2007; Blinn interview.

11   Grower interview; William B. Green interview, 12 February 2002; Gorjian interview, 28 June 2007.

12   Angier, "First Byte." On the use of JPL computers, see C. Kohlhase to F. J. Colella and W. E. Porter, 18 August 1978 (JPL 142, 24/417).

13   Blinn interview; Angier, "First Byte"; David Salisbury, "Computer Art Takes Off into Space," *Christian Science Monitor*, 20 July 1979.

14   Angier, "First Byte"; Salisbury, "Computer Art"; Alvy Ray Smith, "George Lucas Discovers Computer Graphics," *IEEE Annals of the History of Computing* 20, no. 2 (1998): 48–49, and "The Genesis Demo: Instant Evolution with Computer Graphics," *American Cinematographer* 63, no. 10 (October 1982): 1038–39, 1048–50. On the effect of the "Genesis" shot, see Grower interview and Blinn interview. Blinn, Smith, and Kajiya all later worked for Microsoft.

15   Blinn, "Texture and Reflection in Computer Generated Images," *Communications for the Association of Computer Machinery* (*CACM*) 19, no. 10 (October 1976): 542–47; "Models of Light Reflection for Computer Synthesized Pictures," *SIGGRAPH 77* (1977): 192–98; "Simulation of Wrinkled Surfaces," *SIGGRAPH 78* (1978): 286–92; "A Generalization of Algebraic Surface Drawing" [on blobby modeling], *ACM Transactions on Graphics* 1, no. 3 (July 1982): 235–56; "Light Reflection Functions for the Simulation of Clouds and Dusty Surfaces," *SIGGRAPH 82* (1982): 21–29; Blinn interview. On "Blinn's blobs," see Grower interview.

16   Paul Ceruzzi, *A History of Modern Computing* (Cambridge, Mass.: MIT Press, 1998), 235–36; Martin Campbell-Kelly and William Aspray, *Computer: A History of the Information Machine* (New York: Basic Books, 1996), 243. On California and computing, see Fred Turner, *From Counterculture to Cyberculture: Stewart Brand, the Whole Earth Network, and the Rise of Digital Utopianism* (Chicago: University of Chicago Press, 2006).

17   Grower interview.

18   Ibid.

19   Kohlhase interview.

20   Caltech/JPL Conference on Image Processing Technology, *Proceedings*, 3–5 November 1976 (JPL SP-43–30).

21   Green interview. On shared techniques, see Kenneth R. Castleman, *Digital Image Processing* (Englewood Cliffs, N.J.: Prentice-Hall, 1979), 371–77.

22   Kevin Hussey, phone interview, 11 September 2006; Green interview; Kevin Hussey, Bob Mortensen, and Jeff Hall, *L.A. the Movie*, 1987 (JPL audiovisual collection).

23   Hussey interview. For the history of Whitney/Demos, see Gary Demos, "My Personal History in the Early Explorations of Computer Graphics," *Visual Computer* 21, no. 12 (2005): 961–78.

24   James A. Evans memo, "The Reimbursable Program," 28 February 1995 (JPL 259, 50/553).

25   Michael J. Mandel and Mark Landler, "The Entertainment Economy," *Business Week* 14 March 1994, 60.

26   Gorjian interview; Hussey interview.

27   Richard Verrier, "Animators Expanding Their Lines of Work," *Los Angeles Times*, 7 May 2007. For example, the Department of Defense funds USC's Institute for Creative Technologies in order to apply computer graphics and virtual-reality techniques from video games to military training and simulation.

28   DARPA was initially known as the Advanced Research Projects Agency, or ARPA.

FROM L5 TO X PRIZE:
CALIFORNIA'S ALTERNATIVE SPACE MOVEMENT

On an early June morning in 2004, an odd-looking jet aircraft took off from an airstrip in the Southern California desert. Attached to the underside of its red-and-white fuselage was another craft. When the pair reached an altitude of 47,000 feet, the smaller vehicle dropped away. A few seconds later, its pilot Michael W. Melvill ignited a single rocket motor and blasted upwards. After climbing to 328,000 feet, Melvill experienced three minutes of weightlessness before he glided *SpaceShipOne* back to Earth. He landed in front of an enthusiastic throng of some 10,000 witnesses. One spectator held up a sign that read "*SpaceShipOne / GovernmentZero.*"[1]

Melvill's twenty-four-minute flight officially made him an astronaut, a status that NASA gives to someone who has flown higher than fifty miles. More importantly, the flight of *SpaceShipOne* marked the first time that a human reached space in a privately funded and developed craft. Melvill repeated the feat two more times in the fall of 2004, making his third flight forty-seven years to the day after the Soviet Union launched *Sputnik 1*. Following the successful 4 October 2004 flight, *SpaceShipOne's* builder, maverick aircraft designer Burt Rutan, and its patron, Microsoft billionaire Paul Allen, claimed the Ansari X Prize. This was a $10 million purse offered by the Los Angeles–based X Prize Foundation for the first private team to build and launch a spacecraft capable of carrying three people 100 kilometers above the Earth's surface twice within two weeks. Rutan and Allen later donated *SpaceShipOne* to the Smithsonian Institution. Today, it is displayed alongside Lindbergh's *Spirit of St. Louis*, Chuck Yeager's X-1, and spacecraft from NASA's golden era of manned missions in the 1960s in the dramatic entrance hall of the National Air and Space Museum.

The successful flights of *SpaceShipOne* drew international attention to the small town of Mojave, California, home to the Mojave Air and

Space Port and located near Edwards Air Force Base. News reports and aerospace industry articles depicted Mojave as the epicenter of a growing national movement. Since the flight of *SpaceShipOne*, several other NewSpace companies have opened facilities in Mojave. "Innovation is what we do here," boasted Rutan, "because there's not much else to do in Mojave."[2] Known variously as "NewSpace," "alt-space," and "Space 2.0," this group of pro-space and pro-technology enthusiasts, builders, and entrepreneurs aim to privatize space-flight and space-launch activities and, in the process, show that they can do it better and more cheaply than NASA. The "new" and the "alt" in their monikers refer to a new way of doing and thinking about aerospace with practices and principles expressed in opposition to the more traditional styles of NASA and the world's giant aerospace firms.

In some important ways, the attitudes of the NewSpace community resemble another California business culture, that of Silicon Valley and its much-critiqued "California Ideology."[3] This is not surprising—several major players in the private space business first made their fortunes in computer- and Internet-based businesses. In addition to Microsoft cofounder Paul Allen, Elon Musk (cofounder of PayPal) and Jeff Bezos (founder of Amazon.com) started private space firms. In 2002, for instance, Musk launched Space Exploration Technologies Corporation (known as SpaceX), a California-based company that hopes to make regular trips to outer space with its series of Falcon rockets. The NewSpace movement, therefore, straddles the classic California divide between Northern California (Silicon Valley) and Southern California (the aerospace industry).

The roots of the NewSpace movement, however, predate the "dot-com" era by at least two decades. Its history includes the visionary ideas for space settlements and manufacturing that emerged in the early 1970s (which, in turn, were influenced by science-fiction writers like Robert Heinlein), California's counterculture, the grassroots pro-space movement that emerged in the late 1970s, and the promotion of space commercialization by the Reagan administration through the mid-1980s. All of this, of course, must be placed in the context of Southern California's long-standing position at the leading edge of aerospace research, development, and manufacturing; the presence of several NASA centers in the state; and deep cultural and ideological trends in California.

This essay discusses the activities of some of the main actors—people, companies, and institutions—active in the early years of the pro-space movement. My goal is to show how their ideas and activities coalesced in

California and helped form the basis of today's NewSpace movement. In addition, I explore the question of whether the history of other technological regions such as Silicon Valley offer analogies that provide a better understanding of today's NewSpace companies in Southern California.

Dreaming of the High Frontier

For decades, fiction writers and scientists harbored dreams of space-based utopian settlements that might provide the basis for new societies.[4] These futuristic ideas went hand in hand with the schemes for human settlements at the frozen poles or on the ocean floor that proliferated in the early 1960s. They also reflected the tide of optimistic "our-future-in-space" books that filled bookstore shelves after Yuri Gagarin and Alan Shepard rocketed into orbit in 1961.

However, where previous visionaries offered only speculative descriptions of their utopias, Princeton physicist Gerard O'Neill used precise mathematical calculations and informed extrapolations of existing technological trends to develop detailed prototype designs for space settlements. Trained as a high-energy physicist, O'Neill divided his time between Princeton University and California, where he spent months at a time engaged in large-scale experiments at the Stanford Linear Accelerator Center. An instrumentalist in a culture that ruthlessly separated machine builders from experimentalists and theoreticians, O'Neill felt at home in the midst of big engineering projects.[5] O'Neill was also an avid science-fiction fan, especially enjoying works like Robert Heinlein's *The Moon is a Harsh Mistress*. Libertarian-minded pundits have long viewed Heinlein as a "true bard of Southern California" with his "peculiar and unprecedented combination of rocket visions, a tough-minded individualism respectful of the military and iconoclastic free living."[6] O'Neill's later advocacy for privately funded space exploration reflected many of Heinlein's political and social ideals.

Looking for a new career path in the mid-1960s, O'Neill, a lifelong airplane enthusiast, tried to join NASA's scientist-astronaut program. When this did not pan out, O'Neill turned his interest in space in new directions. Believing that the "days of blind trust in science and in progress were past," O'Neill urged his undergraduate physics students to focus on problems relevant to the environment and "the amelioration of the human condition."[7] In the fall of 1969, O'Neill offered a weekly seminar for his best students. To get them thinking about science in a more holistic fashion, he posed a thought experiment by asking: "Is the surface of a planet the right place for an expanding technological civilization?"

For decades, most science-fiction writers and space visionaries had imagined that human expansion into space would happen through settlements on the surface of other planets. However, as O'Neill discussed with his students, getting people and materials off the surface of a planet like Mars, like leaving Earth, would require a lot of energy simply to overcome gravity. Compared with building settlements on another planet, O'Neill thought it made much more sense from an engineering and economic perspective to build them in space.

O'Neill's basic design involved long metal cylinders, rotating to create gravity, which held soil, water, and an atmosphere. Initially, a few hundred people would be boosted into orbit where they would assemble prefabricated living quarters and subsist on dehydrated food. At the same time, several hundred more people would be stationed on the Moon. There, they would begin mining the raw materials needed to build the actual colony. Studies from the Apollo flights showed that the lunar soil was an abundant source of metals like titanium and aluminum, along with silicon that could also be processed to form glass. O'Neill imagined that oxygen from lunar material could be combined with hydrogen brought from Earth to create water. Hypothetical space settlers could construct their long-term habitation by processing lunar materials using solar-powered equipment and shooting it out to a construction site using an electromagnetic catapult that O'Neill helped design called a "mass driver."[8]

O'Neill envisioned self-contained worlds, microcosms of larger earthbound systems. What matured over time were detailed designs for a self-enclosed ecological system that, once built and functioning properly, would be maintained through established engineering and cybernetic feedback principles. It is telling that O'Neill's space settlements as he described them are reminiscent of communities and climates on the West Coast. One image from a NASA study O'Neill helped lead showed a "landscape" strikingly similar to San Francisco, complete with an impressive bridge spanning a brilliant blue bay.[9]

When compared to the scale and cost of the era's other mega-projects, O'Neill's vision and price estimates were not wildly out of line. Apollo had cost about $25 billion, while the space shuttle and the Trans-Alaska Pipeline were each predicted to cost at least $6 to $8 billion. Even more extravagant were Nixon-era plans for achieving national energy self-sufficiency ("Project Independence"), which analysts predicted could cost some $500 billion. O'Neill estimated (using several optimistic assumptions including NASA's own cost projections) that the initial cost for building the first space colony would be in the neighborhood of $30 billion. With a construction time of six or seven years, O'Neill projected the first space settlements might be occupied by the late 1980s. After drawing down the national purse to explore and study the Moon, O'Neill argued it was "now time to cash in on Apollo."[10]

"L5 in '95"

O'Neill's plan for settlements and factories in space, with all its utopian aspects, can best be understood as an amalgam of engineer-like conceptualizations coupled with decades-old ideas about technology, society, and how together they produced modern America. O'Neill's essential vision spoke to long-standing beliefs shared by many Americans about progress, the ability of technology to solve social problems, and the perceived need to seek new frontiers. These were blended with O'Neill's fondness for large-scale engineering and systems thinking and infused with a certain "counterculture libertarianism" and pragmatic environmentalism—a combination that defied easy explanation, confusing some of his critics.[11] But what really sparked public and media interest in O'Neill's ideas was his description of space not as a government-run *program*, but as a *place*. This critical shift in perspective, envisioning space as a home for potential habitation and manufacturing—what O'Neill later called the "humanization of space"—was essential in motivating the first wave of people excited by his technological optimism.[12] It also helped lay the foundation for the NewSpace movement.

Over the next five years, O'Neill refined his concept and presented it at campuses throughout California. Seeking to expand his audience and knowledge base, O'Neill brought a small group of people together in May 1974 for an inaugural meeting on "space manufacturing facilities." The Bay Area–based Point Foundation, started by counterculture icon Stewart Brand (who had lobbied NASA to take a photograph of the whole Earth from space a decade earlier), provided the initial funding for the meeting. This marked the start of Brand's interest in space colonies as a technological and social concept.[13] The *New York Times* put the meeting on its front page and media coverage of O'Neill's idea blossomed in mainstream newspapers and magazines.[14] That same year, *Physics Today* ran a lengthy article by O'Neill that summarized the technical details of his plan.[15] The next summer, Stanford University and NASA's Ames Research Center hosted O'Neill and other scientists, engineers, and students while they conducted a broader study "of how people might permanently sustain life in space on a large scale."[16]

Many of the images and ideas that O'Neill and his followers chose reflected a sensitivity for ecological issues and social diversity blended with a high-tech, megasystems-oriented approach. A considerable amount of this attention came from small fringe groups in California. Berkeley, for instance, was home to The Network, a small group that promoted the spacy ideas of Timothy Leary. After his release from jail on drug charges in 1976, Leary began to advocate a trippy new agenda that he termed SMI^{2}LE, an acronym for "Space Migration, Intelligence Increase, Life Extension." Leary described his ideas in books, articles, and even a comic book.[17] To be fair, Leary's interpretation was far from O'Neill's own ideas and the physicist was careful to distance himself from them.

Nonetheless, thousands of university students and other young adults, many with ties to or interest in the Bay Area's counterculture, were thrilled by the idea that someday they might live in space. In 1975, for example, Keith Henson and Carolyn Meinel, two O'Neill devotees, started the L5 Society in Tucson, Arizona. Previously, they had been vocal opponents of the Vietnam War and supporters of the women's movement. The name Henson and Meinel chose for their group came from O'Neill's proposal to put a space colony at one of the Lagrangian points where gravitational forces are balanced so that objects there remain in relatively stable positions.[18]

L5's membership was relatively small, never more than 10,000 people or so. But it was a vocal group—at times argumentative and prone to internal disagreements—with a strong California-based membership bolstered by local chapters in the Bay Area, San Diego, and Los Angeles. "L5 in '95" was an unofficial slogan the group adopted to express its determination to settle space and end their group with a mass disbanding in orbit. A song—"Home on Lagrange"—composed by two L5 members provides a humorous look at their vision:

> Oh, give me a locus where the gravitons focus
> Where the three-body problem is solved,
> Where the microwaves play down at three degrees K,
> And the cold virus never evolved.
> CHORUS: Home, home on LaGrange,
> Where the space debris always collects,
> We possess, so it seems, two of Man's greatest dreams:
> Solar power and zero-gee sex.
> We eat algae pie, our vacuum is high,
> Our ball bearings are perfectly round.

Our horizon is curved, our warheads are MIRVed,
And a kilogram weighs half a pound.
(chorus)
If we run out of space for our burgeoning race
No more Lebensraum left for the Mensch
When we're ready to start, we can take Mars apart,
If we just find a big enough wrench.
(chorus)
I'm sick of this place, it's just McDonald's in space,
And living up here is a bore.
Tell the shiggies, "Don't cry," they can kiss me goodbye
'Cause I'm moving next week to L4!'[19]

L5 members were not shy about getting involved in the political process. During L5's eleven-year existence, its members debated a range of space-related topics, including lunar mining, space colonies, missions to Mars, and the Strategic Defense Initiative. The group played a role, for instance, in preventing U.S. Senate ratification of the Moon Treaty in 1980. The United Nations' agreement declared that "the moon and its natural resources are the common heritage of mankind" and claimed that "neither the surface nor the subsurface of the moon, nor any part thereof or natural resources in place, shall become property of any State, international intergovernmental or non-governmental organization, national organization or non-governmental entity or of any natural person."[20] These phrases struck some private space-development enthusiasts as possibly preventing opportunities for private space manufacturing and settlement. One result of L5's mobilization to oppose the treaty was the establishment of a national telephone network that could be used to alert members about issues like cuts to NASA missions. L5 members disagreed about the value of the space agency; some supported it while others thought it would derail or delay plans for expanded space activity without Uncle Sam's involvement.[21]

When the L5 Society first formed in 1975, its members had a diverse set of interests. A good deal of attention in its first few years, judging from its monthly newsletters, was given to spreading O'Neill's ideas as well as countering some of the "doomsday" talk found in widely read books such as *The Population Bomb* and *Limits to Growth*. Energy-related ideas and news figured prominently, as did reports on NASA's long-range plans. The space shuttle, then under development, was of considerable interest, as were plans, endorsed by O'Neill, to develop ways to beam solar power back to Earth from orbiting satellites. In this sense, 1970s-era concerns for energy independence, enthusiasm for solar power, and the pro-space agenda converged. The pro-space community also reflected a sense of counterculture utopian ideals, as fringe figures like Lyndon LaRouche and Barbara Marx Hubbard endorsed a renewed space program.[22]

Stewart Brand sparked broader discussion about space settlements and the pro-space agenda. In the mid-1970s, Brand's new magazine, entitled *CoEvolution Quarterly*, published several long articles and contentious opinion pieces about O'Neill's vision for the "humanization of space."[23] Letters from California residents and articles tended to reflect the state's particular form of "western libertarian sensibility."[24] The magazine's extensive coverage became a flashpoint, igniting conflict between technological enthusiasts like Brand and those opposed to the very concept of humans in space. As Brand summarized it: "The man-made idyll is too man-made, too idyllic or too ecologically unlikely—say the ired. It's a general representation of the natural scale of life attainable in a large rotating environment—say the inspired. Either way, it makes people jump."[25]

The volume and tone of the letters that survive in Brand's personal papers attest to the impassioned debate, pro and con, that the idea of space colonies triggered. To some readers of *CoEvolution Quarterly*, the idea of living in space was a logical extension of a "back to the land" lifestyle that eschewed crowded urban environments for communes and wilderness preservation. But for those readers who embraced E. F. Schumacher's "small is beautiful" philosophy and its ideas of "appropriate technology," space colonies provoked horror and outrage. Many counterculture leaders, including some of Brand's good friends, among them poet-farmer Wendell Berry, harshly condemned the whole idea. Brand himself tried to remain neutral, but his correspondence and diary notes show where his loyalty was. After seeing the first space shuttle, he wrote in his journal: "Technology, kiddo. This is to today what the great sailing ships were to their day. Get with the program or stick to your spinning wheel."[26]

Pro-space activism in general received a huge boost in 1978 when the first issue of *Omni* magazine appeared. Slickly produced and bankrolled by soft-core porn king Bob Guccione, *Omni*'s optimistic articles and colorful photoessays offered a veritable window into the technology enthusiast's view of the future along with many articles on paranormal sciences, such as ESP and UFO studies.[27] While the concept that Earth's resources had limits had helped inspire technological enthusiasts to propose alternative and seemingly radical visions of the future, *Omni* brought these ideas to millions of readers in mainstream America.[28] For example, *Omni* featured Gerard O'Neill's work or some other aspect of the pro-space agenda in almost every issue, a trend that intensified when science-fiction writer and L5 advocate Ben Bova took over as *Omni*'s chief editor in 1980.

In the late 1970s, science writer Trudy Bell began tracking the emergence of the pro-space movement, which was then modest in size, but took off in 1980.[29] Her surveys showed that there were some forty-two non-local space-interest groups active in the United States. They claimed some 40,000 members altogether, a number that tripled between 1980 and 1982. The western United States was home to much of this organizational activity; about a third of these groups were based in California. Membership was especially strong in the Los Angeles and Silicon Valley areas. Part of this interest, of course, can be traced to California's long involvement with and deep economic ties to the aerospace industry as well as to the presence there of NASA centers like Ames and the Jet Propulsion Laboratory. At the same time, Southern California has a long history of "fringe" groups with a pro-technology orientation. A classic example is the community of occultists who surrounded John Whiteside "Jack" Parsons and L. Ron Hubbard in the 1940s—Parsons was an enthusiastic innovator of rocket technology who helped found the Jet Propulsion Laboratory while Hubbard, of course, achieved even greater notoriety for inventing Scientology.[30]

However, the pro-space community in the late 1970s and early 1980s tended to be fractious and had a difficult time unifying behind common goals. It also had to overcome some tendencies toward eccentricity among its members. Carolyn Meinel recalled having to tell one true believer: "No, I can't turn your pool table into a starship."[31] The advent of the Reagan administration, with its focus on the military uses of space, tended to amplify debates within local chapters and national groups. The title of O'Neill's seminal book on space colonies—*The High Frontier*—was appropriated by Gen. Daniel O. Graham when he established the High Frontier foundation to promote the Strategic Defense Initiative (and, less notably, to advocate space industrialization).

The pro-space movement produced unusual political bedfellows. For example, Republican politician Newt Gingrich displayed considerable support for space, especially its private business opportunities, as did libertarian outlets like *Reason* magazine. One sign of the pro-space movement's struggle over its agenda can be seen in a report put together in advance of Reagan's 1981 inauguration by the "Citizens' Advisory Council on National Space Policy." This informal group, led by science-fiction writer Jerry Pournelle, who served on L5's board of directors, first met in Tarzana, just outside Los Angeles. It eventually assembled a membership that defied traditional political boundaries—Freeman Dyson (Princeton physicist), Barbara Marx Hubbard (spiritualist and futurist), and Larry Niven (science-fiction writer) were on the membership list with former astronaut Walter Schiarra and future "Star Warrior" Lowell Wood. The committee's report advocated a "vigorous space program" that combined exploitation of space-based resources, entrepreneurial activities in space, and space-based weaponry.[32]

Pournelle's enthusiasm for military and corporate-backed space ventures was resisted by some left-leaning space enthusiasts and L5 members who still supported the original idea of communal space settlements and space-based solar power.[33] Many other space buffs supported the Reagan space agenda in the hopes that military activities might jumpstart more peaceful citizen initiatives, in much the same way that nineteenth-century military forts preceded civilian settlements. These disputes presaged debates about Silicon Valley's cyberculture and its libertarian leanings in the 1990s, when left- and right- wing writers and political leaders united briefly in support of the electronic frontier's new opportunities.[34] Like space commercialization in the 1980s, enthusiasm for the Internet and the World Wide Web a decade later was tinged with utopian and libertarian aspirations as well as hopes for profits, ideals that proponents of the NewSpace movement would also embrace.

"Governor Moonbeam" Discovers Space

In 1977, O'Neill's ideas came to the attention of California governor Jerry Brown. Besides noticing the swell of public interest, Brown was also mindful that aerospace companies (and technology-oriented firms in general) were a mainstay of the California economy. By one estimate, about half of all NASA procurement monies went to the Golden State, for example. Brown had recently asked former Apollo astronaut Russell Schweickart to be his science advisor; he first met O'Neill at meetings facilitated by Brand. Encouraged by Schweickart, Brown advocated a "California Space Program." One part of his plan proposed a California–NASA satellite partnership to improve communications within the Golden State and to facilitate environmental monitoring.[35] Brown's plan, of course, was later lampooned by Chicago columnist Mike Royko, who termed Brown "Governor Moonbeam" for his advocacy. Nonetheless, Brown and Schweickart were committed to making space socially useful and economically relevant.

In August 1977, as the movie *Star Wars* sold out theaters nationwide, Brand, Schweickart, O'Neill, and some 1,100 invited guests from the aerospace and science communities met at the Museum of Science and Industry in Los Angeles for the first California Space Day. The event blended O'Neill's techno-utopianism with presentations from major aerospace firms. Space Day's motto, emblazoned behind the podium, was anti-limits, proclaiming "California in the Space Age: An Era of Possibilities." A working model of O'Neill's mass driver device, which would soon be featured in an episode of the PBS science show *Nova*, sat next to the podium. Timothy Leary, meanwhile, pushed his psychedelic version of O'Neill's vision, saying, "Now there is nowhere left for smart Americans to go but out into high orbit. I love that phrase—high orbit.... We were talking about high orbit long before the space program."[36] More down-to-earth comments came from Bruce Murray, head of the Jet Propulsion Laboratory, oceanographer Jacques Cousteau, planetary scientist Carl Sagan, and O'Neill himself.

Brown's speech abandoned his earlier ascetic language of limits and restricted opportunity, which he had used at his 1975 inauguration. "It is a world of limits but through respecting and reverencing the limits, endless possibilities emerge," he said. "As for space colonies, it's not a question of whether—only when and how."[37] The pro-space ideas Brown put forth were drawn straight from O'Neill's vision—solar power beamed to Earth via satellite, and space manufacturing facilities along with space settlements providing a "safety valve of unexplored frontiers" to accommodate the dreamers and rebels from the pro-space movement. Journalists, of course, noticed the gubernatorial shift in rhetorical direction and wondered if critics would "challenge what appears to be his recantation of Buddhist economics."[38] Outside, laid-off workers waved signs that said, "Jobs on Earth, Not in Space," and one of Brown's own advisors said, "This is disgusting. It's a technology worship session."[39]

The two-day event ended with a trip to Edwards Air Force Base in the Mojave Desert. Some 68,000 people showed up to watch the first successful atmospheric flight of the space shuttle *Enterprise*, which had been built by the California company Rockwell International. (Brown himself donned a clean-room "bunny suit" and toured the craft with astronaut Deke Slayton.) Space Day brought together an odd alliance of counterculture celebrities like Brand and, to some degree, Schweickart (who spoke about the transcendental experience of being in space) with representatives from the federal–corporate space establishment. This hybrid coalition reflected the tensions that were emerging in the pro-space community over military and commercial initiatives in space. The ideas discussed at the event also reflected divergent views—for example,

O'Neill's utopian aspirations for factories and settlements in space contrasted sharply with the space shuttle, a product of Nixon-era incrementalism and (to some) a sop to California's aerospace industry. What was not on the radar then was a middle path that set out a role for small-scale private space-flight companies that, while not perhaps meeting O'Neill's grand ambitions, could challenge the corporate hegemony of large aerospace firms and NASA.

The 1977 event was a high-water mark for California's pro-space movement in terms of attracting a broad base of participants. San Francisco's "April Coalition," an offshoot of California's Space Now Society, organized another Space Day the following year. Bringing together space enthusiasts with antinuclear and environmental advocates, the event rejected a strong corporate presence and instead reflected ideas from the Bay Area counterculture: "There is no time to waste uniting the progressive political groups of the United States to wrest control of the national destiny from the militarists," organizers claimed, "Space is the place for the NEW human race!"[40]

If Not NASA, Then...

Jerry Brown's interest in space-based opportunities presaged the Reagan administration's later promotion of the commercialization of space. As one pro-space booster boasted in 1977, "I'm going to be a billionaire. A lot of us are."[41] Several of the small private space companies that sprang up in the late 1970s and early 1980s called California home. This wave of activity served as a precursor to the later NewSpace firms that clustered around Mojave and the Antelope Valley. It also signified a certain maturing of the pro-space movement from its earlier and untenable focus on bootstrapped citizen settlements in space to shorter-term political and economic goals. When the L5 Society merged with the establishment-oriented National Space Institute—an acrimonious process resisted by many of the original dreamers who had flocked to L5—one observer remarked, "There's lots more to do in space than colonies and settlements."[42]

One of the earliest of these endeavors was Earthport. Started in Santa Barbara in late 1976, this was an offshoot of the libertarian and free-market-driven Sabre Foundation. The goal of Earthport was to study and create "an international commercial space launch site" and, in the process, speed "the transition of space activities from government to private hands."[43] Establishing a place where launches could be done without government regulation or interference was seen a necessary first step toward breaking the monopoly that governments had on access to space.

Over the next few years, Earthport explored possible equatorial launch sites in several countries, including Iran, Liberia, and Kenya, as well as launch platforms in international waters. Another option the project studied was a "world crisis observation satellite," similar in some ways to what the state of California was considering.

Although the Earthport project went nowhere, it did manage to attract a considerable number of high-profile supporters, including Arthur C. Clarke and Robert Heinlein. James C. Bennett was one of the people attracted to the project and he eventually went to work for it. As a student at the University of Michigan, Bennett had been inspired by Heinlein, O'Neill, and New Right libertarianism. He wanted to "extend the narrative of settlement and expansion of America into space," and he helped start an L5 chapter in Ann Arbor.[44]

After moving to California in 1977, Bennett met Phil Salin, a Stanford business student and aficionado of libertarian economist Friedrich Hayek. Salin and his wife Gayle Pergamit had recently started the Center for Space Development, another one of the small California-based groups that was pushing for private space development. The three space entrepreneurs, based in the Bay Area, formed a company, ARC Technologies, with Bevin McKinney, an engineer who led Berkeley's Space Now Society. They later rechristened their small company Starstruck ("stars truck") and sought out backers in Silicon Valley. Michael Scott, a former Apple Computer CEO, made a significant investment and soon took over as Starstruck's president. Meanwhile, the company's technicians developed the Dolphin, a fifty-foot rocket with a hybrid engine—it used liquid as well as solid fuel—that could be launched at sea. After three failures, in August 1984, the California-based company finally launched its first Dolphin.[45] As Bennett recalled, the debut of the space shuttle "got a lot of intelligent people to turn their minds to the problem and that's always the first step. In private space development at that point, there were no rules and no criteria. It was extremely hard to judge the chance of success."[46]

Magazines like *Omni* and *Popular Science* started regularly featuring the fortunes of this future-looking industry in their pages. Buoyed by success, Bennett helped start another enterprise called American Rocket Company (AMROC) a year after the Dolphin flew.[47] Based in Camarillo, on U.S. Route 101 between Los Angeles and Santa Barbara, AMROC devoted its efforts to developing hybrid rocket engines that used a combination of synthetic rubber and liquid oxygen. Bennett's partners in AMROC were engineer Bevin McKinney and George Koopman. Like

Bennett, Koopman had been an avid member of L5 and had left college before finishing his degree. He co-authored parts of *Neuropolitics* with Leary and coordinated stunts for Hollywood movies before partnering with Bennett. Encouraged by the Reagan administration's emphasis on space commercialization, AMROC's goal was to develop low-cost rockets that could boost small payloads into orbit at a fraction of the cost that large aerospace companies charged.

Between 1985 and 1989, AMROC raised and spent some $30 million as the company's one hundred workers constructed engines and a fifty-eight-foot tall, sixteen-ton rocket.[48] However, in the summer of 1989, Koopman died in a car accident while driving back from a rocket-motor test near Mojave. This happened just as AMROC was preparing for its first launch. A few months later, the company's first flight, rechristened the *Koopman Express*, burned on the launch pad at Vandenberg Air Force Base. Although the company fell into bankruptcy, McKinney went on to invent a hybrid rocket–helicopter craft and later co-founded a company called Rotary Rocket that set up shop in Mojave in the mid-1990s.[49] Bennett maintained his interest in a variety of cutting-edge technologies, including nanotechnology and Internet commerce. Meanwhile, elements of the hybrid rocket technology that AMROC developed eventually found their way into Burt Rutan's *SpaceShipOne*, which flew successfully in 2004.

And what of Gerard O'Neill, whose advocacy for private space flight helped catalyze these early pro-space and commercial launch companies? In 1977, he and his wife Tasha formed a nonprofit organization called the Space Studies Institute to advance his vision. A small outfit based in Princeton, New Jersey, the institute supported research on "critical path" technologies to bootstrap space development.

A few years later, O'Neill, in advance of a wave of small space-related start-up companies that emerged during the Reagan era, started a company called Geostar. His plan was to use three geostationary satellites, a complex ground station, and thousands of small transceivers to provide location and tracking information for people and vehicles. As with all his projects, O'Neill thought big. Estimates for building the Geostar system ran as high as $300 million. O'Neill set about raising money and recruiting partners and investors for his venture. At one point, the roster included Nobel Prize–winning physicist Luis Alvarez, former head NASA administrator Thomas Paine, and Bernard Oliver, who had directed the laboratories of electronics giant Hewlett-Packard for years. Despite perennial cash shortages and opposition from various federal agencies, Geostar conducted initial ground tests by 1984 and raised several million dollars in a public stock offering. His idea, described in several patents, can be seen as one forerunner of today's ubiquitous global positioning systems. Innovative and ambitious, O'Neill's company collapsed amid legal battles as his own health deteriorated. In April 1992, after a long battle with leukemia, he passed away in California.

The Power of Prizes

The successful 2004 flight of *SpaceShipOne* was the most visible event to date in the recent history of the private space-flight business. It brought international attention to Burt Rutan, his company Scaled Composites, and the entire private space sector, much of it centered in Southern California. Besides the flight of *SpaceShipOne* itself, the other main story that journalists focused on was the role of the X Prize Foundation and its $10 million purse, which *SpaceShipOne*'s flight had claimed.

The X Prize itself was an indirect result of O'Neill's advocacy for bold new technological advances made independently of NASA and large corporate firms. The X Prize Foundation traces its pedigree back to the early days of flight. In 1919, Raymond Orteig, an immigrant French hotel magnate, offered a $25,000 purse to the first person to make a nonstop flight between New York City and Paris. The prize, of course, was claimed by Charles Lindbergh in 1927 after receiving backing from a group of St. Louis businessmen. In 1980, O'Neill's vision as well as Lindbergh's courage inspired Peter Diamandis, then a freshman at MIT. Diamandis, together with Todd B. Hawley, formed a national organization of university-based pro-space groups called Students for the Exploration and Development of Space. The two men, after graduating, also started the International Space University to help train young people "to take leadership roles in future space exploration and development."[50]

A year after Hawley's death,[51] Diamandis met with Gregg Maryniak, a longtime associate of O'Neill's Space Studies Institute, and several members of the St. Louis philanthropic community. Drawing on the Lindbergh legacy—the aviator's grandson pledged financial support—Diamandis raised $25,000 for a space prize and secured the blessing of sci-fi visionary Arthur C. Clarke. Raising additional money was hard, especially after the dot-com collapse of 2000, until Diamandis met with Iranian-born Anousheh Ansari, a business entrepreneur who had made millions in the telecom business before becoming the world's first woman space tourist. By 2002, Ansari made a considerable financial commitment to Diamandis and the prize was renamed the Ansari X Prize. Diamandis's strategy was to use the prize to promote private entrepreneurship in space-related technologies. It worked. In addition to Rutan's company, some two dozen other groups signed up to compete for the $10 million purse.

The publicity generated by Diamandis and the X Prize Foundation, which set up its main office in the Los Angeles area, prompted a great deal of interest in using prizes to motivate and drive technological innovation. Shortly after *SpaceShipOne*'s first flight, Congress's Subcommittee on Space and Aeronautics held a hearing on whether prizes were a viable way to encourage innovation for space exploration. Diamandis was one of the people asked to testify. Prizes were clearly in the air at that point. A month before the hearing, NASA had held its inaugural Centennial Challenges workshop in Washington to promote prizes for specific space-related technologies ranging from new propulsion systems to improved gloves for astronauts.[52] One of its most popular contests was the Space Elevator Games, a regularly held event cosponsored by NASA and the Spaceward Foundation (based in Silicon Valley) with a multimillion-dollar purse. The most recent of these contests was held near Mojave outside Edwards Air Force Base.

After the flight of *SpaceShipOne*, prizes for space-related feats proliferated. In 2007, for instance, Google, the California-based Internet juggernaut, announced a $20 million prize to the first group that could land a privately developed spacecraft on the Moon, traverse some 500 meters, and send back a lunar broadcast. Meanwhile, the X Prize Foundation announced new awards for advances in genetic sequencing and automotive innovations. The interest in technological prizes was a development, albeit an old one, that visionaries like O'Neill didn't anticipate, nor was it available to early space start-ups like AMROC. Connected to federal agencies or sponsored by deep-pocketed entrepreneurs, these prizes offered a new path for space enthusiasts seeking the high frontier, one that avoided government contracts and involvement with traditional players from the corporate aerospace world.

Space's Netscape Moment?

Why has the NewSpace cohort of entrepreneurs succeeded (thus far) where earlier efforts from a quarter-century ago flamed out? While there is no single simple causal factor, a number of possible reasons emerge. One of them is obvious—money. Flush with tens of millions of dollars in capital, companies like Scaled Composites and SpaceX simply had more resources to draw upon, including funds from California-based venture capitalists. This led to more sophisticated and reliable technologies. This can also be seen in companies' scale of operations—whereas AMROC functioned on a shoestring budget with about one hundred employees, SpaceX employed some eight hundred people in 2008 with operations based in California and a launch site at Kwajalein Atoll in the Pacific.

A second and related factor is that the business connections New-Space entrepreneurs made over the years allowed them to tap into an established network of venture capitalists and "angel investors." These networks are reflected in other ways as well. Elon Musk, CEO of a New-Space company called SpaceX, and Larry Page, one of Google's co-founders, sit on the board of directors for the X Prize Foundation. The extensive media attention that *SpaceShipOne* received also helped facilitate fundraising, acting as a "Matthew Effect" for private space exploration.

Finally, historical context is a huge factor. When people like James Bennett and Phil Salin were trying to establish their fledgling enterprises around 1980, the space shuttle was still unproven. Fast forward ahead two decades and one finds a NASA that has no clear mission for human space exploration and that lost two orbiters to tragic accidents while coming nowhere near the cost and schedule predictions it had made. Coupled with this was a decline in the visionary rhetoric typified by Gerard O'Neill's ambitious ideas for space settlements and space manufacturing. In short, the interest of some pro-space advocates shifted from building utopian space colonies to simply launching people and payloads into orbit while making a profit.[53] Also, although it is hard to prove, one suspects that engineers' dissatisfaction with the traditional aerospace companies of Southern California, with their massive projects and huge bureaucracies, may have motivated some of them to seek out opportunities in the NewSpace realm.

Since the success of *SpaceShipOne*, various observers of NewSpace have drawn attention to the Mojave region as the locus of a new entrepreneurial spirit and concomitant business opportunities. One could argue that Michael Melvill's brief flights over the California desert constituted a "Netscape moment" for the private space industry. "There's often something that catches the public imagination," said technology commentator, investor, and space tourist Esther Dyson (daughter of the famed physicist and O'Neill advocate Freeman Dyson) in 2007.[54] The recent awarding of a major NASA launch contract to Musk's SpaceX company, which beat out bids by industry giants Lockheed Martin and Boeing, offered another success and yet another permutation of the NewSpace business model.[55]

It would be disingenuous to claim that the isolated town of Mojave, marooned in rural California, is anywhere close to an industrial, financial, and academic "city of knowledge" like Silicon Valley, with its universities, government labs, and multibillion-dollar companies.[56] However, there is value in considering historical analogies. While the Mojave area has neither multinational firms nor major universities, the region exhibits some of the basic conditions necessary for promoting a space-friendly high-tech region. This includes available land for building, restricted airspace for testing, good flying weather, isolation (which maximizes secrecy as well as safety), as well as established technology-oriented entities like Edwards Air Force Base and the China Lake Naval Air Weapons Station. In the creation of new regions of technology activity, experience and connections also matter a great deal. Many of the NewSpace movement's leaders had prior experience with successful and profitable Internet and computer companies. One longtime private space enthusiast even noted that, around 2000, starting a space-related company had become a "geeky status symbol" for dot-com billionaires looking for something more than a private jet.[57]

Perhaps a more important analogy is that between the history of Silicon Valley and the Antelope Valley; in both places, narratives of previous eras and founding figures are conducive to mythmaking. Just as Silicon Valley's "creation story" rests on the accomplishments of heroic inventors (Hewlett and Packard, Moore and Noyce, Brin and Page), the deserts of Southern California have been a similar place of birth, experiment, and regeneration for the aerospace industry. The skies over Mojave were, after all, where Chuck Yeager and Neil Armstrong—people with the "Right Stuff"—tested some of the world's most advanced aerospace technologies during the Cold War.

Another regional comparison comes from looking for similar cultural values to those of the NewSpace movement. Social critics once described the Internet and dot-com inspired "California Ideology" as "promiscuously combin[ing] the free-wheeling spirit of the hippies and the entrepreneurial zeal of the yuppies... [brought together by] a profound faith in the emancipatory potential of the new information technologies. In the digital utopia, everybody will be both hip and rich."[58] With roots in Gerard O'Neill's vision and the L5 Society's activism, the modern pro-space movement blended left-wing counterculture ideas about the "humanization of space" with right-wing libertarian beliefs in free markets, less government, and profits to those who dared to push the technological envelope. More recently, proponents of NewSpace combine skeptical views of the federal government (especially NASA) with a belief in the power of private enterprise and a profound enthusiasm for technology's ameliorative economic and social benefits. On one photograph of *SpaceShipOne*, for example, Rutan penned, "See What Free Men Can do."[59]

Like Silicon Valley's computer- and chip-driven entrepreneurs, the rocket dreamers and doers of the Antelope Valley were motivated by profit as well as by predictions of the technological future. If one imagines the aerospace business sector as akin to a vibrant technological ecosystem—a metaphor that Silicon Valley cognoscenti have promoted for some time—then we must also take visionaries like Gerard O'Neill, yesteryear's pro-space activists, and California's long-vanished rocket companies into account. All played a role in shaping the social, political, and economic environment that today's private space firms now navigate.

This essay is based upon work supported by the National Science Foundation under Grant No. SES 0531184. Any opinions, findings, and conclusions or recommendations expressed in this material are those of the author and do not necessarily reflect the views of the National Science Foundation. I would also like to thank people who provided valuable research material or were interviewed for this work. These include: Tasha O'Neill, Freeman Dyson, James C. Bennett, Stewart Brand, Trudy Bell, and Ben Bova.

NOTES

1   John Schwartz, "Manned Private Craft Reaches Space in a Milestone for Flight," *New York Times*, 22 June 2004, A1.

2   John Schwartz, "Private Rocket Ship Earns $10 Million in New Space Race," *New York Times*, 5 October 2004, A1.

3   "California Ideology" was the term used by Richard Barbrook and Andy Cameron in an essay, "Californian Ideology," that was widely cited by critics of information technologies such as the web in the mid-1990s. Their essay appeared in several online versions beginning in 1995; as of October 2010, it was available at http://www.hrc.wmin.ac.uk/theory-californianideology.html. One catalyst for the discussion of this trend was the publication of a libertarian-oriented, cyber-manifesto by Esther Dyson, George Gilder, George Keyworth, and Alvin Toffler; "Cyberspace and the American Dream: A Magna Carta for the Knowledge Age (Release 1.2, 22 August 1994)," *The Information Society* 12, no. 3 (1996): 295–308.

4   For an example, see Asif Siddiqi, "Imagining the Cosmos: Utopians, Mystics, and the Popular Culture of Spaceflight in Revolutionary Russia," *Osiris* 23 (2008): 260–88.

5   Elizabeth Paris, "Ringing in the New Physics: The Politics and Technology of Electron Colliders in the United States, 1956–1972" (PhD diss., University of Pittsburgh, 1999).

6   From 1 July 2007 Op-Ed in the *Los Angeles Times* by Brian Doherty, a writer for the libertarian magazine *Reason*, which is based in California.

7   O'Neill's version of how he became interested in space colonization is presented in the last chapter of his book *The High Frontier: Human Colonies in Space* (New York: William Morrow, 1977).

8   Gerard K. O'Neill, "The Colonization of Space," *Physics Today* 27 (1974): 32–40. Documents related to O'Neill's development of his space-colony ideas are in his personal papers; as of this writing, these are kept by his widow, Tasha O'Neill, who generously allowed me access. Copies are in the author's possession.

9   "Interior View with Long Suspension Bridge," NASA ID Number AC75–1883, available at "Space Colony Art from the 1970s," NASA Space Settlement Mirror Site, Space Settlement Nexus section, National Space Society website, http://www.nss.org/settlement/nasa/70sArt/AC75-1883.jpeg.

10   From 23 July 1975 testimony O'Neill gave to the congressional Subcommittee on Space Science and Applications; reprinted in *Space Colonies: A Coevolution Book*, ed. Stewart Brand (New York: Penguin, 1977).

11   Andrew G. Kirk, *Counterculture Green: The Whole Earth Catalog and American Environmentalism* (Lawrence: University of Kansas Press, 2007).

12   The term appears in a number of articles by and about O'Neill throughout the 1970s; see, for example, Richard K. Rein, "Maybe We Are Alone," *People*, 12 December 1977.

13   Robert Poole, *Earthrise: How Man First Saw the Earth* (New Haven, Conn.: Yale University Press, 2008).

14   Walter Sullivan, "Proposal for Human Colonies in Space Is Hailed by Scientists as Feasible Now," *New York Times*, 13 May 1974.

15   O'Neill, "The Colonization of Space."

16   From the preface of *Space Settlements: A Design Study*, NASA SP-413, ed. Richard D. Johnson and Charles Holbrow (Washington, D.C.: NASA, 1977).

17   See, for example, "Starseed Seminar Aims for Mutation, Migration, Rejuvenation," *L5 News*, October 1976, 11. See also Timothy Leary's books *Neuropolitics: The Sociobiology of Human Metamorphosis* (Los Angeles: Starseed/Peace Press, 1977), and *Exo-Psychology: A Manual on the Use of the Human Nervous System According to the Instructions of the Manufacturers* (Los Angeles: Starseed/Peace Press, 1977). *Neuropolitics* included contributions from science-fiction writer Robert Anton Wilson and space entrepreneur George Koopman (both California residents).

18   Gerard K. O'Neill, "A Lagrangian Community," *Nature* 250 (1974): 636.

19   William S. Higgins and Barry D. Gehm, "Home on Lagrange," 1978. The lyrics originally appeared in *CoEvolution Quarterly* 18 (Summer 1978): 30.

20   Agreement Governing the Activities of States on the Moon and Other
      Celestial Bodies, 5 December 1979, *United Nations Treaty Series*, 1363:3;
      text available at United Nations Office for Outer Space Affairs website,
      http://www.unoosa.org/oosa/SpaceLaw/moon.html.

21   M. Mitchell Waldrop, "Citizens for Space," *Science* 211, no. 4478 (1981): 152.

22   Roger D. Launius, "Perfect Worlds, Perfect Societies: The Persistent Goal of
      Utopia in Human Spaceflight," *Journal of the British Interplanetary Society* 56
      (2003): 338–49.

23   Brand collected these pieces as well as many of the letters he received on the
      subject and published them as his 1977 edited book *Space Colonies*. In addi-
      tion, his professional correspondence, preserved in Stewart Brand papers,
      Stanford University Special Collections, Manuscripts Division, Palo Alto,
      Calif., M1237, series 1, captures the sense of debate that emerged over the
      issue in the mid-1970s.

24   Kirk, *Counterculture Green*, 18.

25   From the preface to *Space Colonies: A CoEvolution Book*.

26   Stewart Brand, mid-1977 journal entry, box 18, folder 6, Stewart Brand papers
      (M1237), Stanford Special Collections, Stanford University.

27   People associated with the magazine in its early days have noted that *Omni*'s
      coverage of the paranormal—encouraged by Guccione and his partner and
      copublisher Kathy Keeton—created difficulties as the magazine tried to es-
      tablish its credibility, especially among corporate advertisers; Trudy Bell, in-
      terview with the author, 8 August 2008.

28   The monthly readership of *Omni*, according to the magazine, was about
      5 million people. Although this may be inflated, a figure of around 1 million is
      not unreasonable. See Eugene Garfield, "Omni Magazine Leads the Upsurge of
      Mass-Audience Science Journalism," *Current Contents*, 12 March 1979, 5–12.

29   An early example is Bell's "Space Activism"; *Omni*, February 1981, 50–54.
      More details on the demographics and size of the pro-space community
      can be found in Michael A. G. Michaud, *Reaching for the High Frontier:
      The American Pro-Space Movement, 1972–1984* (New York: Praeger, 1986).

30   George Pendle, *Strange Angel: The Otherworldly Life of Rocket Scientist John
      Whitesides Parsons* (New York: Harcourt, 2005). For more on cult activity in
      Southern California, see Carey McWilliams, *Southern California: An Island
      on the Land* (Salt Lake City, Utah: Gibbs M. Smith, 1973).

31   Michaud, *Reaching for the High Frontier*, 86.

32   Pournelle later claimed that this group's activities helped catalyze Reagan's
      Strategic Defense Initiative; see Andrew J. Butrica, *Single Stage to Orbit:
      Politics, Space Technology, and the Quest for Reusable Rocketry* (Baltimore:
      Johns Hopkins University Press, 2003).

33   Mark Hopkins, interview with the author, 24 August 2009.

34   My thanks to Peter J. Westwick for stimulating discussions about places in which the left and right coalesced around particular technologies; see also Fred Turner, *From Counterculture to Cyberculture: Stewart Brand, the Whole Earth Network, and the Rise of Digital Utopianism* (Chicago: University of Chicago Press, 2006).

35   Jay Miller, "L5ers Develop a State Space Program," *The L5 News*, April 1982, 2–3.

36   Roger Rapoport, *California Dreaming: The Political Odyssey of Pat & Jerry Brown* (Berkeley, Calif.: Nolo Press, 1982), 186–92.

37   From Brown's 11 August 1977 speech, box 10, folder 10, Whole Earth Catalog records (M1045), Stanford Archives.

38   "Our New, Spaced-Out Governor," *Los Angeles Times*, 5 August 1977, D6.

39   Rapoport, *California Dreaming*, xiv.

40   From letters of 21 and 28 November to Jerry Brown and Stewart Brand, box 12, folder 3, Whole Earth Catalog records (M1045), Stanford Archives.

41   L5 Society cofounder H. Keith Henson, quoted in Ned Scharff, "Too Crowded Here? Why Not Fly Into Space," *Washington Star*, 3 November 1977.

42   Richard Wolkomir, "Missionary Power," *Omni*, May 1986, 47–52, 100.

43   Robert W. Poole to Robert Heinlein, 7 February 1977, Robert A. and Virginia G. Heinlein Papers, MS 95, University of California at Santa Cruz, Santa Cruz, Calif., PERS328-11 (Sabre Foundation/Earthport), available at The Robert A. and Virginia Heinlein Archives website, http://www.heinleinarchives.net/upload/index.php. Santa Barbara in the 1970s was also home to *Reason*, a libertarian magazine now published in Los Angeles.

44   James C. Bennett, interview with the author, 19 July 2007.

45   This was not the first privately funded launch; in September 1982, a small rocket made from surplus military hardware called the *Conestoga I* blasted off from an island near Houston; Robert Reinhold, "Texas Rocket Built on a 'Shoestring' Carries Free Enterprise into Space," *New York Times*, 10 September 1982, A1.

46   Bennett interview.

47   Butrica, *Single Stage to Orbit*, chap. 2.

48   Barry Stavro, "Shoestring Space Race," *Los Angeles Times*, 30 May 1989, 1C.

49   Described by cofounder Gary C. Hudson in "Insanely Great? or Just Plain Insane?" *Wired Magazine*, May 1996, available at Wired.com, http://www.wired.com/wired/archive/4.05/roton.html.

50   "The International Space University," *The Space Times*, March–April 1989, 7.

51   In 1997, his ashes were lofted into orbit, along with those of O'Neill, Timothy Leary, and *Star Trek* creator Gene Roddenberry by a private launch company. See "The Founders Flight," Celestis, Inc. website, http://www.celestis.com/memorial/founders/default.asp.

52   Jack Hitt, "The Amateur Future of Space Travel," *New York Times Magazine*, 1
       July 2007, 40–47, 66, 80.

53   This is not to say that visionary ideals disappeared completely. A 2009 edito-
       rial by Elon Musk, called "Space, the Fiscal Frontier," still expressed a belief
       that it was important for humans to become "multi-planetary"; *The Economist:
       The World in 2010*, 13 November 2009, 150.

54   Leonard David, "Space Entrepreneurs Wait for That Netscape Moment,"
       Space News, 26 November 2007, http://www.space.com/spacenews/
       071126-new-space-markets.html.

55   Peter Pae, "SpaceX Beats Out Lockheed and Boeing for Rocket Contract
       Worth $3.1 Billion," *Los Angeles Times*, 25 December 2008, C1.

56   Margaret Pugh O'Mara, *Cities of Knowledge: Cold War Science and the Search
       for the Next Silicon Valley* (Princeton, N.J.: Princeton University Press, 2005).

57   Rick Tumlinson, founder of the Space Frontier Foundation, quoted in John
       Schwartz, "Thrillionaires: The New Space Capitalists," *New York Times*,
       14 June 2005, F1.

58   Barbrook and Cameron, "Californian Ideology."

59   Peter Westwick and I observed this particular photograph hanging on the
       office wall of sci-fi writer Jerry Pournelle when we interviewed him in 2007.

Whether one considers how real-estate redlining limited nonwhites' access to aerospace jobs, or how underfunded inner-city educational systems left poor children unprepared for technical careers, the history of the aerospace industry is deeply inflected by the class and racial divisions that have often defined communities in Southern California. The essays in this section examine two specific examples.

Zuoyue Wang shows how broader forces converged to shape the local Chinese American community's relationship with aerospace. The growth of the aerospace industry made Southern California a major destination for waves of immigrant Chinese scientists and engineers from both mainland China and Taiwan after the Chinese Communist revolution of 1949 and U.S.–China rapprochement in the 1970s. Like other minorities, Chinese American scientists and engineers have struggled against racism and discrimination. Their experiences, furthermore, perhaps more than other ethnic groups, have been shaped by geopolitical developments. Strategic rivalries between the United States and Communist countries have made them targets of security investigations from the McCarthy era to the present. Here Wang returns us to a distinguishing feature of the aerospace industry, its connection to national defense and the security regime. Despite these cases, the attraction of technical and professional advancement in a socially diverse Southern California has proved irresistible for many Chinese scientists and engineers.

Dwayne Day examines the intriguing intersection of the local indigenous Chumash tribe with the space-launch complex at Vandenberg Air Force Base. This episode represents the latest in a long series of interactions between modern technologies and indigenous tribes in the American West, encounters often brokered by the U.S. military, from repeating rifles and railroads to strategic missiles and satellites. The resulting folklore about a supposed Indian curse at Vandenberg invoked a common trope in Western history, that of the mystical, vengeful Native American. It also, however, resonated with widespread mythologizing about the American space program in general: the conspiracy theories of faked Moon landings, faces on Mars, alien fireflies circling the Mercury astronauts, and so on. In the process, the Vandenberg story highlights the human tendency to attribute the problems of modern technology to mysterious, sinister forces.

Z U O Y U E   W A N G

Engineering a New Space:
Chinese American Scientists and Engineers in Aerospace in Southern California

When the Soviet Union launched *Sputnik 1*, the world's first satellite, on 4 October 1957, it not only took the world into the space age, but also marked a turning point in American science and technology policy. Within days, President Dwight Eisenhower radically changed how his administration solicited science advice and formed science policy. He appointed James Killian of MIT as his full-time science adviser and reassigned a group of science consultants as the President's Science Advisory Committee (PSAC). Although by no means blind believers in technological fixes for social and political problems, PSAC scientists nevertheless advocated in 1960 that American science and technology must "double and redouble in size and strength" in Sputnik's shadow.[1] In response, the federal government increased its support of science education to meet an expected technical manpower shortage, especially in the area of aerospace.

But how real was this manpower shortage? It turned out that whether the gap would materialize depended on what the federal government did or did not do, especially in aerospace. This became clear during the first months of John F. Kennedy's presidency. In April 1961, another Soviet feat in space, the orbiting of Yuri Gagarin, created renewed public pressure on the Kennedy administration. Just a month later, President Kennedy and his advisors deliberated over whether to launch a Moon-landing project; manpower became part of the calculation. When Kennedy was told that without a large space program there would be an oversupply of aerospace manpower, it "took away all the argument against the space program."[2]

The Apollo project absorbed all the existing manpower and generated a huge new demand of its own. In January 1962, Kennedy asked PSAC to study the problem of the technical manpower shortage. The committee came back by the end of the year with a recommendation for increased federal support to universities and students in engineering, mathematics, and the physical sciences, which the National Science Foundation subsequently implemented.[3] By 1963, according to Jerome Wiesner, Kennedy's science adviser and PSAC chairman, roughly every other science and engineering graduate would be expected to "go into NASA activities." When Kennedy asked again "what the new people would be doing if the NASA program did not exist," Wiesner answered, "one can only guess." It certainly made "the technical manpower problem today . . . tight," with serious shortages predicted for 1964–65, when the demand from Apollo would reach its peak. To meet this need would take not only the 70,000 new scientists and engineers produced in the United States each year, but also the four to five thousand immigrant scientists and engineers.[4]

It is not clear whether Wiesner included foreign students who were pursuing science or engineering degrees in the United States in the former or latter category. Either way, his memorandum indicates the crucial importance of attracting immigrant scientists and engineers to the United States to help meet the Apollo-driven demand for technical manpower. Of course, the need for foreign technical manpower did not originate with the Apollo project; there was much talk about the "Cold War of the Classrooms" in the 1950s, even before *Sputnik*'s launch, and many policies had been enacted to attract foreign technical manpower to the United States. But due to its scale and technical nature, Apollo, more than any other single project, jacked up the demand for foreign technical manpower.

Chinese Americans in Science and Technology

Chinese Americans, perhaps more than any other group, benefited from the rising demand for technical manpower. In the late nineteenth century and the first half of the twentieth century, thousands of Chinese students came to the United States to study science and engineering. Most of these students returned home after finishing their studies, in part due to the Chinese Exclusion Acts that were first passed in 1882. But in 1949, with the Communist revolution in mainland China, a majority of the estimated 5,000 Chinese students then in the United States, many of them specializing in science and technology, decided to stay in the United States.[5] By the mid-1950s, these so-called "stranded students" were joined by about 2,300 more Chinese intellectual refugees who had fled Communist China.[6] By then the racist Chinese exclusion laws had been repealed (during World War II), but the discriminatory immigration quota system, which limited new Chinese immigrants to 105 a year, was still in place. Both the stranded and the refugee Chinese were able to gain legal status in the United States only through a number of special congressional and executive decisions. Those decisions in turn were driven by dual Cold War concerns: denying talented workers to the Communists and attracting them to the United States. In 1953, for example, Congress passed and President Eisenhower signed the Refugee Relief Act that, among other measures, allowed stranded Chinese students to stay in the United States permanently and also permitted 2,000 Chinese refugees to enter the country over and above the 105-per-year quota.[7]

A third group of Chinese American scientists came from Taiwan (and to a lesser extent, Hong Kong) in the 1950s and 1960s. Many of these newcomers had been born and raised in mainland China, then fled with their families to Taiwan around the time of the Communist revolution in 1949. Most of them received undergraduate education in Taiwan but came to the United States for graduate training. The backward and often politically dangerous conditions at home provided the push, while the prospect of much better living and working conditions in the United States furnished the pull. In many ways, the migration of Taiwanese scientists and engineers to the United States fit into a pattern of "brain drain" that was common to many developing countries, such as India and South Korea, in this period.[8]

In the 1960s, the immigration of Chinese to the United States was further encouraged by both the continuing Cold War demand for manpower and the push for racial and ethnic equality amid the rising Civil Rights movement. By the end of the 1960s, about 2,000 students were leaving Taiwan for the United States each year.[9] The landmark 1965 immigration reform act increased the annual allotment for Chinese immigrants from about 100 to 20,000 spaces, most of which went to Taiwanese Chinese, including those Taiwanese students in American universities who decided to stay in the United States following graduation. Finally, the reopening of United States–China relations in the early 1970s and the renormalization of diplomatic relations between the two countries in 1979 brought a fourth major wave of migration of Chinese to the United States, this time from mainland China, which was given a separate quota of 20,000 a year. These immigrants were once again led by students who came to the United States mainly to study science and technology, some of whom went into aerospace.[10]

Asian Americans in Aerospace

The exact numbers of Chinese Americans in aerospace are hard to come by, but some data on Asian Americans help piece together a picture of the scale and characteristics of this group. A 1989 report by the U.S. Government Accounting Office (GAO) on female and minority aerospace managers and professionals during the period from 1979 to 1986 provides some useful indicators. The industry employed altogether about 1.27 million workers in 1986, based on census data. The GAO examined closely about half of these employees (678,780 in 1986) because it focused on so-called EEO (Equal Employment Opportunity) data, which gathered more detailed information on the ethnicity and gender of workers at the larger companies.[11] Nationwide, Asian Americans comprised about 3.2 percent (about 38,100 if one uses the census data) of the aerospace workforce in 1986, almost doubling from 1.7 percent in 1979. This increase was slightly faster than the increase in Asian Americans as a percentage of the general population (from about 2 percent in 1979 to about 3 percent in 1986). In this period, total national aerospace employment increased by 58 percent, from 430,383 in 1979 to 678,780 in 1986.[12] The GAO data did not provide further detail on the proportions of various ethnicities in the Asian American category, but one assumes that the general pattern for the group held true for Chinese Americans, who make up the plurality of Asian Americans.

A striking finding of the GAO confirmed that the "glass ceiling" effect that blocked Asian American advancement in corporate America was especially serious in aerospace. Even though nationwide a greater proportion of Asian American aerospace employees had technical training and were in the category of "professionals" than whites, African Americans, or Hispanics, they had the smallest proportion of management jobs. For example, in 1980, according to the GAO's analysis of the EEO data maintained by the federal Joint Reporting Committee, while Asian Americans made up 1.5 percent of the employees in the industry, their share of professionals was 3.6 percent but their share of managers was only 1.0 percent. All minority groups and women were underrepresented in management in terms of their total numbers when compared with white males, but the case of Asian Americans seemed especially acute. Even as the number of Asian Americans in aerospace increased, the pattern seemed unchanged.[13] As the sociologists Lucie Cheng and Philip Q. Yang argued, many Asian immigrant professionals discovered to their dismay that "America seemed to want them for their skills and work ethic as employees but not for their assertiveness and ambition as bosses."[14]

Table 1. Ethnic Distribution of Aerospace Jobs, 1980

| | Percentage of Workforce | | | |
Job Category	Whites	African Americans	Hispanic Americans	Asian Americans
All	81.0	11.6	5.4	1.5
Professionals	89.9	4.4	1.9	3.6
Managers	92.5	4.0	2.2	1.0

Source: GAO, Equal Employment Opportunity: Women and Minority Aerospace Managers and Professionals, 1979–1986 (Washington, D.C.: GAO, 1989), table II.1 on p. 23, http://archive.gao.gov/d26t7/139889.pdf.

There were some relatively bright spots in the statistics for Asian Americans: not only were they "over-represented" in the category of "professionals," but also, as professionals and managers, they earned salaries about 95 percent of those of their white counterparts; in comparison, African and Hispanic Americans made only about 75 to 85 percent of whites' salaries in 1987.[15] Yet, even these numbers highlighted the narrow career paths that seemed open to Asian Americans in aerospace. Due to the nature of the industry, the option of escaping from the glass ceiling by going into self-employment was often not as readily available to Asian American scientists and engineers in aerospace as it was to those in other fields, such as computers or biomedicine. Furthermore, as the sociologist Joyce Tang pointed out, Asian Americans, like other minorities, again faced discrimination when attempting to go into self-employment, for example in the form of bias by consumers.[16]

Yet, despite persistent problems such as underrepresentation in management, there was no denying the dramatic increase of Asian Americans in aerospace. According to EEO data from the 1990 census, there were 143,434 aerospace engineers in the country that year, of whom 11,274, or about 8 percent, were Asian or Pacific Islanders (APIs).[17] By the 2000 census, the number of aerospace engineers nationwide had fallen 23 percent to 110,475, but the number of APIs in the occupation held relatively steady: 10,440 who had two Asian parents, 540 who had one Asian and one non-Hispanic white parent, and 165 native Hawaiians and "other Pacific islanders," totaling 11,145, or about 10 percent of the national total.[18]

Chinese Americans in Aerospace in Southern California

Nowhere was Asian American growth and concentration in aerospace more striking than in Southern California. The Los Angeles area had the largest number of aerospace employees in the country in the early 1980s. In 1979, there were 114,248 aerospace employees in the Los Angeles area, and about 4,570, or 4 percent, were Asian Americans, more than double their average representation in the industry nationwide. By 1986, the number of all aerospace employees in Los Angeles increased by 42 percent to 162,563, while Asian Americans more than doubled their numbers, to about 11,380 or 7 percent of the total regional aerospace employees.[19] The trend continued in later decades. According to the U.S. Census of 1990, in the narrower category of aerospace engineers, the total number for Los Angeles County was 23,523, of which 3,610, or more than 15 percent, were API Americans.[20] Following the post–Cold War retrenchment in the 1990s, the total number of aerospace engineers in Los Angeles county fell to 12,135 by 2000, and the number of APIs (including native Hawaiians and other Pacific islanders) among them also decreased, to 2,780, but their proportion increased to about 23 percent.[21]

The pattern of Asian American employment in aerospace in Los Angeles followed that at the national level in some ways but also differed from it in others. As noted above, the percentage of Asian Americans in Los Angeles aerospace was about double that of the national average from 1979 to 1986.[22] Asian Americans held professional and managerial positions in the Los Angeles area at triple the national rates; they made up about 10 percent of professionals and 5 percent of managers, according to the 1986 EEO data.[23] Such prominence in the industry undoubtedly reflected Asian Americans' higher concentration in the region. Indeed, if one compares their numbers in Los Angeles aerospace and in the regional labor market in general, one finds that all minorities were actually underrepresented in managerial positions and, somewhat surprisingly for Asian Americans, in professional positions as well.[24]

Why was there such a high concentration of Asian Americans in aerospace in the Los Angeles area? There likely were several factors at work here. Rapid industrialization, including the rise of aerospace, and the accompanying economic expansion of Southern California in the post–World War II period created employment opportunities that attracted immigrants from all over the world, but especially from Asian-Pacific countries. While traditional immigration from many Asian countries was still severely restricted due to the discriminatory pre-1965 quota system, many students, especially those from Taiwan and Korea,

were able to find ways to stay and work in the United States. In this regard, Southern California had advantages not only in its booming aerospace industry, but also in its many universities and colleges. The 1965
immigration reform further promoted Asian immigration because it
vastly expanded quotas for the region and favored immigration of family members of those who were already in the United States. Other appeals of Southern California included the area's rich Asian and especially
Chinese cultural traditions and resources, including Chinatown and
many excellent Chinese restaurants, its position on the Pacific Rim, its
status as a major port of entry for Asian Pacific immigrants, and perhaps
most important of all, its pivotal role in trade linking the United States
with the Asian Pacific region. All of these factors helped to make Los
Angeles a favored place for Asian immigrants and Asian Americans to
settle and find employment.[25]

Among Asian American aerospace scientists and engineers, Chinese
Americans not only formed one of the largest groups, but their story also
provides an especially good illustration of how aerospace reshaped
Southern California and vice versa. The presence of Chinese Americans
in Southern Californian aerospace can be traced back to the 1930s, when
a number of talented Chinese students, driven in part by their national-
ist determination to build up China's nascent aviation industry and air
force, came to study aeronautics at the California Institute of Technology
(Caltech). Perhaps the most famous of them was Hsue-sen Tsien (Qian
Xuesen in *pinyin*), who worked with Theodore von Kármán at Caltech
first as a student and then as a colleague. Tsien helped establish Caltech's
Jet Propulsion Laboratory (JPL) and consulted for the U.S. Air Force on
secret military projects during and after World War II. The head of Caltech, Robert Millikan, had recruited von Kármán to Caltech to help convince aircraft companies to stay in the region by promising them a supply
of good engineers. Tsien's return to Caltech as the Goddard Professor of
Jet Propulsion in 1948 after a brief stint at MIT similarly reflected the institute's and the region's ambition to become a leader in the new aerospace field in the postwar period.[26]

As detailed by Iris Chang, Tsien rose as an aerospace scientist in the
1940s but was persecuted as a suspected Communist during the early
1950s and, in 1955, was allowed to return to China, where he assumed
leadership of the Chinese space-and-missile program.[27] In the wake of his
departure, many Chinese Americans seemed to take two lessons from his
experience: one, that Chinese Americans could indeed excel in American
science and technology, and two, that in order to succeed in the United

States, they had to concentrate on their professional achievement and avoid politics at all costs.[28] This legacy, in addition to the effects of racial discrimination and language barriers, may also help account for the relative paucity of Chinese/Asian Americans in aerospace management.

The strategy, however, did seem to lead to success for a number of Chinese American scientists at academic institutions in Southern California, including those who studied aerospace. Yuan Cheng "Bert" Fung, for example, came from China in 1946 to pursue a PhD in aeronautics and mathematics at Caltech but decided to stay in the United States after he completed the degree in 1948. He became the second ethnic Chinese (after Tsien) to hold a professorship at Caltech, made major contributions to the field with his study of aeroelasticity, and pioneered the new field of biomechanics and bioengineering, first at Caltech and later at the University of California, San Diego.[29] Theodore Y. Wu, who followed Tsien and Fung as the third Chinese American professor at Caltech, also worked in fields related to aerospace engineering.[30] Another Chinese American aeronautical scientist, Tung-Hua Lin, came to the United States after designing China's first airplane (using a wood frame) in the 1940s during the war against Japan and stayed on to become an engineering professor at UCLA in 1955. Apparently the first Chinese American faculty member at the university, he made major contributions to the safety of building materials, including metals used in the construction of airplanes.[31]

Representing a younger generation of Chinese American aerospace scientists was Chih-Ming Ho. Coming from Taiwan in the 1960s, Ho received his PhD from Johns Hopkins in 1974 and rose to full professor of aerospace engineering at USC before moving to UCLA in 1991 to help found the new field of micro-electro-mechanical systems research with applications in aerospace. Elected a member of the U.S. National Academy of Engineering in 1997, Ho has been active in scientific and technological exchanges with institutions in Taiwan and mainland China.[32] A 2009 review of UCLA's Department of Mechanical and Aerospace Engineering, for example, counted eight Chinese Americans (and about ten other Asian Americans) among its thirty-five active faculty members. The presence of these prominent Chinese American academics in turn helped attract other Chinese students from Taiwan and elsewhere to Southern California, often to study and work in aerospace. Following the 1965 immigration reform, they would help bring their own extended families to the Los Angeles area.

Following the establishment of diplomatic relations between the United States and China in 1979, an even larger wave of students and immigrants came from mainland China to the United States, where many of them studied science and technology. Most ended up working as scientists and engineers in the United States, some in aerospace in Southern California. The reopening of bilateral relations also led to increased trade in aerospace and opportunities for Chinese Americans in brokering such deals. In the early 1980s, for example, the Los Angeles–based aerospace company McDonnell Douglas entered into an agreement with China both to sell it aircraft and to help it set up facilities to produce its own. For this purpose the company created a subsidiary, McDonnell Douglas China, and appointed Gareth Chang, a Chinese American, its president.[33]

The dynamic mutual reinforcement of the aerospace boom and Chinese immigration from both Taiwan and mainland China eventually helped reshape Southern California. The influx of the new Chinese immigrants led to the rise of new Chinatowns in metropolitan Los Angeles, especially Monterey Park ("Little Taipei"). The city elected the nation's first female Chinese American mayor, Lily Lee Chen, then a social-work manager for Los Angeles County, in 1983. In an interview with the *Los Angeles Times* at the time, Chen explained why she and her husband Paul, an aerospace engineer, decided to move from Seattle to Los Angeles: "The space industry was booming and so was the field of social work.... We were part of something important."[34] Aerospace jobs also brought Chinese immigrants to other parts of Southern California, including the Palos Verdes peninsula, beginning in the early 1980s.[35] According to a study by the sociologist Yen-Fen Tseng, the lure of Southern California continued into the 1990s, when "Taiwanese professionals and executives have...found Los Angeles more attractive because of its engineering jobs in high-tech and aerospace industries and its Asia-Pacific business environment."[36]

As they have settled into Southern California, many Chinese American scientists and engineers in aerospace-related fields have become leaders of local Chinese American communities. Peter Yao, a child when he migrated to the United States with his refugee family in the mid-1950s, later became an engineer and mid-level manager at the aerospace firm Raytheon and in 2006 was elected the first Chinese American mayor of the city of Claremont.[37] Munson Kwok of Aerospace Corporation became president of the Chinese Historical Society of Southern California and one of the founders of the Chinese American Museum in Chinatown.[38] Regional organizations recognized Chinese Americans in aerospace. In 2007, for example, the Chinese American Engineers and Scientists Association of Southern California (CAESASC) honored Heidi

Shyu, vice president of corporate technology and research at Raytheon. Shyu, who had migrated with her family from Taiwan to the United States at the age of ten, became chair of the high-level U.S. Air Force Scientific Advisory Board in 2005 and thus rose to be one of the few women and Asian Americans in a leadership position in aerospace and military research and development.[39]

The increasing importance of Chinese American scientists and engineers was also recognized within aerospace companies in Southern California. In the 1990s, for example, the Aerospace Corporation, a major local firm, joined with several Asian American organizations to establish the "Asian-Pacific Americans of the Year" awards. In 1998 the awards went to, among others, two Chinese American engineers, Dick Chang and James Chang. Dick Chang, an expert on material and structural problems, was originally from Taiwan, received his PhD from UCLA, and started working at Aerospace in 1973. He was active with the company's Aerospace Asian American Association, working on issues related to affirmative action, and in the CAESASC. James Chang, a specialist on damage tolerance and fracture control for aircraft and space vehicles, also came from Taiwan and joined Aerospace in 1983. He was equally active in the local Chinese American community, founding the Chinese Culture Association of Southern California and chairing, at one point, the Southern California Chinese School Council.[40]

Not all Chinese Americans had the same political views, especially when it came to relations between Taiwan and mainland China. Many Taiwanese American aerospace scientists and engineers, especially those who were native-born Taiwanese (in contrast to those who fled to Taiwan in 1949 with the Nationalists) and who were sympathetic to the Taiwanese independence movement, organized the Taiwanese American Aeronautics and Space Association in 1993, a majority of whose members live in Southern California. This organization facilitated technology transfer to Taiwan after the native-born Lee Teng-hui became president in 1988 and especially following the election victory of the pro-independence Democratic Progressive Party (DPP) in 2000.[41] Some of these DPP supporters gave up their U.S. positions to return to work in Taiwan full time. Ching Jyh Shieh, an aerospace engineer who had headed the Southern California Taiwanese Association, for example, moved to Taiwan in 1995 to serve in its space program.[42] In contrast, the Society of Chinese American Aerospace Engineers, founded in 1999 and with many of its members originating from mainland China, declared in its bylaws that it was a nonpolitical organization with the sole purpose of promoting the welfare of

Chinese American aerospace engineers, "following American laws and national regulations governing the restrictions of secrets." It maintained contacts with both sides of the Taiwan Strait.[43]

Of all the aerospace institutions in Southern California, JPL had particular success in attracting Chinese American scientists and engineers, probably in part because its work was largely unclassified and so did not require security clearances that might be difficult for immigrants to obtain. A report in 2004 put the number of Chinese Americans at JPL at three hundred. In recent years the prominent roles they played in the Mars rover and Stardust projects have earned them publicity, both in mainstream American media and in Chinese-language media in the United States, mainland China, and Taiwan. But even in this supposed bastion of meritocracy, sometimes Chinese American scientists felt they suffered from conscious or unconscious discrimination. In 2006, Peter Tsou, for example, complained to Chinese-language media that, although he was the original designer of the Stardust project, which collected comet dust in space, he was relegated to the position of deputy principal scientist while others received most of the credit for its success. Tsou did not hide his disappointment and resentment: "This happened mainly because I am a Chinese."[44]

While, for many Chinese American scientists and engineers, aerospace presented a technological escape from politics, for others, the boundary was far blurrier, especially after the end of the Cold War. In the early 1990s, although the Soviet and then Russian menace decreased, the perceived threat from a rising China increased. Ever since the Tsien case, Chinese Americans in aerospace often worked in the shadow of suspicion of disloyalty, as did their counterparts in nuclear science and other sensitive areas of technology. There have been a few cases of Chinese Americans convicted of violating the law in technology transfer to China in recent years. In 1997, Peter Lee, a Taiwanese-born Chinese American physicist who worked at the Los Alamos National Laboratory and later at TRW Space & Electronics Group in Manhattan Beach, was arrested by the FBI for transmitting secret technology on lasers and submarine detection to Chinese scientists. In a plea bargain, Lee admitted that he leaked classified information to Chinese scientists but insisted that it was unintentional—he was carried away by his enthusiasm for scientific exchange. In view of his cooperation and the fact that the information Lee leaked was soon declassified, Lee was given a very lenient sentence, one year in a halfway house. The event received scant media attention until the nationally publicized case of Wen Ho Lee, another Taiwanese-born Chinese American scientist at Los Alamos who was accused of leaking vital nuclear secrets to China in 1999. That affair, which ended with only a minor conviction of mishandling classified information, ignited what to many Chinese Americans was a new witch-hunt resembling the McCarthy era.[45]

In the 2000s, Chi Mak, a Chinese American engineer in the Los Angeles area, and several of his relatives were convicted of attempting to violate export-control laws, among other charges, by transmitting unclassified data related to submarines to people in China.[46] Once again, there was fear that this and similar cases would be used to cast doubt on all Chinese and Asian Americans. In court, the FBI revealed that it had put thousands of Chinese Americans, from both mainland China and Taiwan, under various forms of monitoring and surveillance for suspicion of military and commercial espionage. Influential Chinese American commentator Chen Shiyao warned in *Shijie Ribao* (*World Journal*), the largest Chinese-language newspaper in the United States by circulation, that such cases would probably limit the advancement of Chinese Americans in defense-related industries in the future, "with implications even for second, third, and subsequent generations of Chinese Americans":

> In the shadow of the so-called Chinese menace, traps are everywhere in U.S.–China scientific exchange. Anyone not careful enough will likely be snared in legal troubles. Will Chinese Americans be sacrificed as pawns in superpower competition? Those Chinese Americans who are in sensitive occupations should learn to behave and protect themselves.[47]

In all likelihood, such cases will make Chinese (and other Asian) Americans think twice before going into aerospace, just as the Wen Ho Lee case affected their attitudes toward working for the nuclear weapons and national labs (and hence increased the appeal of working at less-classified places like JPL). Yet, at a time when the GAO and other federal agencies are warning of a "major workforce crisis in the aerospace industry," the United States can ill afford to lose a major source of aerospace labor, and even less to again make an entire ethnic group suffer injustice due to international politics and the actions of a few individuals.[48]

Conclusion

Like other American scientists and engineers, Chinese American aerospace scientists and engineers in Southern California were profoundly shaped by broader social and political developments, in particular the Cold War arms and space races that created the huge demand for technical manpower in the post–World War II period. Along with other Southern Californians, they saw the fortunes of their industry and often the regional economy rise and fall (and rise again), following the contours of geopolitical developments. Like other minorities, especially other Asian Americans, they struggled against obstacles posed by racism and discrimination. Often their pursuit of professional excellence entailed forsaking political involvement or managerial advancement, whether by choice or necessity. Finally, like all Chinese Americans, they could not always control their own fates when international politics, especially U.S.–China relations, shaped how they were perceived by the rest of American society. The problem has proved an especially serious one for those dealing with sensitive, defense-related aerospace technologies.

In the second decade of this century, as the United States struggled to deal with a severe economic recession and other challenges, China and its scientific and technological progress, especially in space and clean energy, once again captured American national attention. In his state of the union address on 25 January 2011, for example, President Barack Obama characterized competition from China and India as "our generation's Sputnik moment" and vowed that the United States would "out-innovate, out-educate, and out-build the rest of the world."[49] President Obama was careful to call the Chinese achievements a constructive challenge to the United States, and his administration has continued the post-Nixon bipartisan tradition of pursuing scientific collaborations with China, but others took a more negative view of such endeavors. A U.S. congressman, for example, declared that China had stolen American space technology and succeeded in inserting a ban on all scientific and technological interactions with China involving NASA in the 2011 federal budget. Such measures recalled the days of United States–China Cold War rivalry, with potentially negative implications for Chinese American scientists and engineers.[50]

Yet, despite all the obstacles, the attraction of doing cutting-edge science and technology, pursuing professional advancement, and contributing to American national security, coupled with the social, cultural, and environmental lure of a diverse Southern California, has proved irresistible for many Chinese American aerospace scientists and engineers in the past and will likely do so in the future. As they continue to fashion and refashion themselves in the shifting political and economic winds, the struggles of Chinese American scientists and engineers will provide a fascinating case study for historians to explore how science, technology, race, immigration, regional dynamics, and transnational politics interact.

I thank Bill Deverell, Haiming Liu, Peter Westwick, and Min Zhou for encouragement, discussions, and comments on drafts of this essay, and Sara K. Austin for her editorial assistance. This work was supported in part by the National Science Foundation under Grant No. SES-1026879. Any opinions expressed in this essay are those of the author and do not necessarily reflect the views of the NSF.

Notes

1   President's Science Advisory Committee, *Scientific Progress, the Universities, and the Federal Government* (Washington, D.C.: U.S. Government Printing Office, 1960). For more on PSAC, see Zuoyue Wang, *In Sputnik's Shadow: The President's Science Advisory Committee and Cold War America* (New Brunswick, N.J.: Rutgers University Press, 2008).

2   Walter McDougall, *The Heavens and the Earth: A Political History of the Space Age* (New York: Basic Books, 1985), 322.

3   PSAC, *Meeting Manpower Needs in Science and Technology* (Washington, D.C.: U.S. Government Printing Office, 1963).

4   Wiesner to Kennedy, 8 May 1963, in Kennedy Library, President's Office File, Departments and Agencies File, box 85, folder "Office of Science and Technology 1963."

5   Zuoyue Wang, "Transnational Science during the Cold War: The Case of Chinese/American Scientists," *Isis* 101 (June 2010): 367–77.

6   Benjamin Zulueta, "'Brains at a Bargain': Refugee Chinese Intellectuals, American Science, and the 'Cold War of the Classrooms'" (PhD diss., University of California, Santa Barbara, 2004).

7   Zulueta, "Brains," 56. Wang, "Transnational Science."

8   Iris Chang, *The Chinese in America: A Narrative History* (New York: Viking, 2003), 283–311. A shocked Donald Hornig, President Johnson's science adviser, found that almost the entire Korean engineering class that graduated in 1965 went to the United States and most stayed after finishing their graduate training; Wang, *In Sputnik's Shadow*, 256.

9   Chang, *Chinese in America*, 286.

10   Ibid., 314–15.

11   U.S. Government Accounting Office [hereafter GAO], *Equal Employment Opportunity: Women and Minority Aerospace Managers and Professionals, 1979–86* (Washington, D.C.: GAO, 1989), http://archive.gao.gov/d26t7/139889.pdf. The census number is on p. 2, and the EEO number is on p. 25.

12   Ibid., 25, 27.

13   For more on the lack of Asian Americans in aerospace management, see Deborah Woo, *Glass Ceilings and Asian Americans: The New Face of Workplace Barriers* (Walnut Creek, Calif.: AltaMira Press, 2000), esp. chap. 5, "The Glass Ceiling at 'XYZ Aerospace.'"

14   Lucie Cheng and Philip Q. Yang, "Asians: The 'Model Minority' Deconstructed," in *Ethnic Los Angeles*, ed. Roger Waldinger and Mehdi Borzogmehr (New York: Russell Sage Foundation, 1996), 305–34 at 328.

15   GAO, *Equal Employment Opportunity*, 36.

16   Joyce Tang, "Differences in the Process of Self-Employment among Whites, Blacks, and Asians: The Case of Scientists and Engineers," *Sociological Perspectives* 38 (1995): 273–309. Interestingly, she found that immigrant Asian Americans suffered less than native-born Asian Americans in the self-employment market.

17   Bureau of the Census, "Census '90: Detailed Occupation by Race, Hispanic Origin, and Sex," available from U.S. Census Bureau website, http://censtats.census.gov/cgi-bin/eeo/eeojobs.pl.

18   Bureau of the Census, "Census 2000 EEO Data Tool," U.S. Census Bureau website, http://www.census.gov/eeo2000/index.html.

19   GAO, *Equal Employment Opportunity*, 27 (table III.2), 71. The total growth in Los Angeles was slightly behind the national rate of 58 percent, partly because of the explosive increase (4,000 percent) of aerospace jobs in Seattle, the region with the second largest number of aerospace employees behind Los Angeles, from 1,599 in 1979 to 65,002 in 1986; ibid., 71. The report referred to Los Angeles and Seattle "local areas," which in the case of Los Angeles probably meant Los Angeles County, not the city; ibid., 26. On the rise of Los Angeles as an aerospace center, see the other essays in this book and Allen J. Scott, *Technopolis: High-Technology Industry and Regional Development in Southern California* (Berkeley and Los Angeles: University of California Press, 1993).

20   Bureau of the Census, "Census '90: Detailed Occupation."

21   Bureau of the Census, "Census 2000 EEO Data Tool."

22   GAO, *Equal Employment Opportunity*, 27 (table III.2).

23   Ibid., 73.

24   Ibid., 74–75. In contrast, in the Seattle area, the percentage of Asian Americans in managerial positions in aerospace was lower than their percentage in the regional workforce in general, but the percentage in professional positions was higher; ibid., 76–78.

25   On the significance of Chinatowns for the emergence of immigrant Chinese American communities, see Min Zhou, *Chinatown: The Socioeconomic Potential of an Urban Enclave* (Philadelphia: Temple University Press, 1992). On Taiwanese preference for Los Angeles as a destination for immigration, see Yen-Fen Tseng, "Beyond 'Little Taipei': The Development of Taiwanese Immigrant Businesses in Los Angeles," *International Migration Review* 29 (1995): 33–58. On the importance of ethnic food for Chinese immigrants in Southern California, see Haiming Liu and Lianlian Lin, "Food, Culinary Identity, and Transnational Culture: Chinese Restaurant Business in Southern California," *Journal of Asian American Studies* 12 (June 2009): 135–62. For more general studies of Chinese Americans in Southern California, see Min Zhou, *Contemporary Chinese America: Immigration, Ethnicity, and Community Transformation* (Philadelphia: Temple University Press, 2009) and Wei Li, *Ethnoburb: The New Ethnic Community in Urban America* (Honolulu: University of Hawaii Press, 2009).

26   On Millikan and von Kármán's recruitment, see the oral history interview with Theodore Y. Wu by Shirley K. Cohen, 21 February, 6 March, and 12 March 2002, Caltech Archives Oral Histories Online website, http://resolver.caltech.edu/CaltechOH:OH_Wu_T.

27   Iris Chang, *Thread of the Silkworm* (New York: Basic Books, 1995).

28   Zuoyue Wang, "Chinese American Scientists and U.S.–China Scientific Relations: From Nixon to Wen Ho Lee," in *The Expanding Roles of Chinese Americans in U.S–China Relations: Transnational Networks and Trans-Pacific Interactions*, ed. Peter H. Koehn and Xiao-huang Yin (Armonk, N.Y.: Sharpe, 2002), 207–34.

29   Zuoyue Wang, "Yuan Cheng Fung" (unpublished 2003 paper), and interview with Fung by Wang, 20 June 2010, La Jolla, Calif.

30   Wu interview by Cohen.

31   M. Chin, "In Memoriam: Tung-Hua Lin, Professor Emeritus of Civil and Environmental Engineering," UCLA Engineering website, http://www. engineer.ucla.edu/newsroom/featured-news/archive/2007/in-memoriam-tung-hua-lin-professor-emeritus-of-civil-and-environmental-engineering. Chen Qing, "Zhongguo hangkong zhifu Lin Tung-Hua qingshi liuming" (Tung-Hua Lin, the father of Chinese aviation, will live in history), *Shijie Ribao* (*World Journal*), 9 July 2007, B2.

32   UCLA Department of Mechanical and Aerospace Engineering website, http://www.mae.ucla.edu.

33   Michael Parks, "China Opens Up to U.S. Aerospace Companies," *Los Angeles Times*, 30 July 1984, D3. Ralph Vartabedian, "Chinese Engineers in Southland Seek to Learn, Not Play," *Los Angeles Times*, 11 November 1985, D1.

34   Mark Arax, "Lily Lee Chen: Her Roots—and Perhaps Her Political Goals—Lie beyond Monterey Park," *Los Angeles Times*, 14 November 1985, SG 1, 7, 12 at 12.

35   Mark Gladstone, "More and More Asians Merge into Life on the Peninsula: High Income, Low Profile Characterizes Growing Group of Business, Professional Residents," *Los Angeles Times*, 26 September 1982, SB1.

36   Tseng, "Beyond 'Little Taipei,'" 39.

37   "Full Biography for Peter S. Yao," League of Women Voters of California website, http://www.smartvoter.org/2003/03/04/ca/la/vote/yao_p/bio.html; Caroline An, "Peter Yao Elected Mayor of Claremont," *Inland Valley Daily Bulletin*, 30 March 2006.

38   "Dr. Munson Kwok," in *2011 Asian Pacific American Heritage Day,* Los Angeles County Asian American Employees Association brochure, 19 May 2011, http://www.lacaaea.com/AAEAPDF/Heritage_Brochure_05192011.pdf.

39   "Chinese American Heroine: Heidi Shyu," *AsianWeek*, 16 July 2009, http://www.asianweek.com/2009/07/16/chinese-american-heroine-heidi-shyu; "On the Move," *Daily Breeze* (Torrance, Calif.), 4 April 2005, D2.

40   "Three Named Asian-Pacific Americans of the Year," Aerospace website,
      29 June 1998, http://www.aero.org/news/newsitems/asianamer-062998.html.
      The two were apparently unrelated.

41   For more details, see Taiwanese American Aeronautics and Space Association
      website, http://www.taasa-web.org.

42   Vik Jolly, "Fountain Valley Man Fights to Stay Free amid Former Boss' Cor-
      ruption Case," *Orange County Register*, 25 November 2008. See also Ching
      Jyh Shieh (Xie Qingzhi in *pinyin*) and Peng Linsong, *Xie Zhiqing de shengming
      zhendong* [Ching Jyh Shieh's life shaken] (Taipei: Yushang, 2008). In contrast,
      David H. Huang, who was born in mainland China and was a longtime aero-
      space engineer and executive at Rocketdyne in Los Angeles, went to Taiwan
      to serve under the Nationalist government in 1980 but returned to the
      United States in the 1990s following the rise of the DPP. See David H. Huang
      (Huang Xiaozong in *pinyin*) and Yin Zhengci, *IDF zhifu: Huang Xiaozong de
      rensheng yu shidai* [Father of the IDF: David H. Huang's life and times]
      (Taipei: Tianxian Wenhua, 2001).

43   See Society of Chinese American Aerospace Engineers website,
      http://www.scaae.org.

44   Chen Yong, "Zou Zhe: Hunhuang 'xingchen' beihou de guduzhe" [Peter Tsou,
      a loner behind the glory of "stardust"], *Guoji xianqu daobao* [International
      Herald Leader], 23 January 2006, http://news.xinhuanet.com/st/2006-01/23/
      content_4088460.htm.

45   Wang, "Chinese American Scientists and US–China Scientific Relations."
      On the Lee case, see also Dan Stober and Ian Hoffman, *A Convenient Spy:
      Wen Ho Lee and the Politics of Nuclear Espionage* (New York: Simon and
      Schuster, 2001), and Wen Ho Lee with Helen Zia, *My Country versus Me*
      (New York: Hyperion, 2001).

46   David Haldane, "3 Plead Guilty in Chinese Spy Case," *Los Angeles Times*,
      5 June 2007, B3.

47   Chen Shiyao, "Zhongguo dieying chuangchuang zaixian?" [Shadowy China
      spies again?], *Shijie Ribao zhoukan* [*World Journal* weekly magazine],
      13 May 2007.

48   GAO, *U.S. Aerospace Industry: Progress in Implementing Aerospace Commis-
      sion Recommendations, and Remaining Challenges*, GAO-06-920 (Washing-
      ton, D.C.: GAO, September 2006), 9, http://www.gao.gov/new.items/
      d06920.pdf.

49   Barack Obama, "Remarks by the President in State of Union Address,"
      25 January 2011, http://www.whitehouse.gov/the-press-office/2011/01/25/
      remarks-president-state-union-address.

50   See Jeffrey Mervis, "Spending Bill Prohibits U.S.–China Collaborations,"
      Science 332, no. 6029 (29 April 2011), 521, and Zuoyue Wang, "China, Sputnik,
      and American Science," *APS* [American Physical Society] *News* 20, no. 10
      (November 2011): 5, 7.

The Air Force and the Chumash:
The "Curse of Slick-6"

Vandenberg Air Force Base lies on California's Central Coast, about an hour's drive north of Santa Barbara. It is a beautiful spot, where rocket launch pads are lost amid the cragged hills and valleys that flow down to the Pacific Ocean. It is also the source of a long-standing myth resulting from a cultural conflict between the Chumash Indians, who originally occupied the territory, and the United States Air Force. This is a story that remains relatively unknown and is inherently difficult to research, involving as it does two different communities, and types of expertise not usually mingled. A researcher familiar with military history records may lack the skills of a researcher familiar with Native American history and culture, and credentials useful for opening doors for military research may actually close doors to Native Americans. There are also issues of access to materials in both communities. But the intersection of these two groups and issues, normally considered distant and disconnected, is precisely what makes this history interesting.

The West Coast Launch Range, which extends out into the Pacific Ocean from Vandenberg, is one of two primary launch sites in the United States. Vandenberg was established in the late 1950s on the site of a former Army training base known as Camp Cooke. It is on a promontory on the coast, bounded on the south by open ocean. This is advantageous for launching satellites into north–south orbits that fly over the poles. (The military launches its reconnaissance satellites into polar orbits because the Earth rotates underneath them as they repeatedly circle the poles, and so they eventually pass over every part of the planet.) If a rocket bearing a satellite blows up after launch from Vandenberg, the pieces fall in the ocean rather than on occupied land. Florida's Cape Canaveral is unsuited for such launches because rockets taking off there pass over Cuba during their ascent; a failed launch once rained wreckage down on that country.

Most of the launches from Vandenberg are either ICBM test flights sent arcing southwest into the Pacific, or military satellites sent into polar orbit, although some civilian and commercial satellites are also launched from Vandenberg. Google's *GeoEye-1* was launched from Vandenberg, and weather satellites are also launched there. Many of Vandenberg's launches are visible from Santa Barbara and even Los Angeles. However, because the base never launched astronauts, it never received the outside attention that Cape Canaveral has.

Slick-6

Starting in the mid-1960s, the Air Force began construction of a new launch-pad facility at Vandenberg, designated Space Launch Complex 6 (SLC-6), or "Slick-6" for short. (The Air Force had already built other launch pads designated SLC-1, SLC-2, and so on.) The purpose of SLC-6 was to serve as the preparation and launch site for a powerful new rocket known as the Titan IIIM, which was going to launch a small manned military space station known as the Manned Orbiting Laboratory, or MOL. Officially the MOL was to serve as an experimental test platform to determine whether there was any military mission for men in space. But by the later 1960s, the MOL had evolved into a powerful manned reconnaissance satellite. Today, MOL resides in an odd historical purgatory: some aspects of the program have been declassified whereas others, those pertaining to its primary reconnaissance mission, remain highly classified.

In order to build Slick-6, the Air Force needed more land, so the federal government used eminent domain to acquire an area owned by the Sudden family known as the Sudden Ranch. The Suddens reportedly fought this seizure, but they lost and the Air Force took the property, now known as Vandenberg's South Base, and began construction of the largest launch complex on the entire base. The federal government also built a penitentiary on some of the land, and today prisoners herd cattle on the ranchland.

In 1969 the MOL program was canceled as a result of cost overruns, schedule slippages, and technical reviews that indicated that putting men in the same spacecraft with sensitive optical systems was not a good idea. Slick-6 was incomplete at the time, but the Air Force had received enough money to finish it before placing it in mothballs. By 1970, the Air Force had a launch pad that had cost tens of millions of dollars and was no longer needed.[1]

By the mid-1970s the Air Force had decided to use NASA's space shuttle to launch its satellites into orbit. The Air Force and the secretive

National Reconnaissance Office, which built and operated the United States' intelligence satellites, wanted to place its satellites into polar orbit, and so they needed to launch the shuttle from Vandenberg. Existing reconnaissance satellites were already being launched from other launch sites at Vandenberg aboard Titan III rockets, but the plan was to transfer this function to the shuttle, which required a new launch facility.[2] Slick-6 was the obvious launch site for the shuttle—it was, after all, a vast, unused launch facility designed for large and powerful rockets—and so the Air Force began converting the facility to launch the shuttle.

The massive rebuilding effort soon ran into difficulties. There were technical problems, including the potential for explosive gases to build up in the launch-pad flame trench, cost overruns, delays, accidents, and allegations of drug use by construction workers.[3] After the *Challenger* accident in early 1986, the Air Force leadership decided not to launch its satellites on the space shuttle; once again, the Air Force shut down Slick-6 and placed it in mothballs. By this time the government had spent over $3.1 billion preparing SLC-6 to launch two types of launch vehicles, but had never launched a single rocket from the facility.[4]

In 1995 Lockheed used the Slick-6 facility for launching its first Lockheed Launch Vehicle (or LLV, later renamed Athena). This was a very small rocket. Lockheed's engineers placed it on a small corner of the massive pad facility; in pictures it looked like a pencil sticking up from the corner of a desk. The first rocket launched, in August 1995, failed to reach orbit. Two years later, in August 1997, Lockheed tried again, launching another Athena rocket carrying NASA's Lewis Earth-observing spacecraft from Slick-6. The spacecraft entered orbit but began spinning, and all contact was lost only a few days later. A little more than a month after launch, the spacecraft burned up in Earth's atmosphere.

In April 1999, the company tried a third time. This time an Athena II rocket launched from Slick-6 carrying Space Imaging's *IKONOS-1* satellite. Once again, the rocket failed to place the satellite into orbit. By this time, Vandenberg's Slick-6 launch complex had an ignominious reputation: three launches, three failures, and a history of failed projects, cost overruns, and canceled programs dating back over three decades.

The Chumash Indians

In the late 1970s and early 1980s, when the Air Force first started construction at Slick-6 preparing it for the space shuttle, a controversy was raging only a few dozen miles to the south, which soon spilled over to Vandenberg. In 1978 the California Public Utilities Commission and the

Federal Energy Regulatory Commission approved construction of a liquid-natural-gas import terminal north of Santa Barbara at Point Conception. The plan aroused local opposition, including protests by the Chumash tribe. The Chumash had occupied central California for thousands of years, but had suffered demographic collapse and political and economic dislocation. By the 1980s their tribe was politically and geographically fractured. But the rise of the American Indian Movement in the 1960s and 1970s demonstrated and inspired a new level of Native American political activism, including the "Longest Walk" protest of 1978, which highlighted the issue of tribal sovereignty.

The Chumash also protested the shuttle launch pad construction at Vandenberg, although these protests were never as organized or as vociferous as those against the Point Conception facility. Their protests took the form of sporadic demonstrations outside the Vandenberg gate. According to one Vandenberg employee, at times Chumash representatives met with the base commander in full tribal regalia to express their disapproval of the Slick-6 construction. The Chumash protests of the Point Conception and Vandenberg construction projects were based upon the Chumash religious belief that this area of the coast, from Point Conception roughly to Point Arguello (only a short distance north of SLC-6), is part of what the Chumash refer to as the Western Gate. This is the westernmost point of that stretch of the California coast. In the Chumash religion, the Western Gate is where their souls travel after death on the way to the afterlife. They therefore objected to white men building large industrial and military sites on what they considered sacred ground.

By 1983 specific plans for the Point Conception liquid-natural-gas terminal had been approved by the Federal Energy Regulatory Commission. But numerous Chumash protests, other local opposition, and the changing worldwide liquid-natural-gas market led to the terminal project's cancellation in 1985. One year later, Vandenberg's Slick-6 facility was placed in mothballs, not so much because of protests, but rather because of its history of delays and overruns and, especially, the failure of the space shuttle program in 1986.

The Curse

After the Air Force decided to develop SLC-6 for the space shuttle, they conducted in 1974 a survey of a stretch of land that was going to be converted, according to Larry Spanne, a former cultural affairs officer at Vandenberg. Spanne, who was responsible for oversight of the numerous archeological sites on the Air Force base, said that the survey included test excavations at numerous spots in order to determine if any archeological sites were in the way of the construction. Although several Chumash cemeteries were discovered, none of these was near the Slick-6 facility.[5] Later, in the late 1970s and early 1980s, Spanne was part of a contractor team that included Santa Ynez Chumash representatives monitoring construction of space shuttle roads and facilities. According to Spanne, "no human remains or cemeteries were discovered during that multi-year project."[6]

One day, soon after a construction accident at the pad, when a large structure was blown off the rails in a high wind, one of the Chumash elders assigned to the monitoring project remarked, "Larry, that place must be cursed." Spanne interpreted this as an offhand comment and said, "at no time did I hear any Chumash person say that their people had cursed the facility."[7]

At some time, probably when the Air Force began experiencing construction problems at Slick-6 in the mid-1980s, and following the protests, a rumor surfaced that the Chumash Indians had "cursed" the site. The rumor was that Slick-6 was built on the site of an Indian burial ground, and therefore the site was cursed; this explained the delays, the cost overruns and the accidents, and presumably also the drug abuse among the construction workers.

Stories of Indian curses have long been a part of American folklore. To white settlers, Indians seemed to have strange and difficult-to-decipher customs, and it was common to attribute bad luck to a mysterious force created by members of a different culture. In the case of SLC-6, the rumor was also a convenient way of blaming the Chumash for whites' problems—not only had the federal government expropriated sacred Chumash land, the Chumash were being enlisted as scapegoats for the Air Force's failures.

In 2007, Spanne recounted how "over the years I spent many hours attempting to dispel or debunk the rumors, but they persist." The "curse of Slick-6" rumor apparently existed for a long time before it was ever written down. In 1994, Roger Guillemette published a series of two articles about the launch site, which explained that the area was considered sacred by the Chumash.[8] Later, Guillemette wrote a more light-hearted article on the *Florida Today* newspaper's now-defunct *Space Online* website, which jokingly referred to the Chumash's supposed role in the "curse."[9] He intended the reference to be slightly humorous. According to Guillemette, who later became the website's editor, it was the site's most downloaded article.[10]

A few articles appeared in 2006 (one of them written by Phil Chien, who was later exposed for fabricating several parts of his stories, including a source used in a *Wired News* online article titled "Tribal Curse Haunts Launch Pad").[11]

Rumors of the curse also flared up among the contractors involved with the Athena launch vehicles in the 1990s, especially after the first two vehicles launched from SLC-6 failed to reach stable orbit. When Space Imaging prepared to launch the second *IKONOS* imaging spacecraft in September 1999, employees—most likely of Space Imaging—began circulating a doctored image depicting their rocket on its launch pad with a cartoon image of a Native American in ceremonial garb touching the vehicle, apparently blessing the launch (the cartoon image is from a collection of Microsoft Office clip-art graphics and is pasted over an actual photograph; the doctored image was later obtained by Guillemette, who supplied it to this author).

More significantly, at some point, possibly before the September 1999 Space Imaging launch, or several years later when construction work recommenced at SLC-6, a contractor brought a Chumash religious official to the site to "remove the curse." According to one government employee, there are photographs of the ceremony, although he refused to reveal them. According to a different former government employee, the incident created controversy when a group of Chumash Indians who were not involved in the ceremony learned about it and complained to the Air Force, which had never approved the ceremony and was unaware that it had even taken place. (Neither employee wanted their names used for this sensitive information, but one is a current Vandenberg employee and another is a former Vandenberg employee.) The incident soured a generally good relationship between the Air Force and the Chumash.

The rumors about the curse are wrong on several key points, starting with the claim of an Indian burial ground. There is no such burial ground anywhere on the SLC-6 facility. The Air Force performed a careful survey before it began construction in the 1970s and the official environmental impact statement for SLC-6 contained no mention of any cultural or archeological sites in that immediate area. As part of the Western Gate, the area does have religious significance to the Chumash and is connected to their beliefs about death, but it is not a "burial ground" in any sense of the term.

Although the "curse removal ceremony" created controversy at the time between the Air Force and some of the local Chumash groups, who felt insulted, renewed construction at the site after 2000 did not result in any further protests. This can most likely be attributed to active efforts by the Air Force to improve relations with the local Chumash groups, which included granting them access to their traditional hunting and fishing grounds on Vandenberg Air Force Base.[12] The Chumash even went so far as to honor Spanne, the base's cultural resources officer who had worked on the base for nearly two decades, upon his retirement in 2006, thanking him for his efforts to improve relations.[13]

Conclusion: Chasing Rumors

The September 1999 launch of *IKONOS-2* was successful. After that, Boeing converted SLC-6 to launch the company's powerful Delta IV rocket, including its large Delta IV Heavy. Delta IVs were launched successfully from SLC-6 in June and November 2006, a Delta IV Heavy was successfully launched in January 2011, and more launches are currently scheduled. Although the pace of launches is slow, it is likely that SLC-6 will continue in operation for many years to come. As the facility continues to make new history, a great deal of its past history and its relation to the Native Americans who lived on the land remains to be explored.

Chasing the tale of the "curse of Slick-6" poses a difficult challenge for researchers on several fronts. To begin with, it is often impossible to determine approximately when a word-of-mouth rumor begins. Although Roger Guillemette first wrote about the curse rumor in 1999, he had been told that the rumor dated from at least the time when space shuttle pad construction was ongoing (that is, the mid-1980s).[14] In addition, the episode involves research into two communities—Cold War aerospace organizations and Native American groups—requiring different research skills. To compound the problem, the Chumash are not unified, consisting of at least three groups, only one of which has federal recognition; these groups do not get along very well.

The aerospace side of the story, meanwhile, presents the obstacle of military classification. The MOL program remains partially classified, and the decisions leading to the closing of SLC-6 in the shuttle era have not been fully revealed. Most of the remaining secrecy is not directly related to the launch complex itself and therefore is probably not relevant. But it is still possible that more information on this subject exists in some still-classified official history of either the MOL or space shuttle programs.[15]

Finally, the episode evolved in the hazy realm of folklore and cultural stereotypes. Folklore and myths have concrete effects, however, in this case affecting the relationship between the Air Force and the Chumash. The "curse of Slick-6" ostensibly represented the revenge of Native Americans. The "curse" itself, however, was likely a creation of whites blaming Native Americans for problems in aerospace engineering and politics.

The Chumash, in effect, suffered twice: first when the U.S. military built launch pads on their sacred sites, then again when they got blamed for problems. The Air Force's failures cursed the Chumash.

NOTES

1   There are no comprehensive histories of the MOL. An account of the program can be found in: Curtis Peebles, *Guardians: Strategic Reconnaissance Satellites* (London: Ian Allan, 1987).

2   U.S. General Accounting Office, *A Second Launch Site for the Shuttle? An Analysis of Needs for the Nation's Space Program*, report to the U.S. Congress by Elmer B. Staats, Comptroller General, 4 August 1978, GAO No. PSAD-78-57, http://archive.gao.gov/f0902d/106762.pdf.

3   "USAF Studies Shuttle Engine Exhaust Problem," *Aviation Week and Space Technology*, 13 January 1986, 20; "KH-12 Reconnaissance Satellite Planned for Kennedy Launch," *Aviation Week and Space Technology*, 23 June 1986, 17.

4   U.S. General Accounting Office, *Space Shuttle: The Future of the Vandenberg Launch Site Needs to be Determined*, report to the chairman, Subcommittee on Strategic Forces and Nuclear Deterrence, Committee on Armed Services, U.S. Senate, 3 August 1988, GAO No. NSIAD-88–158, http://archive.gao.gov/d16t6/136501.pdf, 8.

5   Larry Spanne, email to Dwayne Day, 7 September 2007. This communication includes a forwarded email from Spanne to several other persons, which contains the details reported here.

6   Ibid.

7   Ibid.

8   Roger Guillemette, "Vandenberg: Space Shuttle Launch and Landing Site, Part 1," *Spaceflight*, October 1994, 354–57, and "Vandenberg: Space Shuttle Launch and Landing Site, Part 2," *Spaceflight*, November 1994, 378–81.

9   Roger Guillemette, "The Curse of Slick Six: Fact or Fiction?" *Florida Today Space Online*, 10 May 1999. (The article, along with *Space Online*'s entire archive, was removed from the paper's website in 2002 during a corporate takeover. The author is in possession of a paper copy.) A small article, titled "The Curse of Slick-6," and written by Phil Chien, appeared in *Popular Science*, August 1999, 28, but did not refer to the Chumash Indian issue, merely the string of bad luck: http://books.google.com/books?id=zeDOJtNcWUsC& dq=phil+chien+curse+of+slick-6&q=curse#v=page& q=curse&f=false.

10   Roger Guillemette, conversation with the author, September 2009.

11   "Tribal Curse Haunts Launch Pad," *Wired News*, 27 June 2006 (removed from the website); "Wired News Writer Faked Info," *Wired News*, 9 August 2006, http://www.wired.com/techbiz/media/news/2006/08/71562.

12   Frances Snyder, "Uncovering History," *Chumash! Magazine*, Summer 2006, 93. This is a short profile of Larry Spanne.

13   Ibid.

14   Guillemette, personal communication with the author, and Guillemette, "The Curse of Slick Six: Fact or Fiction?"

15   According to an Air Force source, there is an official history of the MOL program. However, a Freedom of Information Act request in 2005 to the National Reconnaissance Office resulted in a "refuse to confirm or deny records" response (otherwise known as a "Glomar response," after the Glomar Explorer case).

The two essays in this section address what we might call the footprint of aerospace. The first, by Glenn Bugos, looks at aerospace in the rest of California—namely, Northern California, thus returning to the issue, raised by Patrick McCray's essay, of the relations between the state's often-quarrelsome halves.

Bugos situates his essay in business history and economic geography. Such concepts as factor endowments, knowledge networks, and technology incubators—frequently invoked to explain the development of Silicon Valley microelectronics—apply, and often earlier, to Southern California aerospace. The usual view of these two industries, and of the state itself, is that they are starkly divided, Southern California and aerospace on the one hand, Northern California and Silicon Valley on the other, and never the twain shall meet. Bugos instead highlights overlap and interchange: between institutions, technologies, and culture. Of institutions that crossed the divide, the Bay Area hosted aircraft firms from the Loughead brothers and Hiller Aviation to Lockheed (again) and Loral, and the Ames Research Center provided key research expertise. As for shared technologies, aerospace demand for microelectronics helped drive the growth of Silicon Valley, and clean-room expertise, developed for aerospace firms, was applied to microchip fabrication. Finally, aerospace contributed to the celebrated Silicon Valley culture, through the government engineers and military inspectors who cross-pollinated Northern California aerospace firms and provided a model for the information networks so prominent later in Silicon Valley.

Bugos's analysis suggests the costs and benefits of industrial agglomeration. When weighing where to locate the Ames Research Center, officials considered the advantages of distance, and hence independence, from existing aircraft industry and from established aeronautical departments, such as that at Caltech. Does agglomeration lead to efficiencies and information-sharing, or to inbreeding and stagnation? The future of Southern California—and of Silicon Valley—will tell.

And, finally, aerospace left its mark on the land itself. Wade Graham's essay describes what one might call the aerospace ecology: how suburban development to house aerospace workers shaped land-use policy, how the need to protect factories and homes from flooding drove the engineering of the Los Angeles basin, how their need for power built hydro-electric networks, and how the air and water pollution from all these plants and people ultimately impelled environmental remediation. The environmental legacies of aerospace will linger long, affecting distant generations, and extend far, reaching well beyond Southern California. Graham's account underscores how aerospace fundamentally reshaped not only Southern California's physical terrain but also its human landscape. Any accounting of the aerospace century in Southern California must reckon with its human as well as its environmental costs.

GLENN E. BUGOS

Aerospace in the Rest of California:
The View from Silicon Valley

Aerospace was not restricted to Southern California. Throughout the rest of California, aerospace activity was intense enough to influence, and to show the influence of, the regions in which it occurred. Strategic Air Command airbases in the Central Valley, for example, notably shaped family life and small business in their communities during the 1960s. Likewise, regional dynamics affected airport operations in the 1950s around San Francisco and Oakland, where air fleets were maintained and air cargo began departing and arriving from around the Pacific Rim.

Aerospace has been similarly significant in the history of Silicon Valley, perhaps the most studied of all industrial regions. Silicon Valley never dominated America's aerospace industry; no more than 5 percent of the nation's aerospace workforce was ever located in Silicon Valley, even at the peak of the region's aerospace activity in the early 1960s. Nor did aerospace ever dominate Silicon Valley; at most, again in the early 1960s, it represented less than a quarter of industrial employment in the area. Yet aerospace was a driving force in the history of Silicon Valley, especially in the 1950s and 1960s when the American military bought much of Silicon Valley output. And technologies emerging from Silicon Valley firms during the 1970s and 1980s—electronic components intended for use in many industries—had a revolutionary effect on the technology of aerospace worldwide.

The aerospace industry, however, is important not only for driving the economy but also for creating and reflecting the regional work culture of Silicon Valley. Many have tried to define this work culture by highlighting, among other traits, teamwork, conspicuous production, and an acceptance of failure.[1] One trait of this culture, emphasized here, is that customers get heavily involved in the engineering and industrial process. In Silicon Valley today, customers of industrial components tend to be technically savvy, persistent, and willing to rely upon their suppliers.

Suppliers, in turn, allow their customers greater involvement in their operations. As a result, the roles played by customer and supplier remain fluid, especially when it comes to driving innovation. This particular trait is a legacy of the 1950s and 1960s, when aerospace ruled Silicon Valley.

The traditional approach of business historians to industrial districts has been to focus on the supply of commodities or ideas. Some districts arise out of existing local advantages, known as factor endowments, then continue because skilled labor is drawn to those districts and moves fluidly within them. Boosters of aviation in Los Angeles, for example, first emphasized its favorable flying weather and airports and later touted its trained workforce, which gave the industry momentum. In many industrial districts, firms remain small. In others, large, vertically integrated firms emerge—like U.S. Steel in the Pittsburgh metals region, Colt in the Connecticut firearms region, Lowell mills in the Massachusetts textile region, or Hughes, Lockheed, and Douglas in the Los Angeles aerospace region—which then support an ecosystem of suppliers.[2] However, regions built on factor advantages have not historically sustained themselves, and large firms have persisted as anchors only when they diversified. In any case, the factor endowment model does not explain the growth of Silicon Valley. None of the industries now rooted in Silicon Valley depended on natural factor endowments, with the possible exception of access to cheap hydroelectric power and a livable climate that attracted knowledge workers. Silicon Valley was dominated by large firms—Intel, Hewlett-Packard, National Semiconductor, Sun, Cisco, Oracle, now Google, but these companies seldom enjoyed complete control over production. Thus, neither the geography of Silicon Valley, nor the influence of dominant firms, shaped the character of industry there.

Another version of the factor endowment argument emphasizes universities as economic drivers rather than large firms. This assumes a linear model of innovation: basic research leads to applied research that in turn leads to industrial innovation. And in fact, Stanford University, at the epicenter of Silicon Valley, has been persistently inventive, and its engineering school has encouraged students to become entrepreneurs.[3] Most universities teach a diversity of subjects, so regions built around them do not get tied to any particular technology. Thus, the mining and food chemistry industries created Stanford's earliest millionaires; then, as those industries were eclipsed in the global economy, Stanford produced entrepreneurs fluent in vacuum tubes, silicon semiconductors, digital storage, personal computers, internetworking, biotechnology, and now nanotechnology. Universities have certainly seeded the development of other industrial regions, as did MIT and Harvard around Route 128. As a matter of policy, when a nation or state wants to create a new industrial region, they almost always start near an established university. But, unlike Caltech and UCLA, which have long had aeronautics departments that produced a population of aerospace experts,[4] Stanford was late to focus on the field. Not until 1958 did Stanford have a department of aeronautics and astronautics, and not until the 1980s did Stanford or the University of California at Berkeley have aerospace departments of national prominence.[5] Stanford's direct impact on the aerospace industry in Silicon Valley—as a supplier of engineering labor or aeronautics research—was small.

A newer approach to industrial districts focuses on industrial culture —persistent business practices and non-firm institutions (like families or guilds or angel investors) that serve to perpetuate certain styles of working. AnnaLee Saxenian first emphasized the importance of industrial culture in contrasting the firm-centered style of innovation along Route 128 near Boston with the more startup-driven culture of Silicon Valley.[6] In Silicon Valley, economic actors are interdependent. They are willing to rely on other firms for important parts of the technology they produce. Few Silicon Valley firms are vertically integrated in their control over their product. While they constantly innovate, innovation is often found in their conference rooms, where outside salesmen pitch new components to an audience attuned to the technological possibilities those parts open up. Many Silicon Valley firms run research laboratories not to invent new materials and devices, but rather to test new components and perform systems integration. Silicon Valley firms consider themselves good customers in that they understand the importance of innovation coming from their suppliers.

This article will focus on three examples of the fluid boundaries between customer and supplier that shaped the aerospace industry in Silicon Valley. First I will look at the impact of the NASA Ames Research Center, which served as an important supplier of aviation expertise to the Southern California firms in its earliest years and, in its later years, served as a customer infusing Silicon Valley technologies into America's space program. Second, I will examine airframe and satellite firms, whose impact on the region arose from their approach to manufacture. Practitioners of more traditional forms of aircraft manufacture, Hiller Aircraft in Palo Alto and the U.S. Navy maintenance facility in Alameda, had an arm's-length relationship with their suppliers, and thus little lasting impact on the region. By contrast, two satellite firms that invested in specialized manufacturing facilities and pursued more complex projects—Lockheed in Sunnyvale and Philco-Ford in Palo Alto—created a supplier ecosystem in Silicon Valley similar to that of the Southern California airframe manufacturers. Third, I will explore the resident inspectors of the military customers and the influence they had on component manufacturers that dominated the region. The inspectors served as cross-pollinators, spreading information the firms needed in order for the government to get the technology it wanted.

The NACA Making an Intelligent Customer

The National Advisory Committee for Aeronautics (NACA), the predecessor to NASA, broke ground for its second laboratory in December 1939, as the United States was preparing for World War II. The laboratory was located at the Army Air Corps airfield in Sunnyvale, California, famous as a dirigible base (and later known as Moffett Field). Ames Aeronautical Laboratory was dedicated to Joseph Sweetman Ames, founding chairman of the NACA and the architect of early aeronautical research in the United States. The NACA focused on solving engineering problems that no single firm could. Government customers of aircraft—initially from the military—staffed the NACA committees that tried to define the major technological barriers to fulfilling the government's aeronautical needs. The NACA advocated for the government customers of aircraft by analyzing the problems that aircraft manufacturers faced.[7]

The NACA also did fundamental research—theoretical investigations when those were necessary, but also testing of parts designed in-house and parameter variation studies. The NACA invested in building wind tunnels, conducting long duration flight tests, and compiling useful operational statistics. They supplied the results freely, in open publications, so all aircraft firms could use them to improve their designs. The NACA also helped military agencies solve intractable problems with specific aircraft, especially during World War II. But most of the firms that hoped to manufacture those aircraft were in Southern California. Why, then, did the NACA not build its second laboratory in Los Angeles, where the users of its expertise worked?

The NACA had already decided that its second laboratory should be on the West Coast. By 1939, four-fifths of American aircraft manufacturing occurred within two hundred miles of either the East or West Coast (about half each). Los Angeles had already staked its claim as the leading center of aeronautics on the West Coast, which was a long way from the wind tunnels of the Langley Aeronautical Laboratory, the first NACA laboratory, which opened in 1920 in the Virginia tidewaters.

Throughout the 1930s, leaders of the aircraft industry in Southern California encouraged the NACA to build a laboratory there. GALCIT, as the Guggenheim Aeronautical Laboratory at the California Institute of Technology in Pasadena was known, was a leading center of academic research, led by theorist Theodore von Kármán. In the mid-1930s, von Kármán, with considerable support from local congressmen, asked the military to fund the expansion of the GALCIT wind tunnels to serve the more immediate testing needs of local manufacturers.[8] General Henry "Hap" Arnold of the Army Air Corps and a member of the NACA objected. He thought neither basic nor applied research would be well served by so cozy a relationship between a university and the manufacturers of his airplanes.

In response, the NACA proposed its own West Coast laboratory. The question of where it should be built sparked intense political maneuvering. Even before Congress decided to fund construction of the facility, the NACA had decided that Moffett Field in Sunnyvale, California, was the best location. The Navy had done an extensive survey of aviation sites around the nation in 1931 when looking for a base for its dirigibles and had identified the advantages of Sunnyvale. (Moffett Field had been occupied by the Army since the 1935 crash of the Navy dirigible *Macon*.) The NACA relied on that survey, supplemented with visits to twenty other potential sites, when it concluded in 1939 that Moffett Field was the ideal place for its new laboratory.[9]

Smith DeFrance, whom the NACA had already selected as the engineer-in-charge responsible for building the new laboratory, visited the Sunnyvale site in March 1939, when he was in the area staffing an NACA exhibit at the Golden Gate International Exposition. In assessing the disadvantages of the site, he estimated that construction costs were 25 percent higher than in Virginia, that labor unrest was the norm, and that there was very little middle-class housing nearby. He considered the Virginia tidewater a more desirable place to live and raise a family.

The presence of Stanford University, only a fifteen-minute drive away, was a neutral factor. It offered access to libraries and specialized laboratories, but it was not then the powerhouse it would become in the 1950s. William F. Durand had built up an impressive research program in fluid mechanics at Stanford in the 1910s and 1920s, but by the 1930s aeronautics had stagnated as a special field of engineering study. Only three Stanford professors worked with the NACA: Everett Lesley and Elliott Reid continued Durand's work on propellers, and Alfred Niles studied aircraft structures. The University of California, an hour away across the bay, hardly figured in the NACA's appraisal. Berkeley also had a strong general engineering program, but its aeronautics program focused on mechanical engineering. The NACA laboratory in Virginia, likewise, relied little on nearby universities.

Among the advantages of the site were that high-quality well water for boilers could be obtained from Palo Alto, the Army shops were well tooled, a railroad main line ran nearby, with a spur into Moffett Field, and the local harbors were of adequate depth. Most important, electric power arrived at Moffett Field through the Newark substation, which was directly connected with seven new hydroelectric plants in the Sierras. DeFrance declared, "for little expense we would be able to obtain all the power necessary."[10]

However, the only way that Congress, and especially the congressman representing the district of the existing NACA laboratory, would fund the construction of a new laboratory was if the pork barrel was open to all, so the location was not specified in the funding legislation. Charles Lindbergh, then a member of the NACA Main Committee, agreed to chair the site-selection subcommittee required by Congress. Fifty-four cities submitted proposals to host the laboratory. Other leading proposals came from Mather Field near Sacramento, March Field in Riverside County, North Island in San Diego County, the Ordnance Depot near Ogden, Utah, and Lowry Field in Denver. (Notably, the proposal for Moffett Field lacked the flourish of cities with more active air enthusiasts. The local communities had been able to raise $100,000 to buy the land that became Moffett Field in 1931, but for whatever reason, boosterism never took wing in the Bay Area.) Under the urgency of the coming war, the subcommittee took only forty-five days to receive and review proposals. In the process they compiled a useful survey of the vitality of aerospace industry in major cities on the eve of World War II.[11]

In the end, Lindbergh reaffirmed the NACA's decision to locate the laboratory at Moffett Field. One reason was the region's factor endowments. The Bay Area had ample electrical power, and vast tracts of flat empty land along the bay that permitted safe flight-testing. At Moffett Field, the Army air base was well established, and the Army leadership very welcoming. There was also the right mix of skilled labor for the NACA. Not aeronautical engineers; they would initially transfer from Langley or be hired straight from universities around the country, following national searches. Nor was the labor force skilled in building airframes; it was far cheaper for the Southern California aircraft manufacturers to supply any special-purpose aircraft directly to the NACA. At no point did the NACA extol the presence of an aircraft industry around Mountain View. Rather, the NACA would rely on the shipbuilding trades located around Hunters Point and Marin County to weld the massive hulls of the wind tunnels; on the suppliers of machinery to the food industries to manufacture the electrical and mechanical controls of the tunnels; and on the same makers of precision instruments who supplied the local manufacturers of vacuum tubes. There is a saying that Silicon Valley happened where it did because you could get one of anything made there. Indeed, one of the strongest ties between the NACA and the area that became Silicon Valley was that both drew on local manufacturers for their special-purpose machinery.

Furthermore, the NACA leadership was keenly aware of its place in the ecosystem of aeronautical knowledge and valued the distance that Sunnyvale offered from both industry and academia. Sunnyvale was close enough that Southern California firms could ship up a model for a test within a day or fly their engineers there within three hours. But Moffett Field was not so close that firms would station engineers to look over the shoulders of NACA engineers. As for academic researchers, neither Stanford nor Berkeley dominated education in aeronautical engineering as did Caltech. NACA engineers would be free to try any approach to defining and solving a problem without fear of offending a local theoretician. That said, Stanford was relatively well represented in the ranks of the Ames laboratory, its graduates choosing not to go directly into industry or research. Three young graduates of Stanford, none with doctorates—H. Julian Allen, Russell Robinson, and John Parsons—worked for the NACA and helped in the site-appraisal effort. As a result, in Sunnyvale the NACA found the right geographical distance from the pull toward both applied and basic research. In that regard, it also reflected the industrial culture of Silicon Valley.

NASA Ames Channeling Silicon Valley

Smith DeFrance, who served as center director from Ames's founding in 1939 to 1965, attracted some the brightest aeronautical engineers, encouraged them to build test facilities to prove their ideas, then gave them freedom to pursue useful work. For example, Lew Rodert directed an urgent program on de-icing systems that won the U.S. National Aeronautics Association's Collier Trophy in 1946. Although Rodert's team applied their findings to developing a de-icing technology using hot air from the engine piped to the wings, his research was more notable for taking a systems approach to icing and analyzing all the ways that ice accretion might down an airplane. R. T. Jones tested his theories of the swept wing, and in the early 1950s led a group that developed engineering tools that firms could use to get aircraft through the problematic airflows of the transonic regime. Harry Goett led a research effort in subsonic and supersonic aerodynamics that solved myriad problems in jet flight in the 1950s, such as the design of air ducts. And H. Julian Allen proposed his concept of a blunt body shape for re-entry vehicles, then devised a series of hypersonic and high-heat tunnels to test the technologies that enabled nuclear-armed nose cones and later astronaut capsules to return safely to Earth. Each of these research efforts reflected the NACA's interest in stepping back from immediate engineering irritants and in helping government customers of aircraft solve problems encountered by all their suppliers.

This workforce also mapped to what became the Silicon Valley ideal—young, well paid, technically proficient, and obsessed with conspicuous production. In 1950 the average age of the workforce was twenty-nine, and during the Apollo years it rose to thirty-five. Aircraft and missiles then were cutting-edge technology and NACA engineers were recognized, around town and nationally, as leading America's future. NACA engineers were encouraged to move between research topics, and between testing and theory, and to prototype quickly. It was a fast-paced industry, with Ames engineers competing with engineers from the other NACA and military centers. The committee culture of the NACA, and the branch organization within the Ames laboratory, also reflected what Henry Lowood has called the "republic of engineers" mentality. In this culture, which Lowood documented at Varian Associates, bosses did not lead and manage their teams so much as they represented the interests of their teams within a flattened hierarchy. This came to typify a Silicon Valley style of workplace organization.[12]

From 1940 until 1957, Ames was the largest employer in Silicon Valley dedicated to aerospace, though it was never really large. Employment at Ames ramped up to 1,400 civil servants in 1958, then peaked at 2,245 civil service authorizations in 1967. The number of contract staff started to grow in the early 1960s and continued to expand until it equaled the number of civil service allocations in the 1980s. By 2005, NASA Ames had more than $3 billion in capital equipment, a research staff of 2,300 people, and an annual budget of more than $800 million. The center has had a significant and continuous, though hardly dominant, economic impact on the San Francisco Bay Area.[13]

Ames remained one of the smallest NASA centers and the most university-like in its aspirations. When Ames became part of the new National Aeronautics and Space Administration in 1958—one of ten field centers located around the country—it continued its NACA mission of research in new sciences and component technologies. Thermal protection research for re-entry vehicles represented Ames's clearest role on NASA's critical path. Even during the Apollo years, Ames was more likely to do research itself than to channel innovations from Silicon Valley into the space program. The really big procurements for the Apollo program, even those from Silicon Valley, were managed directly by the new space-flight centers in Huntsville and Houston.

With the ramp-up in space funding, though, Ames also became a vehicle for spreading government funds throughout Silicon Valley. Soon after 1958, Ames built a small-business office specifically to find ways in which local firms could supply its research needs. In the mid-1960s, it hosted the group that doled out most of NASA's future-oriented research grants to universities and think tanks. By 1971, it had a very active minority-business program through the Small Business Act. By not abandoning its NACA culture during the enthusiasm for Apollo, Ames was well positioned for NASA's transition to a post-Apollo era. Into the 1970s the culture of NASA Ames continued to reflect that of Silicon Valley, characterized by a focus on collaboration to leverage proven strengths, a desire to nurture new disciplines, a willingness to work cheap and fast, a need to match demonstration with theory, and a view further into the future of space exploration.[14]

Building on its expertise in human factors and pilot workload research, Ames became NASA's lead center in basic life-sciences research, which included radiation biology, adaptability to microgravity, and exobiology. This work had little to do with the gene-splicing boom that defined biotechnology in the 1980s, another major Bay Area industry, though Ames scientists worked closely with Silicon Valley firms specializing in biomedical instrumentation. Ames aerodynamicists, meanwhile, explored the complex airflows around rotorcraft and devised the first tilt-rotor aircraft, while others modeled airflows using new supercomputers and created the field of computational fluid dynamics. Ames bought its supercomputers elsewhere, though it was the launch customer for engineering workstations like those made by Silicon Graphics. NASA's investment in teleoperations and telepresence spurred the creation of three-dimensional graphics, head-mounted displays, and early virtual-reality technology. To link these computers together, Ames engineers pioneered internetworking, adopting open-source technologies like TCP/IP (a set of internet protocols) and the Unix operating system, and using tools from the Silicon Valley firms growing around it. When the internet was commercialized in 1996, a quarter of the world's data flowed through a router at NASA Ames.

NASA Ames, more recently, has drawn new types of university and corporate researchers into space exploration by developing the NASA Research Park at Moffett Field. In 1994, during the Base Realignment and Closure process, NASA Ames became the federal custodian of Moffett Field. NASA Ames converted five hundred acres of that land into a space for collaborative research and educational facilities to train a future aerospace workforce. More recently, the Center has engineered new types of small and modular spacecraft, working with the commercial space firms that began popping up around Silicon Valley in the 2000s. NASA leaders talked more actively about its NACA heritage and how NASA engineers could supply the expertise to help the emerging commercial rocket firms supply the vehicles that NASA needs.

Airframe and Systems Manufacturing

Aerospace is seldom seen as dominant in Silicon Valley because few firms in the Bay Area functioned as prime contractors or airframe manufacturers. In the period before World War II, however, about forty firms manufactured complete aircraft in the Bay Area, including the Loughead brothers, who got their start on the San Francisco waterfront. Many set up shop following the air meet of 1911 at the Tanforan airfield, near present-day San Francisco International Airport. The meet focused on military uses of the airplane. Flying conventional Wright and Curtiss aircraft, pilots there demonstrated for the first time bomb dropping, landing on a ship, and airborne wireless telegraphy. Each day 100,000 spectators jammed the meet, and organizers offered $2,750 in prizes for amateur aircraft makers who completed a half-mile course. Many amateurs turned entrepreneur, working out of garages, crafting airplanes one at a time out of wood by hand for wealthy enthusiasts. The more successful firms, like the Lougheads, were lured southward by active boosterism.[15] By the 1930s Los Angeles was the epicenter of aircraft engineering; young people who wanted to make their mark in the industry naturally headed there. None of the airframe firms that started in San Francisco survived into the postwar period.

One of the few airframe firms active in the region in the postwar period never found the right balance between high-tech research and lower-tech mass manufacturing. Hiller Aircraft Corporation started in a Berkeley garage in 1942 and moved to Palo Alto right after World War II. Hiller was the third company in America to build a successful helicopter. The cheap, reliable Hiller 360 helicopter (also known as the UH-12) proved popular in agribusiness around California. Hiller built a manufacturing plant about six miles north of Ames, and the company flourished through the 1950s. Employment peaked at 2,000 in 1960, mostly in the manufacturing trades. Stanley Hiller invested in, and got research contracts for, many new types of helicopters—flying jeeps, ducted-fan flying platforms, ramjet helicopters, the X-18 vertical takeoff and landing aircraft, and an aerial crane with jet engines at the rotor tips. Many of these were tested and fine-tuned at Ames, which used its full-scale wind tunnel to develop expertise in rotorcraft and aerodynamics at slow landing speeds. But prior to the Vietnam war, manufacturing contracts were sparse, and Hiller proved unable to convert its research projects into military orders. In 1964, devastated by losing the Army OH-6 contract to a desperate but successful bid by Hughes Aircraft, Hiller sold itself to the Fairchild Stratos Corporation and shut down its Palo Alto operations. The Hiller workforce was quickly absorbed into Lockheed and other local manufacturers.[16]

Across the bay in Alameda, a port serving the city of Oakland, the U.S. Navy built its Alameda Naval Air Station. In January 1941, the Assembly & Repair Department there began overhauling aircraft stationed on aircraft carriers, and by the end of the year, it employed 1,900 personnel and repaired fourteen aircraft a month. Employment peaked in 1945, with more than 9,500 civilian employees. The department did no aircraft design, nor did they fabricate new aircraft, but they represented 237 trades and were able to manufacture any part of an aircraft. The station encompassed more than 2 million square feet of shop space, including a foundry, pattern shop, plating shop, parachute loft, clean rooms, paint shops, and weapons testing areas. By 1958, the department had manufactured 1,305 jet and 881 reciprocating engines. The renamed Naval Air Rework Facility Alameda remained busy through the Vietnam War, and into the 1980s repairing Lockheed P-3C submarine chasers based at Moffett Field, then declined as the Navy moved maintenance work to cheaper areas. It was shut down in 1997. Because the facility manufactured many of its own parts, and bought others directly from aircraft manufacturers in other parts of the country, its impact on the industrial culture of the Bay Area was slim.

Of the aerospace firms in Silicon Valley in the postwar period, Lockheed has been by far the most significant. Lockheed established its Missiles and Space division in Sunnyvale in 1956, on what had been 275 acres of bean field. Though on the southern border of Moffett Field, this location was chosen less for its proximity to Ames than for its distance from

Los Angeles. As with the NACA, the geographical separation from Los Angeles proved to be a factor endowment. Lockheed management saw that the big new missile contracts of the early 1950s went to firms with expertise in electronics and systems engineering rather than the airframe firms. Lockheed set up a missiles group at its headquarters in Burbank, but found it hard to recruit electronic engineers from back east. So Lockheed decided to make a clean break from Burbank and build a massive new facility in Silicon Valley.[17] It also built a smaller facility in the Stanford Industrial Park to do advanced research on guidance technology. The strategy worked, and soon after construction began, Lockheed Missiles and Space won an enormous contract to build the Polaris submarine-launched ballistic missile for the Navy. It soon added to its backlog of high-profile work a series of Corona reconnaissance satellites for the Air Force. By 1960, more than 20,000 people worked for Lockheed in Sunnyvale—roughly ten times more than at NASA Ames and at Hiller. The population of Sunnyvale likewise exploded to 53,000 in 1960, five times more than in 1950, with most residents working for firms that supported the Lockheed plant.

In the rapid build-out of the Lockheed campus every local heating, ventilation, and air-conditioning contractor learned how to build the filtration systems for air and water that eliminated dust and contaminants, which could doom a system in the microgravity of space. Construction of clean rooms—which became the basic factory of Silicon Valley firms, whether in semiconductors or biotechnology—remained relatively cheap in Silicon Valley. The Ames Aeronautical Laboratory seldom made more than one of anything. The Lockheed plant, by contrast, was in the business of mass manufacturing and bought from companies willing to invest in materials research. Furthermore, Lockheed engineers influenced the way work was done in many supplier firms. In the 1960s the defense department asked Lockheed to procure more subsystems directly from its subcontractors—subsystems the military had previously bought directly—thus making Lockheed responsible to its military customers for the reliability procedures used by those suppliers.

By 1966 the Lockheed plant grew to 24,000 workers and remained more-or-less at that level until it peaked in 1990 with 28,000 workers. The number of aerospace workers in the entire Bay Area in the mid-1960s was 90,000, which is why many people think of Lockheed when they think of aerospace in Silicon Valley. During that time, submarine-launched ballistic missiles remained its major product, from the Polaris to the Poseidon to the Trident. The Agena multi-mission satellite bus supported NASA's interplanetary missions, the Navy Seasat series, and reconnaissance satellites. Lockheed built the Hubble Space Telescope and the thermal protection tiles used on the space shuttle. By 2003, a decade after the end of the Cold War, however, its workforce had declined to 6,000 and Lockheed receded from its prominence in Silicon Valley.

Space Systems/Loral has had a more notable impact on the industrial culture of Silicon Valley, primarily by enabling access to space for new digital communication technologies. It started in 1957 in Palo Alto as the West Coast laboratory of an established East Coast manufacturer, Philco Corporation, which was looking to diversify into electronic components. The U.S. Army Signal Corps hired Philco in September 1958 to build its Courier series of active repeater satellites, which demonstrated that high-volume communications could be relayed through space. The Courier was also the first satellite powered by solar cells. With other contracts to build satellite command and tracking networks, by the mid-1960s Philco's Palo Alto operations had 2,500 employees. Ford bought the Philco operations in 1961 and, while it continued to work on ground-based networks, its main focus shifted to bigger and more complex communication satellites for military customers. Philco-Ford launched the first geostationary weather satellite, the *SMS-1*, in 1974 and moved into the commercial satellite industry with the Intelsat V series. In 1990 it was acquired by Loral, to become Space Systems/Loral. Its modular 1300 satellite platform, refined in 1989, was stabilized on three axes, optimized for geostationary orbit, and powered by ever-larger solar panels. It has remained the platform on which they integrated different types of electronics—for digital television and radio, global positioning, two-way radio, broadband internet, air-traffic control, weather and imaging, and other types of surveillance. From 1994 through 2008 it manufactured more than 131 satellites, almost ten a year, at a campus of twenty-five buildings in Palo Alto. Though its workforce seldom rose above 2,000, Space Systems/Loral into the 1990s enabled a variety of spin-off firms nearby, which developed electronics to mount on its satellites.

Cross-Pollinators in a Region of Component Manufacturers

Entrepreneurship in Silicon Valley historically depended upon social networks linked together by cross-pollinators and intelligence gatherers—people who made it their job to connect people and firms in ways that went beyond traditional relationships between supplier and purchaser. Today, the cross-pollinators are professional service firms. Lawyers specializing in mergers and acquisitions, investment bankers looking to syndicate funding among a variety of money pools, and venture capitalists seeking synergies among portfolio firms all serve as conduits for transferring knowledge between firms. In the 1950s and 1960s, though, cross-pollinating among Silicon Valley firms was done by government engineers.

Historians Bill Leslie and Christophe Lécuyer have done a remarkable job explaining how military procurement set the stage for the growth of Silicon Valley. Leslie has shown how dozens of firms in Silicon Valley in the 1950s and 1960s depended upon government contracts, then shifted to commercial products as government funding dried up. Lécuyer has described how government contracts allowed these companies to invest in manufacturing processes that made electronics both cheap and reliable, and thus ultimately useful in commercial markets.[18]

Vacuum tubes and microwave devices preceded semiconductors as the dominant Silicon Valley technology, and some of the largest employers in Silicon Valley in the 1950s were West Coast operations of East Coast firms that supplied commercial markets—like Westinghouse, Sylvania, Raytheon, General Electric, and Zenith. But the firms that came to typify Silicon Valley were homegrown and dependent on military contracts. Varian Associates and Litton Engineering built vacuum tubes for guided missiles. Ampex in the early 1960s controlled 80 percent of the data-recorder market for airplanes.[19] Hewlett-Packard started by making industrial test equipment primarily for aerospace firms in the 1950s and 1960s. The launch-control facility at Kennedy Space Center and mission control in Houston used Hewlett-Packard technology in the worldwide network of tracking and communication stations.[20] Into the semiconductor era, the performance and reliability requirements for the integrated circuits needed for the Apollo program allowed Silicon Valley semiconductor firms to learn, at government expense, how to improve their manufacturing techniques. Fairchild Semiconductor and Intel were two integrated-circuit firms that benefitted from the largesse of the Apollo program. All these firms were the survivors; they competed with dozens of similar firms in the same niches, many of which disappeared through either merger or failure. They had little interest in becoming prime contractors. Their strategy was built on supplying components to prime contractors to integrate into larger systems. For them, a good word from a military officer to a prime contractor was the key to sales.

Edwin Hartman clearly played the role of cross-pollinator. Hartman was an aeronautical engineer and director of the NACA Western Support Office from 1946 until it was merged into the Jet Propulsion Laboratory oversight office in 1964. Hartman reported to the director of Ames, and spent a lot of time in the Bay Area, but his office was in Santa Monica, and his territory was the entire West Coast. He traveled constantly to visit airframe and component manufacturers. Often he asked about work the NACA had done for a manufacturer, making sure that it proved useful. His principal task, though, was to survey the state of the art in manufacturing techniques for aircraft, missiles, and aerospace components. If he found a problem unique to one company, he could suggest a solution from a supplier that had perfected a part or a method. If he uncovered a problem shared by many companies, he might suggest that the NACA investigate a solution. He wrote countless memos-to-file that, for historians, paint a vivid picture of the capabilities of each firm in California during the 1950s, and that, for NACA leaders back at headquarters, guided them on where to allocate their research work.[21] Hartman's ability to connect suppliers with those who needed a part or skill did much to refine the capabilities of the West Coast aerospace industry.

Into the 1950s and 1960s that cross-pollinator role was played by what the military called resident inspectors, or what a private firm might call an expeditor. Resident inspectors were young military officers educated in engineering who would likely be using the very equipment they had inspected on the battlefield after their two-year rotation ended. They hailed from any of the three services, depending on which service dominated the backlog of procurements from that factory. They were supported by an office of civilians, which in 1961 managed fourteen prime contracts and more than 130 subcontracts.[22] In Southern California, dominated by large airframe manufacturers, a resident inspector might be stationed at a single factory or even at one product line in that factory. In a place like Silicon Valley, where the contracts were smaller, one inspector visited many firms.

The inspectors' job was to visit factories and see for themselves that milestones were met. They wrote memoranda to the Pentagon desk officers overseeing development of a specific aircraft and to the officers following a particular technology, like magnetic recorders. In the 1950s, most aircraft components were supplied as government-furnished equipment, and these resident inspectors bore responsibility for assuring that the equipment worked right before it was passed upstream for the prime contractor to install in the complete aircraft. Furthermore, in the 1950s, the defense department invested in redundancy, meaning they might sign development contracts with many firms, hoping that one would succeed. In an era of redundancy and government-furnished equipment, the resident inspectors held much sway over which entre-preneurial firms the government invested in. In cost-plus-fixed-fee contracting, the government owned the intellectual property, so the in-spectors felt free to cross-pollinate their firms with information about the state of the art across many firms. Silicon Valley firms tended to wel-come a visit by their resident inspectors.

In the 1960s, resident inspectors were supplemented by the expedi-tors of the airframe firms, often in Los Angeles, that served as prime con-tractors. More aircraft subsystems were managed by a prime contractor as contractor-furnished equipment and the Pentagon funded fewer re-dundant contracts. As a result, more components were developed specif-ically for one system. Information about the state of the art in component manufacturing flowed more often through company proprietary channels, from Northern to Southern California. When it came to aerospace tech-nology, Silicon Valley firms had less opportunity to talk among themselves. The technology emanating from Silicon Valley—miniaturization of com-puting, software modules, computer workstations, and visualization—continued to shape aerospace technology. But aerospace no longer helped shape the work culture of Silicon Valley.

Aerospace Shaping of Silicon Valley Industrial Culture

Government aerospace and defense money drove the fortunes of many early Silicon Valley firms. These profits generated jobs and then profits that firms could reinvest in new products and thus justify a high level of industrial research. These profits also created pockets of expertise in technologies and processes that, when defense demand lagged, some Sil-icon Valley firms succeeded in transforming into products for civilian markets. But money and momentum behind specific technologies alone did not generate the sustained innovation that has characterized Silicon Valley since the early 1950s; persistent cultural traits do.

The notion of an involved, intelligent customer is central to the broader Silicon Valley work culture, and that notion was instilled through aerospace work done in Silicon Valley in the 1950s and 1960s. The Ames Research Center has served explicitly as a conduit for new technology be-tween aerospace firms and their government customers. The military res-ident inspectors likewise represented a government customer involved in all facets of their suppliers' business. Similarly, the Navy gave Lockheed Missiles and Space enormous latitude to impose technical surveillance on its suppliers, in the process broadening the ecosystem of Silicon Valley firms capable of manufacturing to government specifications.

This also influenced the relationship between north and south. Only two Northern California firms, Lockheed Missiles and Space in ballistic missiles and reconnaissance satellites and Space Systems/Loral in communication satellites, ever challenged the primacy of Southern California firms in airframe design and systems integration. Both firms were founded in the golden age of Silicon Valley aerospace, the 1950s, and eventually emerged as the leaders in their respective aerospace vehicles. Many other Silicon Valley firms, not primarily identified as aerospace firms, very profitably served as suppliers of electronic goods to the aerospace firms that clustered around Los Angeles. Avionics, in fact, grew more prominent over time and electronic parts were updated far more often than the airframes that hosted them. Few Silicon Valley firms ever became so dependent on aerospace electronics that it affected the culture of Silicon Valley. Military and aerospace funding has gone through boom-and-bust cycles over the past half-century, as has interaction between firms in the northern and southern parts of California. What has endured is the work culture born of the aerospace boom in the 1950s, which has defined Silicon Valley as an industrial region.

NOTES

1   Chong-Moon Lee and William Miller, *The Silicon Valley Edge: A Habitat for Innovation and Entrepreneurship* (Palo Alto, Calif.: Stanford University Press, 2000); *Understanding Silicon Valley: The Anatomy of an Entrepreneurial Region,* ed. Martin Kenney (Palo Alto, Calif.: Stanford University Press, 2000).

2   Allen J. Scott, *Technopolis: High-Technology Industry and Regional Development in Southern California* (Berkeley: University of California Press, 1993).

3   Stuart W. Leslie, *The Cold War and American Science: The Military-Industrial Complex at MIT and Stanford* (New York: Columbia University Press, 1993); Rebecca S. Lowen, *Creating the Cold War University: The Transformation of Stanford* (Berkeley: University of California Press, 1997); C. Stewart Gillmor, *Fred Terman at Stanford: Building a Discipline, a University, and Silicon Valley* (Palo Alto, Calif.: Stanford University Press, 2004).

4   Clayton R. Koppes, *JPL and the American Space Program: A History of the Jet Propulsion Laboratory* (New Haven, Conn.: Yale University Press, 1982); Judith R. Goodstein, *Millikan's School: A History of the California Institute of Technology* (New York: W.W. Norton, 1991); Paul A. Hanle, *Bringing Aerodynamics to America* (Cambridge, Mass.: MIT Press, 1982).

5   Brian Cantwell, "From Durand to Hoff: The History of Aeronautics at Stanford University," 28 April 2008, available at "Fiftieth Anniversary Symposium and Celebration" page, Stanford University Department of Aeronautics and Astronautics website, http://aa.stanford.edu/events/50thAnniversary/media/aahistory.pdf.

6   AnnaLee Saxenian, *Regional Advantage: Culture and Competition in Silicon Valley and Route 128* (Cambridge, Mass.: MIT Press, 1994).

7   Glenn E. Bugos and John W. Boyd, "Accelerating Entrepreneurial Space: The Case for an NACA-Style Organization," *Space Policy* 24 (2008): 140–47.

8   Alex Roland, *Model Research: The National Advisory Committee for Aeronautics, 1915–1958*, NASA SP-4103, 2 vols. (Washington, D.C.: NASA, 1985), 1:155–60.

9   Edwin Hartman, *Adventures in Research: A History of Ames Research Center, 1940–1965*, NASA SP-4302 (Washington, D.C.: NASA, 1970), 17–22; *Twenty-Fifth Annual Report of the National Advisory Committee for Aeronautics, 1939* (Washington, D.C.: U.S. Government Printing Office, 1940), 38–39. On the U.S. Navy review of potential dirigible sites, see William F. Trimble, *Admiral William A. Moffett: Architect of Naval Aviation* (Washington, D.C.: Smithsonian Institution Press, 1994), 233.

10   Smith J. DeFrance, "Memorandum: Report of Investigation of Building Conditions at Moffett Field, Sunnyvale, California," 31 March 1939, 3, in "22–1 Site for Ames, 1939," folder 1 in box 1, Records of the Ames Research Center, 1939–1967, National Archives and Records Administration, College Park, Md.

11   "Special Survey Committee on 20–3 Aeronautical Research Facilities," folder 2 in box 1, Records of the Ames Research Center, 1939–1967.

12   Henry Lowood, *From Steeples of Excellence to Silicon Valley: The Story of Varian Associates and Stanford Industrial Park* (Palo Alto, Calif.: Varian Associates, Inc., 1988).

13   NASA Ames Research Center, *Economic Benefits Study: NASA Ames Research Center and NASA Research Park in Silicon Valley*, prepared by Bay Area Economics and AECOM Planning and Design (Moffett Field, Calif.: NASA Ames Research Center, 2010).

14   Glenn E. Bugos, *Atmosphere of Freedom: Sixty Years at the NASA Ames Research Center*, NASA SP-4314 (Washington, D.C.: NASA, 2000).

15   Michael Adamson, "Industrial Clusters: San Francisco from the Gold Rush to the Cold War" (presentation, San Francisco Chapter of the National Association of Business Economics, 6 May 2009).

16   Jay Spenser, *Vertical Challenge: The Hiller Aircraft Story* (Seattle: University of Washington Press, 1992). Stanley Hiller kept his prototypes; these later formed the basis of the Hiller Aviation Museum near the San Carlos airport, which celebrates the history of aviation in Northern California.

17   *Forty Years of Leadership: Lockheed Missiles and Space Company, Inc., 1954–1994* (Sunnyvale, Calif.: Lockheed Missiles and Space Company, 1994); and Tony Fettig et al., *A Chronology of LMSC History* (Sunnyvale, Calif.: Lockheed Missiles and Space Company, 1992); Graham Spinardi, *From Polaris to Trident: The Development of US Fleet Ballistic Missile Technology* (Cambridge, Mass.: MIT Press, 1994).

18   Christophe Lécuyer, *Making Silicon Valley: Innovation and the Growth of High Tech, 1930–1970* (Cambridge, Mass.: MIT Press, 2006); Stuart W. Leslie,

"How the West Was Won: The Military and the Making of Silicon Valley," in *Technological Competitiveness: Contemporary and Historical Perspectives on Electrical, Electronics, and Computer Industries* (Piscataway, N.J.: IEEE Press, 1993), 75–89; Thomas Heinrich, "Cold War Armory: Military Contracting in Silicon Valley," *Enterprise and Society* 3 (2002): 247–84.

19   On Varian and Ampex, see Glenn Bugos, "The Aerospace Impetus to Silicon Valley," *Journal of the West* 36 (1997): 97–104.

20   [Hewlett-Packard], "Journey Into Time," *Measure,* February 1969, 2–5; [Hewlett-Packard], "The Giant Step," *Measure,* September 1969, 2–5.

21   This is based on Series III: Confidential Reference Memorandums, 1940–1962, NASA Western Support Office Papers, 1939–1969, record group 255, National Archives and Records Administration, Pacific Region, Laguna Niguel, Calif.

22   "San Francisco-Oakland Procurement District," box K204–603, U.S. Air Force Historical Research Agency, Maxwell Air Force Base, Montgomery, Ala.

Blueprinting the Regional City:
The Urban and Environmental Legacies of
the Air Industry in Southern California

"Aerospace and California were made not just for each other but by
each other," in the words of writer David Beers.[1] Aircraft manufacturing played an outsize role in the growth of California—
especially its southern half—beginning with World War I; the huge
impulse of World War II made the region dominant in the U.S. air industry, a dominance sustained through the end of the twentieth century.
One legacy of this symbiosis has been pollution, including the contamination of groundwater throughout the region with toxic chemicals, heavy
metals, and other persistent pollutants (Southern California now has the
largest cluster of Superfund sites with contaminated groundwater in the
country), and significant soil and air pollution.

The industry's record of pollution in the region, while extensive, locally intensive, and still a long way from being remedied, is not unique—
neither in the context of the U.S. aerospace industry generally, especially
in its military-linked forms, nor of manufacturing in Southern California,
where pollution is widespread, intensive, and complex. The air industry
certainly participated in the industrial development of Southern California, and played its part in the lamentable story of environmental
degradation and pollution that bequeathed its residents the worst air
quality in the nation and some of the worst instances of water and soil
pollution. But this legacy reflects a general lack of concern in the United
States about negative environmental impacts before the rise of the environmental movement in the 1960s rather than a failure specific to the
region or industry.

The deeper and more complex environmental legacy of the industry
lies in its driving role in the extraordinary urban and economic expansion
and social transformation of the region. I want to consider the environmental history of the air and space industry in Southern California
through multiple optics: its local, discrete impacts, its regional ones, and

its super-regional ones, focusing especially on the interconnection between urban, environmental, and social patterns. The aircraft industry located preferentially in Southern California primarily because of two regional characteristics: 1) a decentralized urban pattern, made possible by a vast program of infrastructure provision at public expense, including roads, water, electricity, seaports, airports, railroads, sewers, flood control, and drainage; and 2) the availability of a nearly endless supply of open land for building manufacturing and testing facilities, ancillary businesses, and worker housing, allowing the industry to create its own urban forms, including entire communities, from the drawing board.

By linking the industry's legacy of pollution with its legacy of urban structuring and development, I want to begin to consider how the industry participated in a distinctive cultural formation in Southern California, one whose attitudes toward the environment, business, and lifestyle helped create its success and, just as surely, its failure to sustain its communities, its landscape, and eventually itself within the region.

The Air-Minded City

For decades, the factors most often advanced to explain the air industry's extraordinarily fast takeoff in Southern California were the region's natural advantages—chiefly its clement weather, allowing year-round flying and outdoor airplane manufacture. But several careful studies have shown that this consideration, while it played some role in location decisions, was less important than it may have seemed.[2] First, the area's natural characteristics were never unique—many other parts of the country could claim similarly mild climates and did not attract aircraft builders—nor were they decisive—the industry thrived first in the inclement Northeast, and continues to be dominated by the inclement Northwest. Indeed the region's ballyhooed year-round sunshine is often replaced by dense fog, especially in the coastal areas from San Diego to Santa Monica where aircraft companies located. And by the 1940s, severe smog from air pollution made flying in Los Angeles at times dangerous.

Second, Southern California suffers from natural *dis*advantages that make it an uncompetitive manufacturing site in a national market: the mountains and deserts known as the "great wall of California"[3] isolate it from eastern population centers as well as sources of raw materials such as timber, coal, and iron. High transportation costs, made worse by railroad monopolies, handicapped most industrial enterprises—for example, coal might cost five times as much in Los Angeles as in the East.[4] The economic base rested on the recruitment of migrants, the attendant real-estate development, and agriculture. For these reasons, Los Angeles long lagged behind smaller cities in industry: in 1930, after decades of break-neck population growth, it was the fourth most populous city in the United States, but ranked only ninth in manufacturing.[5]

What overcame these handicaps was a concerted effort on the part of the region's interlocking civic, business, media, political, and military leadership to stimulate growth through industrialization. This elite, often referred to as the "booster complex," addressed the region's natu-ral disadvantages by creating new types of governmental agencies with their own, dedicated funding mechanisms (principally bond elections), such as proprietary harbor, power, and water departments, to enable cities to reach beyond their boundaries to secure resources;[6] it also sought to identify and attract industries that could overcome the re-gion's natural disadvantages. It fixed on cinema and aircraft early in the twentieth century: these products were highly profitable and easy to ex-port, and the industries were mobile, able to take advantage of an es-sentially limitless supply of relatively cheap open land near the region's population centers—land that the booster complex would sell to them.[7]

With crystal-clear visions of making Los Angeles the "Detroit of the aircraft industry," the boosters' watchword was "airmindedness."[8] The Los Angeles chamber of commerce, for example, created an aviation de-partment very early on, in the 1930s. Boosters supported air businesses wherever they saw the chance, whether in the form of financing, con-tracts, or public promotion through sponsorship of airmeets. Most im-portantly, they understood the catalytic role of airfields in anchoring aircraft builders. A chamber of commerce publication asserted in 1929: "In the past an airport has been just a tract of land, usually difficult to get to and at some distance from the roar of the city. [In the future] we will probably see considerable development around these [fields]. Each will produce a community of no small importance . . . solid settlements of industry, commerce, and private residences."[9] The groundwork had already been laid: in 1929, there were fifty-three airfields within thirty miles of downtown Los Angeles—and many of these would become those "solid settlements" that together came to constitute a new kind of multimodal, regional city.

The project was bolstered by the booster complex's concerted effort to gain defense contracts. The effort was, however, not united; instead, there was fierce competition between "Darwinian" cities, between cities and their suburbs, and between government entities within one region, such as the county and the city of Los Angeles, to woo industry and secure federal military contracts. Success went to the interests best able to cobble together alliances of firms, academic institutions, and governments—alliances the historian Roger Lotchin called the "metropolitan-military complex."

This competition took advantage of and accelerated the region's distinctive decentralization—a legacy from the scattered Spanish colonial outposts, which formed the nuclei of dispersed urban nodes by the turn of the twentieth century. Planned decentralization was official policy in the city of Los Angeles as early as the 1908 zoning law separating industrial and residential uses.[10] On the regional scale, the original map of dispersed, separate nodes was ratified and replicated during Southern California's first industrial flowering—oil pumping and refining. The oil fields of south Los Angeles and north Orange Counties spawned dozens of workers' towns.[11] By the 1920s, these nodes were linked by 1,100 miles of electric railways. By the 1930s, Southern California had the ingredients for even more regional growth: well-established industrial decentralization, extraordinary population growth, high levels of car ownership, cheap electricity, an emerging highway network, and burgeoning telephone and radio networks. The entrepreneurial land-development sector took advantage of these features, making its business plan the anticipation of demand, following electric railway tycoon Henry Huntington's belief that speculative developments would draw migrants. The formula was quite literally custom made for the air industry and turned its success into the region's success. The Big Six aircraft manufacturers, all of which had started out in tiny rented spaces in districts within a few miles of downtown Los Angeles, soon spread out to locations near outlying airports where there was room to grow: at Burbank, Santa Monica, Inglewood, and El Segundo.[12] In addition to the Los Angeles area, San Diego County attracted a dense skein of aircraft manufacturers by the close of World War II.[13] Los Angeles aircraft and parts production increased from $5 million in 1929 to $80 million in 1939; the rest of Southern California added $20 million, totaling 44 percent of U.S. aircraft production.[14]

When another war seemed likely, U.S. defense procurement followed in existing grooves. California, having prepared the ground, reaped a bumper harvest, receiving more defense dollars than any other state, and drawing an unprecedented migration of workers: employment increased by 75 percent from 1939 to 1943. By 1940 aircraft manufacturers employed more people in Southern California than any other industry; by 1941 nearly half the region's manufacturing jobs were in the air business and 13,000 new industrial workers arrived in Los Angeles every month.[15] By

1943, there were 400,000 defense workers in Los Angeles County—one-quarter of the entire workforce. The multiplier effect was huge: the number of workers in Los Angeles County grew from 900,000 in 1940 to 1,450,000 in 1943—a 60 percent gain—as the number of manufacturing workers tripled. They earned some of the highest wages in nation: 141.2 percent of the national average per capita income.[16] Faced with labor shortages, manufacturers "extend[ed] the long arm of the assembly line to the outlying reaches of the labor market," according to James Wilburn, locating plants throughout the region in proximity to existing population centers. Lockheed alone occupied 250 buildings in the area.[17] Yet existing housing could not begin to accommodate the need.

Prior to the war, the development of land for worker housing, whether for oil, aircraft, or other industries, proceeded largely on an ad hoc basis. Developers purchased vacant or agricultural land and subdivided it into small, inexpensive parcels; purchasers would either build their own structures or hire contractors to do the construction. Much of the housing was cheap and accretive.[18] Rarely were the subdividers the same as the builders. In the wartime buildup, the vast population influx spilled everywhere: into the city of Los Angeles, outlying cities, and unincorporated areas. The numbers of workers newly concentrated in previously undeveloped areas are mind-boggling: Lockheed's plant in Burbank had 18,569 employees in 1941; more worked at Vega nearby in the San Fernando Valley. By 1943, the Lockheed-Vega cluster, including ancillary suppliers, employed 72,000 war workers, with another 15,500 elsewhere in the valley.[19] The old model of ad hoc residential building could not hope to supply these workers with housing. A new kind of development, modeled on the industrial buildup itself and abetted by local and federal government, absorbed the enormous influx of people.

Increasingly, airframe manufacturers worked with federal authorities and private developers to apply the mass-production methods of the industry to building entire communities from scratch. Critical to their efforts was a kit of new federal financing tools—1941's Lanham Act, which provided $1.3 billion for war-worker housing in areas of shortages;[20] Title VI of the Housing Act, which guaranteed federal loans up to 90 percent of project value for private housing developments in shortage areas; and revised access rules for rationed materials—all meant to encourage private construction of inexpensive single-family houses on small lots, in large subdivisions.[21] In 1940, Douglas Aircraft broke ground on a tract of 1,100 houses on unincorporated Los Angeles County land near Long Beach, about two miles from its plant then gearing up to build

B-17 bombers.[22] Two miles from the Douglas plant at Santa Monica's Clover Field, another developer built Westside Village, a tract of 885-square-foot homes carefully optimized for space, with kitchens with modern appliances (to eliminate the pantry) facing the backyard, in up-to-date suburban fashion. The builders used a continuous-flow assembly line to assemble parts provided by nearby suppliers, producing high volumes of homes at great speed, high quality, and a low price: $3,290, for $190 down and $29.90 a month. Not far from the North American and Douglas plants at Mines Field, Westchester, a tract of 3,230 homes, for 10,000 people, took shape from 1942 to 1944.[23] These developments constituted an industrial revolution in homebuilding, a decade before Levittown.[24]

The postwar Los Angeles that emerged was a regional city, with its nodes sown from the principal aircraft plants and grown into surrounding, purpose-built communities: North Hollywood–Burbank–Glendale (Lockheed, Vega), Santa Monica–Mar Vista–Culver City (Douglas, Hughes Aircraft), Inglewood–Westchester–El Segundo (North American, Douglas El Segundo, Northrop), Downey (Vultee), and Long Beach–Huntington Beach (Douglas Long Beach). These spreading clusters traced a ring roughly fifteen miles in radius around Los Angeles City Hall,[25] linked by an emerging system of freeways—again, primed by federal funding—and serviced by regional shopping centers surrounded by enormous surface parking lots built by developers. Modern Los Angeles had taken shape.

Poison in the Garden

The first-order environmental effects of this extraordinary regional buildout were severe. There was little measurement or documentation at the time, owing to the general lack of environmental awareness, but anecdotal evidence suggests the impacts. Emissions from the aircraft plants and their suppliers, which employed the highly toxic processes of metal plating, painting, synthetic chemistry, and so on was completely unregulated, with considerations of easy and quick disposal generally placed above those of public health. Air pollution emanated from the chlorinated compounds and volatile organics used in the paints, solvents, and other fluids important to aircraft manufacture, and from hydrocarbons used as fuels and lubricants. These and other chemicals were habitually disposed of into storm drains or poured on the ground, where they entered the water supply. Highly toxic chromium compounds from the San Fernando Valley, Burbank, and Glendale aircraft plants were found downstream in the Los Angeles River in 1941. At that time, Los Angeles River basin groundwater provided one-fifth of the city's water.[26]

As the region's largest industry by far, aircraft manufacturing had an outsize environmental effect. But it was not unique: pollution from other sources was ubiquitous and severe. In terms of air quality, pollution had been a problem in industrializing Los Angeles from early in the century— one day in 1905 the pall of smoke was so dark it was mistaken for an eclipse. While the aircraft industry must have contributed its share over the years, there was a much larger impact from other sources. The Los Angeles Basin was thick with oil fields, refineries, tank farms, and pipelines, none designed to minimize emissions. A broad range of other polluting activities and businesses included coal and oil burning, smelting, foundries, cement plants, diesel locomotives and trucks, trash incineration, and hundreds of square miles of orchard smudge pots that kept the region's huge and valuable citrus and avocado industry safe from winter frosts. In the World War II build-up after 1939, visibility in the area noticeably worsened. Smog was called a "serious menace" to aviation, and there was talk by Monrovia officials of moving the city's airfield. On 26 July 1943, a stinging pall settled over the city, cutting visibility to three blocks. The *Los Angeles Times* called it a "gas attack," as though the Japanese had dropped poison bombs on the city. Officials blamed it on a Gas Company plant on Aliso Street that manufactured butadiene, an ingredient of synthetic rubber, but closing the plant failed to solve the problem.[27] The problem was cumulative, the result of rampant industrialization without regard to consequences, in a region with a natural temperature inversion. One of those consequences—a direct effect of decentralization—was the dependence on automobiles, growing in step with the region's growth, contributing principally air pollution but also water pollution, and exacerbating these effects by impelling petroleum extraction and refining activities in the region.

Water pollution was especially severe along the Los Angeles River corridor where most of the region's industry had been sited by Los Angeles City and County zoning policies. The automobile industry was a huge presence: Ford built a plant in Long Beach in 1927, Willys-Overland built another in Commerce the same year, Chrysler built nearby in 1932, Studebaker opened in 1936 across the river in Vernon; three steel plants opened to serve the auto plants. The tiny city of Vernon had three hundred industrial facilities by 1927, including glass and aluminum makers, paper mills, and the Union Stockyards, a vast collection of feedlots and slaughterhouses. All of them polluted the river. The railroad yards near downtown Los Angeles contributed their share. Oil-field brines were dumped in the river near Long Beach. Sewage flowed into the river along its length, leading to frequent beach closures.[28]

Ratcheting pollution led to the beginning of pumping restrictions that would eventually end the use of Los Angeles River water. Yet the city was well on the way to replacing this supply. Just as it had with the Owens River aqueduct in 1913, and spurred in good part by the demand and growth led and fed by the aircraft industry, regional leaders had worked with the federal government to establish a regional water agency to bring in supplies from outside, anticipating future growth just as Henry E. Huntington had advised. The Metropolitan Water District's Colorado River Aqueduct was finished in 1941, just when the chromium wastes were found in the Los Angeles River. One consequence of importing water from the Owens and Colorado Rivers was unfortunately to increase flow into the groundwater basin, with much of it finding its way into the Los Angeles River—magnifying the problem of polluted surface flows. (Average flows in the river in 1960 were twice what they were in 1902.) As development paved the San Fernando Valley, the combination of a greater impervious area, and thus greater storm-water flows, and a saturated groundwater basin increased flooding of homes and businesses along the river. The floor of Lockheed's Burbank plant went underwater in the floods of 1941, reinforcing calls for the U.S. Army Corps of Engineers to lock the Los Angeles River in concrete—which it proceeded to do. This in turn allowed even more building encroachment into the river's immediate floodplain and reinforced the vicious circle of development, ever-increasing demand for imported water supplies, flooding, and pollution.

The dispersed pattern of low-density, extensive land development had direct environmental impacts: the loss of and paving over of farmland and habitat and the consequent diversion of the natural hydrology into the storm-drain system. Mitigating the impact was the fact that the Los Angeles Basin had already been altered by a century and a half of intense grazing, irrigation, and farming, so that the few remaining relatively intact biotic communities in the lowlands were already confined to steep sites and the occasional undisturbed wetland.

The Imperial City

There were, however, more widespread, and in many ways more interesting, second-order environmental impacts of the regional city—those felt beyond the city itself.[29] The most notorious is the result of the region's history of securing water supplies from ever-more-distant sources—the Owens Valley, then the Colorado River—thus tying a watershed encompassing parts of seven states and originating as far away as the Wind River Range of Wyoming into the environmental balance of

Southern California. The aircraft industry, while not the primary reason for these appropriations, was a beneficiary, and its own catalytic role in driving population growth and regional build-out created the demand that justified them. The water importations enabled the complete build-out of the region. When Colorado River water first arrived in 1941, brought by Southern California's first regional super-agency, the Metropolitan Water District, it had almost no takers; to increase "demand" the agency annexed areas beyond its original municipal members. The district offered copious amounts of inexpensive water to San Diego and agricultural areas throughout the five-county region (Los Angeles, Orange, San Bernardino, Riverside, and San Diego Counties) to induce development. The agency's regional *pax aquatica*, called the Laguna Doctrine, traded the acquiescence of its member cities and districts in its operations for the promise that water supply would never become a limitation on local growth decisions.[30] During the boom years from 1942 to 1954, the agency's service area grew from 770 square miles to more than 4,500, and its boundaries described the outlines of Southern California's spectacular, sprawling growth. Today it stretches from Mexico to Ventura County and serves sixteen million people.[31]

Water was just one factor in making Southern California a supercity or, to borrow from Gray Brechin's characterization of its rival San Francisco, an imperial city. In their search for electrical power supplies, regional agencies reached out first to the Southern California mountains, then to the Sierra Nevada (the Edison hydropower system), then the Colorado River (the Bureau of Reclamation's Hoover Dam, followed by the Parker and Davis Dams). Defense industry electricity demand helped justify a proposal for a hydropower plant on the Owens River.[32] World War II, which has been called an "electric war," imposed huge strains on the regional power system: Edison's demand surged 94 percent from 1939 to 1944. Even before Pearl Harbor, anticipation of wartime demand in Los Angeles led the company to begin building a new generator at Hoover Dam and a new transmission line to carry its power.[33] Like the Seattle–Tacoma region with its subsidized electricity from Grand Coulee Dam, Southern California's access to cheap hydropower was an obvious advantage and draw to the air industry. Later, the region's tentacles reached deep into other states in search of coal and sites for power plants, which together came to provide almost half of Southern California's electricity: Mojave Generating Station in Laughlin, Nevada, Navajo near Page, Arizona, and Intermountain in Delta, Utah, 490 miles from Los Angeles. These power plants, tied to the Southern California grid by thousands of miles of transmission cables, are merely the most visible strands in a vast web: Southern California became a super-regional force, sucking in water and electricity, and also metals, coal, lumber, minerals, and farm products from a hinterland that included most of California as well as most of the states west of the Continental Divide, and sending out engineers and builders to construct highways, dams, turbines, and aqueducts to bring in more water and power, raw materials, and food. Thus the metabolism of the Southern California regional city fundamentally structured and entrained the resources and economies of much of the western United States. Indeed, Southern California, driven by the air industry, reorganized the nation: pulling in federal tax money in the form of defense contracts, and with the dollars pulling in people—engineers, planners, scientists, technicians, designers, and workers and their families, followed by the millions attracted by the broad multiplier effects of the air business's prosperity—and ultimately shifting the nation's population, economic, and political balances westward.[34]

Building the Cold War City

At the end of World War II, Southern California builders accounted for 60 to 70 percent of the U.S. airframe industry.[35] The business saw an initial crash of employment when the conflict ended, but its fortunes soon revived: defense spending rose as the confrontation with the Soviet Union escalated and the focus of the Pentagon and the air-defense industry shifted toward jets and rockets, launching a new technology race. For decades, independently of the procurement swings occasioned by American electoral cycles, that race sped ever faster, propelled by international events and domestic anxiety: the explosion of the Russian A-bomb in August 1949, war in Korea in June 1950, the launch of *Sputnik 1* in October 1957. Aircraft became aerospace, to the benefit of Southern California, which continued its well-honed practices of civic boosterism and political support for procurement contracts, aided by an ever-more-cozy relationship between industry, government, the military, and academia. Caltech, for example, strengthened its orientation toward rocketry, and its Jet Propulsion Laboratory emerged as an important aerospace center and spun off companies such as Aerojet.

Employment in the air-and-aerospace industry in Los Angeles County continued to grow in the 1950s, rising from 100,000 in the early 1950s to 275,000 in 1955[36] and driving a continuation of the pattern of dispersed urban growth seen in the war years. What was different in the postwar era was the scale of growth: the planned community building of the early 1940s had been mostly limited to large neighborhood-sized tracts; Westchester, a mini-city with its 3,230 homes, was a harbinger of things to come.

In 1950, next to the neighborhood built in 1942 for war workers near the Douglas Long Beach plant, another housing development was planned, the biggest yet undertaken in America. Platted on 3,500 acres of farmland, Lakewood would comprise 17,500 houses, each 1,100 square feet, in one of several floor plans carefully sequenced so that no two adjacent homes were identical. Private developers secured $100 million in federal mortgage financing to fund a full-scale industrial assembly line to build houses: at full tilt, it produced one hundred a day, five hundred a week; construction was finished in three years. When the sales office opened, 25,000 people were waiting, according to D. J. Waldie in his memoir *Holy Land*. The builders used well-seasoned old-growth Douglas fir from the forests of the Pacific Northwest, cut to what later generations have long wistfully called "true dimension"—a 2 × 4 actually measured two inches thick by four wide, instead of the shaved members that replaced them once the old growth was clear-cut. Lakewood was laid out as a grid over the old fields, of lots fifty feet wide by one hundred feet long, set on streets forty feet wide; from the curbs there were precisely seven feet of lawn to the sidewalk, with the house set back twenty feet from that. "This pattern," wrote Waldie, "of asphalt, grass, concrete, grass—is as regular as any thought of God's." Living in the homes, he wrote, "would . . . require orderly lives."[37] Many of the homes' inhabitants worked at Douglas building the F3D Skyknight fighter, a workhorse in the Korean War. The Marine Corps donated a stripped Skyknight hull to ornament a Lakewood park.

It may have seemed perfectly planned, an earthly paradise. Yet, as Waldie relates, this city born of no limits had limitations. The developers had provided sidewalks, schools, and parks, yet Lakewood was all residential, except for the massive shopping center at its core—the functional center of a centerless place. Other parts of urban life were absent: there were no cultural institutions and no cemetery, and churches and synagogues had to be improvised at first. There was a nowhereness, a randomness of place in new suburbs whose existence had been ordained only by the blueprints of developers, architects, and government bureaucrats: "Before they put a grid over it, and restrained the ground from indifference, any place was as good as any other," Waldie recounts. He talks of the miniaturization of the world within the unchanging grid, of how each house became "its own enchanted island" in a sea of others, and how, as islanders, "the extent of our concern" reached only the immediate tract, or the block, or, as residents aged, to the houses they could see from their own.[38]

Separateness was at the core of the raison d'être of Lakewood and places like it: even if in twentieth-century Southern California people left the central city following jobs in industry, the movement away from the city was no less a flight *from* something—not the industrial city, as it had been in the East, but other people, especially certain kinds of other people. Los Angeles's vaunted status as "the white spot" of America, an attraction to white migrants from early on, had been eroded by the influx of Southern blacks, first during the Depression and then during the war. Drawn by the promise of defense jobs, blacks poured in: as many as 10,000 per month during the height of the buildup. Largely to comply with FDR's order to cease discrimination in war industries, aircraft firms employed a peak of 7,186 blacks in July 1944, only between 3 and 7 percent of their workforces.[39] And because racial covenants excluded them from the majority of subdivisions and communities, blacks remained confined to certain areas, mostly in the central city and outlying industrial districts—approximately 5 percent of the city's residential area. By war's end, their population had doubled within these tight bounds and had spilled over into downtown's Little Tokyo, its Japanese residents having been shipped to internment camps. The situation there was so severe that the city's housing authority reported "families piling up to a congestion of four, five, and six persons per bedroom. In one case a family of 5 was living in a dirt-floored garage with no sanitary facilities whatsoever. In an abandoned store front and two nearly windowless storage rooms in Little Tokyo 21 people were found living—and paying approximately $50 a month for these quarters."[40] Residents of adjoining neighborhoods responded by tightening racial restrictions or moving out. The 1948 Supreme Court decision outlawing housing discrimination began the slow erosion of color lines and accelerated the process of white flight from central city neighborhoods to new, peripheral suburbs, which even after 1948 were advertised implicitly as restricted to white people. The sales brochures for Waldie's subdivision proudly trumpeted its "race restrictions," which kept it a "100% American Family Community," "the white spot" of Long Beach.[41]

In 1953, the city of Long Beach announced its intention to annex Lakewood. Some residents responded with a drive to incorporate the development as a municipality, and their opposition led to a very public battle, which ended in Lakewood's incorporation in 1954. Containing seven square miles, 105 miles of streets, and 70,000 residents, it was the largest unincorporated community in the United States to incorporate in that era. It received national attention for its spectacular, nearly instant growth and the way it seemed to redefine the future of American urbanism. The vote had been fed by fear that the city's order would be disturbed by outside decisions to locate within its boundaries undesirable businesses, facilities, or housing—and therefore undesirable people. The decision to incorporate was swung by an innovative agreement reached with Los Angeles County to contract for the same services the county provided unincorporated areas: road building and maintenance, the health department, building inspection, libraries, school services, the animal pound, tax collection, the fire department, and the sheriff for law enforcement.[42] This arrangement became known as the Lakewood Plan, and it spread like wildfire: two years later, four more Los Angeles County communities became cities following the plan; in 1957, five more followed and twenty-three were in the process of incorporation. Thirty cities incorporated in the space of the next two years, compared to the previous 106 years, over which period a total of forty-five cities had incorporated in the county.[43] All around Lakewood miniature municipalities sprouted: Pico Rivera, Paramount, Montebello, Cerritos, Bellflower, Bell, Bell Gardens, Hawaiian Gardens, Maywood, Cudahy, Commerce, and so on; the San Gabriel Valley followed suit, filling south Los Angeles County with grids of streets and houses covering hundreds of square miles. These cities are best understood as urban multiplier effects of aerospace, part of the diversification and growth of the regional economy and population built on top of the aerospace foundation.

Many decisions to incorporate were no doubt encouraged by the 1955 passage of a state law allowing counties to levy a 1 percent sales tax on unincorporated areas—a strong financial incentive to incorporation.[44] But the new cities were wisely adopting an ingenious and powerful new technology: the Lakewood Plan constituted a new organizational system that allowed small communities that would otherwise have had no chance of affording cityhood's services and payrolls to hive off from the lack of self-determination that was unincorporated Los Angeles County. They could put up walls and exercise control over zoning—all important in keeping out the undesirable—while maintaining low tax rates. As further inducement, the new cities received a proportion of local sales tax: thus the shopping centers that developers built their housing tracts around provided a coveted tax base and a replacement for the diversified downtown business district of traditional urbanism. The Lakewood Plan fulfilled the "Grand Plan," postwar Southern California's audacious blue-print for growth unlimited by natural, political, or financial constraints—where the Metropolitan Water District provided the water, Southern California Edison and municipal utilities like the Los Angeles Department of Water and Power provided the electricity, and counties provided the rest—so that land developers could turn the indifferent ground into grids, and money.[45]

Since 1954, all but one of the cities incorporated in Los Angeles County have adopted the Lakewood Plan. Eighty percent of cities incorporating in California adopt it, bringing the total number of California cities based on it to 30 percent. It is emulated all over the United States.[46]

The Logic of Metastasis

In his 1993 *Harper's* magazine article, "The Crash of Blue Sky California," the writer David Beers described growing up in the 1960s near Sunnyvale, south of San Francisco near the town of San Jose, in an agricultural valley that had been transformed into an aviation insta-city by Lockheed, which built a plant there employing 25,000 workers. They were soon joined by thousands of others who worked for Varian making radar systems, or Hewlett-Packard making computers, or at nearby Stanford University researching the technologies that fed the industry. The town was a carefully laid-out suburban paradise, with schools, parks, hospitals, and, at its center, a mall. Single-family homes on small lots fronted irrigated lawns that betokened the cheerful tenor of the aerospace suburb: "A culture whose fertile crescents were sunny suburbs like our own. A relentlessly optimistic, blue-sky culture whose people, like things in general, were always looking up." In school, Beers was fascinated by the products of his father's firm—the gleaming white rockets and missiles, like the submarine-launched Polaris—though his father, a former Navy carrier jet pilot, couldn't reveal just what job he did for Lockheed. To display alongside the poster of the white missile on his wall, his mother, Catholic like Waldie's, gave him holy cards. "And so the images that informed my mind as a child were airfoils and angel wings, blast-offs and holy ascensions, all mingled in a coherent iconography." On television he watched *The Jetsons* "suburbanize the Milky Way."[47]

This "blue-sky culture" in the valley that became Silicon Valley was akin to that of many other California valleys populated by the urbanistic footprint of the air industry—the rest of them in the southern part of the state (indeed, it can be argued that Silicon Valley, due to its aerospace roots, is the part of Northern California most like Southern California, physically and culturally). In the San Fernando Valley, Lockheed boomed, building the U-2 and the SR-71 "Blackbird" at its Burbank Skunk Works, and the population wave rolled westward into new mega-developments like Panorama City and Tarzana, where farms had been just an eyeblink earlier. Farther west, in Chatsworth and Canoga Park, another cluster of defense firms pulled in big federal contracts, among them Rocketdyne, TRW, and Litton, leading to more residential development. Rocketdyne's pitch for workers included the slogan "Work Close To Home."[48] Aerojet led the way in the San Gabriel Valley, setting up shop in Pasadena, then Azusa, near Pomona, where it was joined by Convair. Outside San Diego, by 1961 Convair was making Atlas missiles at Kearny Mesa. North of Los Angeles, in the Mojave Desert, Lockheed was lured by Los Angeles County authorities, in what Roger Lotchin labeled a "Machiavellian maneuver to dispossess" the city of Los Angeles of its near monopoly, to do some of its testing at Muroc Dry Lake, close to the growing hive of military aerospace facilities at Edwards Air Force Base.[49]

Through the 1950s and 1960s, industrialization and decentralization continued apace, led by aerospace: in the mid-1950s, 55 percent of manufacturing jobs in Los Angeles County were in aerospace; in 1960, the number in San Diego County was an astonishing 75 percent; in 1962, Los Angeles and Orange counties together counted 43 percent of their manufacturing jobs in the aerospace sector—a decline in percentage which derived from the strong overall growth in manufacturing in the region.[50] By 1967, a half-million people in Southern California worked in defense-related industries.[51] Then, the skies began to darken. The end of the 1960s saw a drop in weapons spending, a cyclical low in commercial aircraft purchases, and most importantly, the end of the space race and the Apollo program, leading to huge aerospace layoffs.[52] In the rest of United States, the gathering decline of traditional industry picked up speed after the oil shocks and increased global competition of the 1970s. Southern California's traditional Fordist assembly-line industry—autos, tires, steel, and consumer durables—suffered the same fate: its "almost complete destruction" since 1965, in the words of Edward Soja.[53] Yet, in spite of periodic contractions in defense spending, aerospace in Southern California drew on its layered strengths of organization, expertise, innovation, and patronage to maintain high levels of employment, giving the region a resilience in manufacturing that only a handful of other Sun Belt, defense-linked areas shared.

Allen Scott has sketched how the "logic" of the decentralization led by the air industry worked. First, drawn by the dynamic of cheaper land at the urban periphery, newly established and expanding industries decide to locate in outlying areas—in the case of air businesses, in places with airports, surrounded by cheap, undeveloped land. This dispersal does not result in evenly spaced dots on the regional landscape, however, because other firms tend to settle near the pioneers in "agglomerations" or clusters, taking advantage of the economies of proximity—in labor, supplies, and services. Public and private entities quickly follow, providing infrastructure such as transportation and worker housing. In time, housing "fully envelops the place of employment.... creating—for a time—a collectively immobile complex of interrelated production and labor market activities." A prime example is the San Fernando Valley, which was home to 403,000 people in 1950, mostly in the eastern portions near the aerospace agglomeration at North Hollywood–Burbank–Glendale; by 1960 it had more than doubled, to 841,000, spreading toward the west along the new 101 freeway, drawn toward a new agglomeration near Van Nuys Airport and an emerging one in Chatsworth and Canoga Park.[54]

Over time, a combination of factors encouraged air industries to seek bluer skies. One was what Lotchin calls "the process of urban strangulation," whereby residential development hems in air facilities and conflicts with their operations. This process led to the incident in 1954 when an Air Force jet crashed into a neighborhood in Signal Hill, near the Air Force's base at the Long Beach airport, destroying six houses and killing nine people; today there is no Air Force presence there. Suffocation by the encircling city is one factor in the decrease in airports in Los Angeles County, from fifty-seven in 1940 to twenty in 1952.[55] Scott posits that the economies of agglomeration increase for a time, then begin to decline as increased demand pushes up land prices and wages. In addition, "negative overspill effects such as congestion, overbuilding, pollution, rising noise levels," and what he delicately terms "changes in local socioeconomic character and ethnic composition" begin to diminish the attractiveness of the place for doing business and living.[56] A primary example of such perceived "environmental" deterioration—defined subjectively by each participant as a shifting sum of urbanistic, social, and economic factors—is the replacement of green pastures with the concrete jungle. This process has proven difficult to stop, even when communities resort to municipal incorporation to slow development. Mike Davis has related how, by 1970, more than one-third of the surface area of the Los Angeles region had been encased in concrete and asphalt, for freeways, streets, parking lots, and driveways, a total of 3 billion tons of pavement, or 250 tons per person.[57]

In response to this urbanization, businesses resume their "leapfrog" pattern of outward movement, followed by homebuilders, and the older, inner-ring agglomerations decline, and in some cases "decompose," according to Scott. This pattern was followed in the decline of airframe manufacturing near Santa Monica, Playa del Rey, El Segundo, and Long Beach; followed by the decline of the North Hollywood–Burbank–Glendale cluster in the 1980s and 1990s. These were partially offset by the rise of aerospace firms in Chatsworth and Canoga Park, and in Orange County. And expansion has leapfrogged even farther out, to San Diego and Ventura Counties: between 1979 and 1987, industrial employment, led by aerospace, grew 82.4 percent in Ventura County, but only 10.1 percent in Los Angeles County.[58] The Los Angeles County growth, furthermore, occurred primarily in the less urbanized deserts of Antelope Valley.

The geographic dynamic of the air industry in Southern California is inseparable from the social dynamics that affect its managers, workers, and communities. The pressures of population and economic growth set in motion social changes that counted as "negative overspill effects" to many people in those aerospace communities. The growth formula that built Lakewood and countless suburbs like it—affordable housing, high wages, and racial segregation—began to break down in the 1960s, for a variety of reasons: ebbing manufacturing jobs, rising property prices, school desegregation, and race riots. The Watts riots of 1965 roughly coincided with the second wave of white flight from the second-ring suburbs to ever-more outlying ones. Post-1965, even while the shrinking aerospace sector shifted from blue-collar to white-collar jobs, regional industry overall was "restructuring" from high- to low-wage employment, fed by and feeding on an influx of millions of immigrants from the developing world—on the order of five million people. Lakewood Plan cities such as Huntington Park and Maywood, which were 80 percent white in 1965, shifted to 90 percent Latino by the mid-1990s.[59]

The next South Los Angeles riots, in 1992, also roughly coincided with a wave of white flight, and, crucially, with the post–Cold War defense contraction. Beginning in 1989, tens of thousands of defense jobs were eliminated in the region. Rockwell cut a thousand more when it closed its Long Beach operation in 1992, by which time McDonnell Douglas had cut another 21,000, in part by moving assembly lines to St. Louis and Salt Lake City. As went aerospace, so went manufacturing as a whole: in Van Nuys, General Motors closed its plant, taking with it 2,600 jobs. By 1992, more than seven hundred manufacturing plants left or expanded outside the state. Between 1988 and 1993, 800,000 California jobs vanished, half from

Los Angeles County.[60] Joan Didion cited these figures in her trenchant memoir, *Where I Was From*, in which she linked the scandal in 1993 involving the Lakewood Spur Posse, a clique of high school boys, several of them star athletes, who were charged with sexual crimes against underage girls, to the crash of blue-sky California. Lakewood and towns like it were, she wrote, "California's mill towns, breeder towns for the boom. When times were good and there was money to spread around, these were the towns that proved Marx wrong, that managed to increase the proletariat and simultaneously, by calling it middle class, to co-opt it." They were "organized around the sedative idealization of team sports," and therefore of adolescent males, learning on the football field the values they would need in a mill town, to be "married and mortgaged, in harness to the plant, a good worker, a steady consumer, a team player, someone who played ball." When times were bad, it was these kids whose behavior signaled the breakdown like flares.[61]

This wave of white flight left the Los Angeles Basin altogether, skipping to the third- and fourth-ring suburbs of the Santa Clarita and Antelope Valleys of northern Los Angeles County, and to booming subdivision landscapes in Ventura, San Bernardino, Riverside, Orange, and San Diego Counties, and also to what constituted a fifth ring—outside the region altogether. In the wake of 1989, hundreds of thousands of white Californians moved out of the state, to the Pacific Northwest, Intermountain West, Nevada, Arizona, and beyond. The region's black community saw a similar exodus, notably to the South, with many formerly black-majority cities and communities falling below that threshold in the same period.[62] With this outmigration came a growing alienation from the Los Angeles left behind: in the mainstream imagination, Los Angeles began to take on a dystopian image, limned in movies like *Colors*, *Blade Runner*, and *Boyz n the Hood*, in which a militarized, mostly white police force armed with the home-grown technologies of the aerospace industry patrols the streets and skies of a chaotic, violent, mostly black and Latino inner city—the "carceral city" in Davis's words, the "militarized technopolis" in Soja's.[63] Inner-city black artists such as Compton's N.W.A captured the battle between residents and the police in hard-edged rap records like 1988's *Straight Outta Compton*. Perhaps the most iconic perspective on the place and time was provided in the 1993 film *Falling Down*, in which Michael Douglas plays a white, suburban aerospace engineer laid off from his job who, stuck in traffic, leaves his car on the Hollywood Freeway and wanders through a third-world Los Angeles populated by Latino gangsters, Korean shopkeepers, and white supremacists, and descends into a maddened rampage of violence that ends in his death in the Pacific Ocean.

As the aerospace industry expanded outward through the region, it brought its direct environmental footprint with it. The agglomeration in the San Fernando Valley, where groundwater pollution had already become a public health issue in the 1940s, continued to dispose of highly toxic chemicals in situ as it expanded and spread northward into the Los Angeles City neighborhood of Sylmar and westward toward Van Nuys. Groundwater contamination, mostly attributed to the air industry by federal and state agencies,[64] is severe: three Superfund areas have been identified in the valley, with elevated levels of volatile organic compounds such as trichloroethylene and perchloroethylene, a component of rocket fuels, hexavalent chromium, and 1,4 dioxane.[65] Government documents list Lockheed, Pacific Airmotive, Weber Aircraft, and many other air businesses as among the presumed sources of the contamination—but also list many unrelated businesses, including the Walt Disney Studios.[66] Similarly, two Superfund groundwater pollution sites exist in the nearby San Gabriel Valley, in El Monte and Baldwin Park, also with prominent aerospace firms listed among the presumed polluters, including Aerojet and Lockheed—but they are but a few on a long roster that includes Chemlawn, Chevron, and a host of other industrial concerns, from air-conditioner manufacturers to dry cleaners, that used chlorinated compounds and either leaked them or disposed of them into the soil.[67]

The list of Superfund sites in the region includes several landfills where industrial concerns dumped their wastes, a former synthetic rubber plant, chemical blenders, oil refiners, and the Jet Propulsion Laboratory in Pasadena, which for many years disposed of highly toxic chemicals in burn and seepage pits on its property near the bed of the adjacent Arroyo Seco stream, a major tributary of the Los Angeles River.[68] A survey of active remediation sites in Los Angeles County shows that groundwater pollution reflected the type and intensity of industrial activity, and recorded, in an unfortunate register, a map of the industrial landscape of the region over the past half-century: Jet A fuel and chlorinated compounds near LAX; much aerospace-related contamination in South Los Angeles, albeit more from steel-drum recyclers and other non-aerospace industries; hydrocarbon contamination in Carson and the South Bay–Harbor area, with their density of oil wells, refineries, and tank farms.[69] A complete list would fill this book.

The most spectacular case of aerospace pollution came from the Santa Susana Field Laboratory, a 2,850-acre site nestled in the sandstone peaks and bowls of the Santa Susana Mountains, which bound San Fernando Valley on the northwest. First used for firing rocket engines by North American Aviation's Rocketdyne Division in 1949 (whose previous tests had been conducted in their parking lot at Mines Field),[70] the site was operated by the U.S. Air Force from 1954 to 1973, and then until 2000 by NASA, to test-fire thousands of motors, including the Navaho, Atlas, Jupiter, and Thor engines, and space-flight rockets from the Apollo missions to the space shuttle main engine.[71] For decades, residents of the communities that stretched below the site felt the powerful shaking and saw the night sky lit up by blasting rocket engines. In addition, Rocketdyne and the Department of Energy conducted nuclear research there, running ten different reactors. For more than a generation, Santa Susana was a critical locus of Cold War science, which left a legacy of highly concentrated contamination. Many tons of toxic materials spewed, leaked, or were deliberately disposed of into the soil. In the early years, on-site incineration in burn pits and pouring into seepage pits was accepted practice. In 1959 an experimental sodium reactor experienced a partial fuel meltdown, emitting radioactive gases, which may have escaped into the atmosphere.[72] The EPA has estimated that more than 500,000 gallons of trichloroethylene are under the site, and has also listed "a variety of radionuclides," perchloroethylene, metals, and petroleum hydrocarbons as primary contaminants.[73] Residents of nearby communities have long suspected that the contamination has entered the water supply (the laboratory contains the headwaters of Bell Creek, the western source of the Los Angeles River, and overlooks the site of Chatsworth Reservoir, now drained) and has caused abnormal levels of cancers in residents and former site workers. Investigation and remediation of these environmental impacts are ongoing, complex, and highly contentious, involving an alphabet soup of federal and state regulatory agencies. A date of 2017 has been set for completing cleanup, but there are few reasons to expect this deadline to be met.

At Santa Susana as elsewhere, regulation is catching up with the toxic legacy of industry. As is characteristic of our society, such efforts are reactive, belated responses to disasters. In 1947, six years after chromium was found in the Los Angeles River, a regional group was formed to investigate water pollution in the waterway; the same year, five years after the Black Monday smog incident, the Los Angeles County Board of Supervisors formed an Air Pollution Control District, the country's first such agency, over the determined resistance of the business community. In subsequent years, Orange, Riverside, and San Bernardino Counties followed suit; twenty years later, the four entities merged into the South Coast Air Quality Monitoring District (AQMD), a regional regulator with quasi-judicial powers that oversees nearly as many Californians as the Metropolitan Water District, around sixteen million.[74] The AQMD has made impressive progress against pollution sources, being the first regulatory agency in the nation to mandate catalytic converters on cars, pushing for cleaner fuels, and requiring the inventory and disclosure of all emissions.

It is perhaps an unintended consequence of industry's freewheeling ways that its legacy includes the birth of such a super-agency—one of seventy-two agencies with environmental permitting authority in the region, by one count—whose mandates have been widely cited by businesses as among the reasons they chose to leave Southern California, or the state of California altogether.[75] This diaspora has exported some of Southern California's environmental footprint to a wide swath of other states, resulting in the urban, social, and environmental restructuring of a large part of the western United States. Lockheed provides one example: started in Hollywood in 1926, it bought Burbank's Union Airport in 1940 and moved operations there, starting the Skunk Works in 1943; by the 1980s, executives moved its headquarters about twenty miles westward down the 101 freeway to Calabasas, an affluent "blue-sky" suburb newly built in the next valley over from the San Fernando Valley; in 1992, aerospace activities ended at the Burbank facility, and the Skunk Works moved to Palmdale in the Mojave Desert; in 1995, the company merged with Georgia's Martin Marietta Corporation, moving most of its production to its Sunnyvale, California, and Marietta, Georgia, plants, and becoming one of the world's largest arms makers, a multinational headquartered in Bethesda, Maryland, closer to its Washington, D.C., patrons on Capitol Hill and in the Pentagon.

Conclusion

Viewed from one perspective, the history of the air industry in Southern California has been like that of a rocket engine: blue-sky California burned brightly, lighting up the night sky before fizzling out. A series of time-lapse images taken from an overview—say from low Earth orbit—would show a more complex sequence: its burn was like a series of brushfires jumping out from a central blaze, each wind-blown firebrand landing some distance away in dry brush, igniting it and spreading until it consumed the fuel, when an ember blew away and ignited another spot fire, until eventually all burned out—leaving behind a vastly altered human and physical landscape. To some, this changed landscape is more a bad dream than the paradise promised early in the twentieth century. The artist Lewis Baltz spoke for this sense of disappointment in words accompanying his photographs of "the new industrial parks near Irvine, California" in 1974–75: "Los Angeles offers the most dramatic instance of the unbridgeable abyss between America's classes, cultures, races, and individuals, between its Utopian fantasy and its dystopic reality.... I always believed that God would destroy LA for its sins. Finally I realized that He had already destroyed it, and then left it around as a warning."

He and others were wrong, if understandably upset at having been sold a bridge. Los Angeles and Southern California never really fulfilled the image that the air and development industries promised: a land of high-paying jobs, of ideal homes in racially and economically homogeneous garden suburbs, of greener pastures under bluer skies. In certain places, for certain moments, for certain people, the image was reality. But it is clear in retrospect that the *pax aeronautica* could not have lasted, as it was sustained on the industries' entrepreneurial knack for always moving to greener pastures, which precluded a commitment to place. There has been something weightless, if not quite transcendent, about the air business from the outset: an uncanny ability to abstract itself from place, and therefore from consequence—like David Beers's boyhood Polaris poster, in which the gleaming white, nuclear-armed missile is poised just after breaking the surface of sea, headed up to heaven, with no suggestion of its deadly cargo, no acknowledgment of the horrific consequences of its use. It is this ability, or compulsion, to escape from the consequences of one's activities in place and time, something inherent in the business model of the air industry and the mind of blue-sky culture, that made the rocket-like, ultimately uncontrollable growth of Southern California not only possible but ineluctable. As a culture, Americans have long been drawn more strongly by the urge to go than the urge to stay and tend the garden. Belief in the promise of virgin soil is an enduring part of the American paradigm of faith in new beginnings and limitless possibilities, in technology, optimism, and pragmatism. This belief has begotten blue-sky cities on the North American continent for more than four hundred years. In recent years we have rediscovered the need to take care of the places we have made, as there are fewer and fewer green pastures left. But we are only halfway there, and Southern California, in characteristically dramatic form, has been left wobbling in a kind of wake turbulence from the passage of the aerospace rocket over the last century. The challenge now, to strain the metaphor, is to bring back the blue skies to the regional city it built by regreening the pastures left behind, one Lakewood at a time.

And news of the Southern California aerospace industry's death is premature: on 27 May 2010, the *Los Angeles Times* reported that the Air Force successfully test-fired the X-51 WaveRider hypersonic plane near Point Mugu, briefly reaching 3,500 miles per hour. Under development for some time, the revolutionary aircraft was built by Boeing's Phantom Works in Long Beach and Rocketdyne (now a division of Pratt & Whitney) in Canoga Park, and tested at Edwards Air Force Base in the Mojave.[76]

Clearly, the fire still burns.

Notes

1   David Beers, "The Crash of Blue Sky California: The Aerospace Industry is Dying, and With It a Way of Life," *Harper's Magazine*, July 1993.

2   Los Angeles Community Analysis Bureau, *The Aerospace Industry as the Primary Factor in the Industrial Development of Southern California: The Instability of the Aerospace Industry, and the Effects of the Region's Dependence on It,* The Economic Development of Southern California, 1920–1976, vol. 1 (Los Angeles: Community Analysis Bureau, 1976); Greg Hise, *Magnetic Los Angeles: Planning the Twentieth-Century Metropolis* (Baltimore: Johns Hopkins University Press, 1997); Roger Lotchin, *Fortress California 1910–1961: From Warfare to Welfare* (New York: Oxford University Press, 1992).

3   Community Analysis Bureau, *The Aerospace Industry,* vii.

4   Ibid., viii; Carey McWilliams, *Southern California: An Island on the Land* (Santa Barbara, Calif.: Peregrine Smith, 1973).

5   Community Analysis Bureau, *The Aerospace Industry,* viii.

6   Stephen Erie, *Globalizing L.A: Trade, Infrastructure, and Regional Development* (Stanford: Stanford University Press, 2004), 43–88.

7   Lotchin, *Fortress California,* 71.

8   Hise, *Magnetic Los Angeles,* 117; Lotchin, *Fortress California,* 74, 76.

9   Quoted in Hise, *Magnetic Los Angeles,* 117.

10 Becky Nicolaides, "'Where the Working Man is Welcomed': Working-Class Suburbs in Los Angeles, 1900–1940," in *Looking for Los Angeles: Architecture, Film, Photography, and the Urban Landscape,* ed. Charles Salas and Michael Roth (Los Angeles: Getty Research Institute, 2001), 77.

11 Ibid., 78.

12 Hise, *Magnetic Los Angeles,* 127–9.

13 Convair (Consolidated-Vultee, which built the B-24 bomber and Catalina and Coronado flying boats), Solar Aircraft Co., and Ryan Aeronautical Co. clustered at Lindbergh Field; Rohr Aircraft was based farther south, at Chula Vista.

14   Community Analysis Bureau, *The Aerospace Industry*, 5. Compare Hise, who reports that the West Coast increased its share of U.S. aircraft production in the 1930s from 14 percent to 40 percent; *Magnetic Los Angeles*, 129.

15   Hise, *Magnetic Los Angeles*, 129.

16   Community Analysis Bureau, *The Aerospace Industry*, 5–6.

17   James R. Wilburn, "Social and Economic Aspects of the Aircraft Industry in Metropolitan Los Angeles During World War II" (PhD diss., University of California, Los Angeles, 1971), 49.

18   Nicolaides, "Working-Class Suburbs in Los Angeles," 78.

19   Hise, *Magnetic Los Angeles*, 129.

20   Ibid., 119.

21   Ibid., 134.

22   D. J. Waldie, *Holy Land: A Suburban Memoir* (New York: St. Martin's Press, 1996), 25, 45.

23   Hise, *Magnetic Los Angeles*, 121, 142–47.

24   Ibid., 137–40. Hise has argued that this model upends the conventional story that explains Southern California's dispersed urban pattern as a result of unplanned "suburban" housing development on the urban fringe. Instead, in Southern California industry led the way to decentralization, with housing close behind in a "highly planned" process of deliberate dispersal. Ibid., 10, 11, 125, 148, 151.

25   Ibid., 132, 190.

26   Blake Gumprecht, *The Los Angeles River: Its Life, Death, and Possible Rebirth* (Baltimore, 1999), 118, 123.

27   South Coast Air Quality Management District, "50th Anniversary of Smog War," May 1997, http://www.aqmd.gov/news1/Archives/History/marchcov.html.

28   Gumprecht, *Los Angeles River*, 123–24.

29   Southern California in the twentieth century recapitulated in its own terms the regional and super-regional organization of space achieved by Chicago in the nineteenth century, as recounted by William Cronon in *Nature's Metropolis: Chicago and the Great West*, and by San Francisco in the late nineteenth and early twentieth centuries, as recounted by Gray Brechin in *Imperial San Francisco*.

30   Robert Gottlieb and Margaret FitzSimmons, "Bounding and Binding Metropolitan Space: The Ambiguous Politics of Nature in Los Angeles," in *The City: Los Angeles and Urban Theory at the End of the Twentieth Century*, ed. Allen Scott and Edward Soja (Berkeley, Calif.: University of California Press, 1996), 198.

31   William Fulton, *The Reluctant Metropolis: The Politics of Urban Growth in Los Angeles* (Point Arena, Calif.: Solano Press Books, 1997), 104–8.

32   Lotchin, *Fortress California*, 151–52.

33 William Myers, *Iron Men and Copper Wires: A Centennial History of the Southern California Edison Company* (Glendale, Calif.: Trans-Anglo Books, 1983), 192–93.

34 Markusen et al., *Rise of the Gunbelt*; Bruce Schulman, *From Cotton Belt to Sunbelt: Federal Policy, Economic Development, and the Transformation of the South, 1938–1980* (Durham, N.C.: Duke University Press, 1994).

35 Lotchin, *Fortress California*, 188, 251.

36 Community Analysis Bureau, *The Aerospace Industry*, 9.

37 Waldie, *Holy Land*, 59.

38 Ibid., 3, 13, 111, 135.

39 Wilburn, *Social and Economic Aspects of the Aircraft Industry*, 170, 180.

40 Ibid., 184–87 at 186.

41 Waldie, *Holy Land*, 160.

42 Historical sources at City of Lakewood website: http://www.lakewoodcity.org/about_lakewood/community/default.asp.

43 Charles F. Waite, *Incorporation Fever: Hysteria or Salvation; An Excerpt from a Report on Incorporation and Annexation in Los Angeles County, Prepared for the Falk Foundation* (Los Angeles: Los Angeles Bureau, Copley Newspapers, 1952).

44 Ibid.

45 Gottlieb and FitzSimmons, "Bounding and Binding Metropolitan Space," 190.

46 Los Angeles County Sheriff's Department, "Contract Law Enforcement," http://la-sheriff.org/lasd_services/contract_law/index.html.

47 David Beers, "The Crash of Blue Sky California," *Harper's*, July 1993, 68–80.

48 Hise, *Magnetic Los Angeles*, 214.

49 Lotchin, *Fortress California*, 189, 192–3.

50 Ibid., 65.

51 Ibid., 4.

52 Beers, "The Crash of Blue Sky California," 73.

53 Edward Soja, "Los Angeles, 1965–1992: From Crisis-Generated Restructuring to Restructuring-Generated Crisis," in *The City*, ed. Scott and Soja, 439.

54 Allen Scott, "High Technology Industrial Development in the San Fernando Valley and Ventura County: Observations on Economic Growth and the Evolution of Urban Form," in *The City*, ed. Scott and Soja, 277, 281, 284, 303.

55 Lotchin, *Fortress California*, 254.

56 Scott, "High Technology Industrial Development," 301, 305.

57 Mike Davis, "How Eden Lost its Garden: A Political History of the Los Angeles Landscape," in *The City*, ed. Scott and Soja, 171.

58 Scott, "High Technology Industrial Development," 288, 297, 305.

59 Soja, "Los Angeles, 1965–1992," 442, 446–47.

60   Joan Didion, *Where I Was From* (New York: Alfred A. Knopf, 2003), 108–9, 130–34.

61   Ibid., 115.

62   Soja, "Los Angeles, 1965–1992," 448.

63   Ibid., 449.

64   Arthur Heath (Environmental Program Manager I, Remediation Section Chief, California Regional Water Quality Control Board), interview with the author, 17 May 2010, Los Angeles.

65   Metropolitan Water District of Southern California, "Upper Los Angeles River Area Basins," in chap. 4, "Groundwater Basin Reports," of *Groundwater Assessment Study*, Report Number 1308, September 2007, 13, http://www.mwdh2o.com/mwdh2o/pages/yourwater/supply/groundwater/gwas.html.

66   Scorecard: The Pollution Information Site, "Who Is Polluting Your Community? Superfund Sites in Your Community That Have Caused Contamination of Drinking Water," http://www.scorecard.org/community/cmy-npl-sites.tcl?dw=t&fips_county_code=06037&zip_code=90027&name=LOS%20ANGELES.

67   Heath interview, 17 May 2010; "Who is Polluting Your Community?"

68   Marla Cone, "Jet Propulsion Lab Added to Superfund List," *Los Angeles Times*, 15 October 92; Patti Paniccia, "The Devil's Advocate," *Los Angeles Times Magazine*, 25 July 2004, 16; Peter Westwick, *Into the Black: JPL and the American Space Program, 1976–2004* (New Haven, Conn.: Yale University Press, 2007), 169–70.

69   Heath interview, 17 May 2010; State of California, California Natural Resources Agency, Department of Water Resources, "Watermaster Service in the West Coast Basin, Los Angeles County, July 1, 2008–June 30, 2009," September 2009, http://www.water.ca.gov/watermaster/sd_documents/west_basin_2009/westcoastbasinwatermasterreport2009.pdf.

70   See http://www.rocketdynearchives.com.

71   Archaeological Consultants, Inc. and Weitze Research, "Historic Resources Survey and Assessment of the NASA Facility At Santa Susana Field Laboratory, Ventura County, California," prepared for National Aeronautics and Space Administration, May 2008, rev. March 2009, 3-1–3-45. http://ssfl.msfc.nasa.gov/documents/historical/NASA_Historic_Resources_ Survey_2009.pdf.

72   "Sodium Reactor Experiment," *Wikipedia*, last modified 15 July 2011, http://en.wikipedia.org/wiki/Sodium_Reactor_Experiment#Run_14_.28July_12_to_July_26.2C_1959.29; cleanuprocketdyne.org.

73   U.S. Environmental Protection Agency, "Site Overview | Santa Susana Field Laboratory (SSFL) | U.S. EPA | Region 9 |Superfund," last updated 2 June 2011, http://yosemite.epa.gov/r9/sfund/r9sfdocw.nsf/7508188dd3c99a2a8825742600743735/27aebc3de0dac08888257515005dbdef!OpenDocument.

74   South Coast Air Quality Management District, "50th Anniversary of Smog War"; Gottlieb, "Bounding and Binding Metropolitan Space," 218.

75   Gottlieb, "Bounding and Binding Metropolitan Space," 188, 198.

76   "Hypersonic Aircraft Shatters Aviation Records," by W. J. Hennigan, *Los Angeles Times*, 27 May 2010.

Afterword

Commentators are, at times, rightly charged with giving their own papers rather than responding to the work of others who have labored to bring fresh information, novel insights, and provocative interpretations before an audience. I shall try to avoid such a gaffe here, but my reactions to the rich body of research and reflection the foregoing essays have delivered do arise from decades of research on U.S. technology, business, and industrialization, focused for the past seven or eight years on Cold War–era aerospace innovations. Given how immensely Southern California has figured in the aircraft and space industries' trajectory, it is a genuine treat to witness scholarly attention being paid, at last, to greater Los Angeles as an industrial district that has operated for two generations at the cutting edges of knowledge and capability. I will commence with a few contextualizing remarks about post-1940 Pacific coast industrialization, then turn to questions and research issues triggered by individual contributions, closing with a set of agenda items that may be of value to students and scholars seeking to continue the research so well begun here.

For half a century, the metal-trades journal *American Machinist* periodically surveyed the distribution of machine tools (cutting and forming devices, such as lathes and presses, respectively) across the United States. Such tools were fundamental to automobile, aircraft, engine, machinery, and ship production, as they fashioned the myriad parts necessary for assembly. They are also a useful indicator of metalworking development. Midway through the Great Depression, the Pacific coast accounted for just 3 percent of America's machine tools; 60 percent of those had passed their tenth birthdays, the trade's rule-of-thumb benchmark for optimal replacement timing. The war changed the coast from Seattle to San Diego, as we know, and by 1945 the Pacific states housed 202,000 light and heavy tools, doubling their national share (to 7.2 percent) in a much-enhanced, war-derived manufacturing base. This burst of outfitting was soon curbed as peace brought contraction. By 1949, nearly half the region's tools at war's end had disappeared, as shipbuilding nearly vanished and aircraft manufacturing shrank sharply. The coast's national share fell back to just under 4 percent, but the average age of the "surviving" tools was much lower—only 28 percent had reached the ten-year mark. Then, with the Korean War, commenced a long settling-in process for the industrial far West, which counted some 250,000 machine tools in 1953; 224,000 in recession-plagued 1958; then 311,000 as spacefaring topped 1963's agenda; and 429,000 in 1968, as military aircraft demand redoubled the Apollo program's effects. In addition to this growth in absolute numbers, the *rate* of machinery demand's growth on the Pacific edge outpaced that elsewhere in the entire United States, for by the late 1960s California, Washington, and Oregon neared a 12 percent national share, tripling their 1949 levels in twenty years. Southern California led the parade, holding over 200,000 machine tools as the Vietnam War ground on.[1] Such dramatic, long-term expansion of heavy industry is not the usual story line for narratives about the Los Angeles region, an error this collection will go a long way toward correcting.

In his editor's introduction, Peter Westwick notes that "aerospace affected the balance between white-collar engineering jobs and manufacturing [jobs], and hence the socioeconomic makeup of Southern California," a point reinforced by Stuart Leslie's illustrations, which show engineering buildings as large as or larger than production spaces. This surge in demand for degree-toting designers, along with highly skilled technical and production workers, is surely related to the creation of the area's endless reaches of middle-income suburbs, and perhaps also the conservative politics that balanced employees' high-risk work situations. One canceled contract could send thousands to the freeways seeking new positions; a major slowdown could, and did, force career changes for much larger numbers. Westwick also observes that "hardheaded business leaders seeking to maximize profits" intersected with "engineers who pushed the technological envelope" for airplanes and spacecraft. Exactly so, but we could profit from work that looks closely at situations in which these two visions resonated and others where they clashed.

D. J. Waldie's description of Douglas as "an organization that seemed to be composed of dense layers of managers in short-sleeved white shirts who had a disturbing inability to manage" is especially salient here. What were the characteristics of good managers in aircraft and space sectors? How were these assets discovered, how was their performance assessed, and how and when did top managers communicate the "dos and don'ts" of the workplace to those who worked for them? Clearly, managing in environments of constant pressure for technological innovation was different than running a plant weaving standard textile fabrics, but in what ways, exactly? M. G. Lord offers a valuable hint when she notes that her father "never doubted the urgency of his work," especially on Apollo. If urgency distinguished aerospace life, what implications did the end of such urgency in the post-moonwalk, post-Vietnam mid-1970s have for Southern California managers' and workers' relationships to one another and to their jobs? Did Reagan-era projects, so crisply outlined by Mihir Pandya, lack the intensity that accompanied building first-generation jets and rockets, and if so, with what consequences? Echoing Waldie's critical sensibilities, Lord also scores the dreadful treatment of women in air-and-space companies and projects. It would be helpful were researchers to expand on her insights with broader studies, inquiring whether this pattern was specific to aerospace, to Southern California, or to Southern California aerospace. A complementary question set might be: What sort of masculinities did competitive innovation foster among air-and-space workers and managers? Who formed the "Right Stuff" crew, what were the pocket protector tribe's gender practices, and what of those of virtuoso machinists?[2]

Anita Seth re-opens the difficult question of aircraft industry unionization from the 1930s into the Cold War, noting that Lockheed management believed "unionization to be inevitable" and so opened the door to negotiations in 1937. So why did Lockheed's Robert Gross take such a different position from James Kindelberger at North American Aviation or Donald Douglas, who both fought labor organizers tooth and nail? Sherman Mullin, in tracing Gross's career, provides raw material for a tempting hypothesis—Gross came to aircraft building from finance and was not an engineer, like so many of his colleagues and rivals. Somehow (precisely how?) this conditioned a different attitude, perhaps reinforcing a preference for ensuring a healthy bottom line over a founding entrepreneur's lust for power and control. Seth also raises the important issue of racism by managers and within unions during the "Good War," a national shame. In Philadelphia, for example, the federal government had to seize the transit system to achieve integration among trolley drivers; and whites' violence against black workers was so viral at Sun shipyards that government orders created a separate "Negro Yard" to get Liberty-ship production back on track. In this light, what can be discovered about long-term patterns of discrimination in the air-and-space industry, and to what degree was this consistent with or distinct from practices in other Southern California sectors?

Mullin's reminder that "Lockheed employment fell drastically, from the wartime peak of 94,000 to 14,500 by the end of 1947" echoes my machine-tool counts and calls our attention to the perils of peacetime in Southern California following six years of sustained capacity expansion amid comprehensive (though not wholly effective) consumption controls. An intensive study of regional adjustment to the war's end would be valuable (not least if conducted with comparative work on the fallout for the air-and-space industry from the Korean truce and the Vietnam and post-Apollo drawdowns in the early 1970s). Decline is of course much less fun to write about than ascent, but understanding decay and failure remains a critical task for historians. On another comparative line, is this aerospace-driven feast-or-famine cycle deeper and more dramatic in Southern California than in other industrial centers? If so, with what consequences for the surrounding communities and nonaerospace businesses?

We also know that military tool, aircraft, engine, and ship orders fell off steadily from late 1944, before the mass cancellations of the summer of 1945. Following World War II, aircraft and metal-trade industry journals often discussed the new specialized companies and job shops that displaced engineers and skilled workers were creating.[3] In time some of these and their successors likely became part of the subcontracting networks for Los Angeles's 1980s aerospace production system that Pandya reviews, but their history remains to be charted. Others may plausibly have moved toward electronics (including aircraft avionics), as some early and mid-1950s firms that developed numerical controls for machinery were located in Hollywood and Burbank.[4] Some may have become members of the area's high-performance-automobile mechanics' fraternity.[5]

Mullin also delivers two pithy comments that should spark our imaginations. First, "airframes began shrinking as a fraction of the total cost of the aircraft" by the 1950s, and second, "designing and producing missiles and satellites required very different capabilities than making aircraft." Given these conditions, what implications for both business and region flowed from the slide in shares of the contract dollar devoted to airframes and also from the declining numbers of planes being constructed in any given model? What were the "different capabilities" needed for space work and to what degree did labor markets respond with migrations, retraining schemes, or wage and salary "auctions" as firms bid for skills in short supply? My guess is that a production shift to missiles displaced machinists in favor of sheet metal and electronics workers, and that systems design and electrical engineering overtook mechanical and aeronautical engineering as key assets. However, we should not overlook the resonances between air and space work, notably the necessity of flexible capacity, integration of complex components, and the ability to rapidly redesign artifacts in response to testing and use (that is, implementing the dreaded Engineering Change Requests).

Pandya's recounting of early 1980s aerospace projects in the region is truly breathtaking: the B-1 and B-2 bombers, the F-18, the F-5 fighters, the Navy's P-3 Orion, and the C-17 transport; along with commercial planes: the MD-80, DC-10, and MD-11 from McDonnell Douglas, and the L-1011 from Lockheed. Major defense contractors boomed, with full work schedules at Loral, Western Gear, Litton, General Dynamics, Ford Aerospace, Hughes Aircraft, Northrop, and TRW, with major subcontracts at Xerox, Goodyear, Unisys, Honeywell, General Motors, and General Electric plants in the metropolitan area (not to speak of the Jet Propulsion Laboratory [JPL], as Zuoyue Wang reminds us). A host of issues about California politics, labor markets, technological innovations, and the military-industrial complex should be investigated for this last Cold War decade, not least because there was a massive contemporaneous collapse of traditional eastern and midwestern manufacturing sectors following the Volcker recession induced by credit strictures that snapped the inflationary surge of the late 1970s.[6] Amid this carnage, the Los Angeles area's aerospace employment rose over 40 percent between 1979 and 1986, reaching 162,000, with another 200,000 regional jobs involved in other aspects of military production and services. This surge encouraged migration, including at a minimum Wang's Chinese engineers, Koreans[7] (many of whom started small businesses), and Latinos (who were not as significant in the 1950s labor force), in part to build homes and business facilities and work in service sectors generated by the aerospace concentrations and by their own increasing numbers. As Leslie's aerospace construction transformed the desert into working spaces as well as subdivisions for living, what roles did this generation of immigrants play in populating and vitalizing the region's economic peripheries?

Both Dwayne Day and Patrick McCray evoke the notion of myths within the regional aerospace complex, some "long-standing," others feeding futurist dreams. Glenn Bugos too cites origin myths in his comparative portrait of Silicon Valley aerospace and the valley as a whole. So wouldn't it be fascinating to identify the core myths of Southern California's aerospace culture and explain what work (maintaining boundaries, solidifying identities, and so forth) they performed for different segments of historical and contemporary engineering, management, labor, and political communities? Again, to put these patterns in context, how do they square with those attendant on Florida or Houston rocket-launch cultures, or those at Boeing's Seattle base? As before, are the local myths and cultural assumptions a regional phenomenon or part of a broader "faster, farther, higher" cultural flying circus that stretched across the nation and beyond? How did these animating beliefs change across the last six decades, which of them remain intact, and in either case, why?

In showing how aerospace initiatives influenced Hollywood innovations, Westwick brings us to the contentious but illuminating issue of spin-offs. This process has at least two key vectors: the adaptation of military-sponsored innovations for direct commercial use and the reconfiguration of such innovations for unanticipated applications. For the first class, we can cite the transition of jet engines from fighters and bombers to Boeing 707s (though not without substantial redesigns), the application of electronic computing capabilities to business problems, the appropriation of the Air Force's numerical control of metal-cutting for routine manufacturing, or the "civilianization" of Plexiglas. Westwick's unexpected account of how JPL flight-trajectory simulations lay the groundwork for computer animation most likely falls into the second. Since the 1970s, NASA has routinely emphasized those innovations that moved from space to land, in printed reports and now in an ongoing web presence "featuring successfully commercialized NASA technology."[8] Always enmeshed in political debates about whether space expenditures did anything for the regular economy, NASA undertook to show that government units could do creative things in territories where markets did not yet exist and where venture capital would not or could not venture. Given this, what spinoffs emerged from Southern California aerospace, if we look beyond the private rockets McCray documents to techniques, capabilities, processes, applications, and products stretching out of experimental development into specialized markets?[9] This question takes us back to the still-unexplored role of the thousands of subcontractors, who were ideally positioned to move knowledge developed in aerospace work toward other ends.

Housing the industry (not the housing industry) centers Leslie's evocative analysis of William Pereira's monumental projects, leading us toward another cultural theme. To what extent might the built environment in air-industry centers embody and express something like an "aerospace aesthetic," and is this regionally inflected in Los Angeles, as compared with similar complexes like McDonnell in St. Louis or NASA's Johnson Space Center in Houston?[10]

Leslie also argues that we should work to preserve these late modern industrial spaces, drawing on Matthew Roth's trenchant argument that, in Leslie's paraphrase, "what makes a place worth saving...is not how good it looks but why it mattered." Frankly, though, while it seems plausible to re-purpose a brick textile mill as high-ceilinged condos, it is rather more difficult to imagine new uses for multimillion-square-foot aerospace plants. Here lie substantive challenges for regional architects and planners, challenges worth embracing. Considering the preservation, analysis, and interpretation of significant artifacts from the aerospace decades should join that agenda. Not discussed here, and perhaps in process already, would be a version of the industrial heritage projects developed elsewhere in the nation and abroad. Revisiting what it was like to work at companies that designed and fabricated aircraft and missiles should be as valuable a museum experience as stepping back farther in time at the Lowell National Historical Park or the Henry Ford complex.

Two final items drawn from *Blue Sky Metropolis*, and my wish list for explorations yet to come, will conclude my remarks. In reviewing Bay Area aerospace and industry on the southern peninsula, Bugos rightly notes that government contracting "drove the fortunes of many early Silicon Valley firms." However, in his view, these flows of funds and the technical expertise and momentum they supported do not explain "the sustained innovation that has characterized Silicon Valley...persistent cultural traits do." To what degree can this cultural explanation for durable creativity be applied to Southern California aerospace, dominated by giant firms, not anchored by garage inventors and electronics specialists? It's certainly worth a look, as among the traits Bugos highlights were the technological "cross-pollination" that roving government inspectors facilitated and engineers' "notion of an involved, intelligent customer" being a partner in development. These were surely standard in Southern California aerospace. Perhaps scale is not as strong a determinant as process; research building on Bugos's insights may help us test this proposition.

Last, the environment dimensions and costs of aerospace may not be as profound as in coal mining, but Wade Graham rightly concludes that the industry's decline yielded "a vastly altered human and physical landscape."

Graham highlights the key roles of specialized agencies for infrastructure development, of the booster elite (and complex), and of the Darwinian competition for securing industrial enterprises with government contracts. Alliances built among firms, regional institutions, and national government units, including but not restricted to the military, transformed Southern California's systems for providing water, power, housing, and transportation, but without concern for the pervasive unintended consequences that would ravage the region's highly diverse environments.

Taking account of the basic land, air, and water dimensions of environmental history and moving through them to evaluating the human "landscape" is an immensely creative prospect. Bridging the human damage that post-1970 industrial decline entails and the toxic residues that abandoned buildings and untreated wastes bequeath can create a more holistic portrayal of the social expenses uncounted in corporate ledgers, expenses that only seem to surface when relocation or failure arrives. What then is distinctive about the aerospace aftermath in Southern California, compared with the Pittsburgh region (which has revived as a smaller, service-sector city) or Detroit (which has not)? There is a great difference between the rhythm of rise and fall and that of rise, fall, and reinvent. Is reinventing in view for the former aerospace districts? Based on what visions and resources? Moreover, what has aerospace production revealed, highlighted, or problematized about Southern Californians' relationships with their environments, their embeddedness in them, and the contours and characteristics of their materiality? The NASA blue planet photograph, still adorning the cover of my yellowing Whole Earth Catalog, helped animate Earth Day and a generation of activism. How did these initiatives intersect with the region's aerospace industry and its challenges to environmental constraints?

This set of essays has done much to re-emphasize the postwar force of air-and-space manufacturing in the Los Angeles region; yet some silences remain, worth researchers' time and energy. As suggested above, it would be valuable for historians to move outside the big firms, which Pandya has so thickly listed. Los Angeles had more air-and-space start-ups than Silicon Valley had computer hardware and software specialists, and earlier, too (a wholly unsupported assertion that would be "good to test"). Who were those guys? (They were surely almost all guys.) Did they create associations of subcontractors, instrumentation designers, or precision-machining operations? What batteries of skills did they deliver to the industry, along with their versatility? In this vein, we could use some fine-grained studies of aerospace process and practice, following a missile design through tests, failures, negotiations, re-designs, and—not uncommonly—failure (perhaps one component would be more manageable). Failure is not the same thing as decline, and studies of wrecked enterprises or projects that died from competition or in-competence, were killed off by canceled contracts, or were just super-seded by the rapid pace of innovation, would be a healthy corrective to broad-brush tales of progress and decay.

As aerospace history has not been heavily populated with critical voices, we should recognize the crucial role that "unbelievers" play in get-ting our histories to accord with actors' incomplete knowledge, pervasive anxieties, and grand ambitions two generations ago. Unbelievers discount heavily the progress talk that crowds trade and technical journals, recog-nize the political special pleading that program managers master, and try to rough out cost-benefit analyses for complex projects. They ask, for ex-ample, if failed projects really do create capabilities that are valuable in years ahead. Unbelievers are good people to have on the team.

Scholars of Los Angeles aerospace extending the many ideas and provocations this collection presents would, however, do well to add some categories of sources to their lists. Although I have just complained about trade and technical journals, they remain invaluable sources, es-pecially when authors forgo enthusiasm for giant steps and technical rev-olutions to discuss the many shortcomings of new technologies as they are being integrated with older systems and bewildered managers. Gov-ernment reports, hearings, and special commissions produce masses of paper, some tiny fraction of which is germane to the core issues raised here, but that fraction is invaluable. Finding it is the diligent (perhaps ob-sessive) scholar's reward. Scholars of regional development generally spend little time in military (or NASA) archives, but for aerospace searchers, this is fundamental. The Air Force, to take one example, con-tracted for a huge number of project histories starting during World War II (when it was the "Army Air Corps" and then the "Army Air Forces," as it imagined an independent future) through the 1970s at least.[11] From air base construction to jet plane manufacture, the histories bring an im-mediacy to their readers, for they were, first, secret and stunningly frank; and second, rich with contemporary documents reproduced as evidence for judgments and conclusions. Now they are in large measure declassi-fied and available. That said, a broad horizon for additional in-depth re-search on Southern California's aerospace growth engine and on the consequences of that engine's failure has been delineated by the authors of this volume. That the Huntington is sponsoring programs for collecting archives and oral histories only reinforces the relevance of these essays to a wider project and their salience in inscribing its key concerns. Onward and upward...

Notes

1   See Philip Scranton, "Machines on the March: Technology and the Spatial Transformation of American Metalworking, 1945–1970," in *Histoires de Territoires*, ed. Laurent Tissot (Neuchatel: Editions Alphil—Presses Universitaires Suisse, 2010), 401–32.

2   A contemporary glimpse of machinists' assumptions and practices, about politics, gender, technology, expertise, and much else, can be had by visiting the Practical Machinist website, which sponsors hundreds of ongoing conversations among working, retired, and novice metal workers; "Forums," http://www.practicalmachinist.com/vb/index.php.

3   The journals also gave considerable space to the often-bizarre diversification efforts corporations undertook after losing their war contracts. These represented generally unsuccessful precursors of the 1950s conglomerate experiments. See Diana Henriques, *The White Sharks of Wall Street: Thomas Mellon Evans and the Original Corporate Raiders* (New York: Scribners, 2000).

4   "Special Report: Factory Controls in Production," *Factory Management and Maintenance* 116 (February 1958): 137–48.

5   Robert Post, *High Performance: The Culture and Technology of Drag Racing, 1950–2000* (Baltimore: Johns Hopkins University Press, 2001). See also David Luckso, *The Business of Speed: The Hot Rod Industry in America, 1915–1990* (Baltimore: Johns Hopkins University Press, 2008).

6   Metalworking was hit particularly hard by this slump, as paging through issues of *American Machinist* will demonstrate. To my knowledge, no comprehensive study of manufacturing's global shifts during the 1980s has been undertaken, though some local and regional studies and research on individual firms were initiated at the time. As a quarter-century has passed, understanding the dynamics of the Rust Belt collapse and the Pacific coast industrial expansion may be timely.

7   See Nancy Abelman and John Lie, *Blue Dreams: Korean Americans and the Los Angeles Riots* (Cambridge, Mass.: Harvard University Press, 1997).

8   See, for a typical print version, NASA, *Spinoff 1998: An Annual Publication,* (Washington, D.C.: GPO, n.d.). The NASA Spinoff website may be found at http://www.sti.nasa.gov/tto/.

9   My sense is that few aerospace spinoffs enter consumer markets, but I am of course open to instruction on this point. It is the case, however, that Tang wasn't made for the space program, but rather was first marketed in 1957 by General Foods to the consumer market, not very successfully. NASA adoption made the stuff popular. See "Tang: The Drink of Choice among Gemini Astronauts," 19 January 2009, The Open End website,

http://theopenend.com/2009/01/19/tang-the-drink-of-choice-among-gemini-astronauts/.

10   Interestingly enough, in 1986 a shadowy scientific advisory group, the Jasons, moved its regular meetings discussing the scientific dimensions of military policy from La Jolla's Bishop's School, which "found it could make more money running tennis camps," to General Atomic's massive new facility. One reason was that it had a "Sensitive Compartmented Information Facility . . . a window-less, locked, guarded, electromagnetically-shielded room for discussing top secret work." See Ann Finkbeiner, *The Jasons: The Secret History of Science's Postwar Elite* (New York: Viking, 2006), 147.

11   See Jacob Neufeld, *United States Air Force: A Guide to the Monographic Literature, 1943–1974* (Washington, D.C.: Office of Air Force History, 1977).

Selected Bibliography on
Southern California Aerospace

Allen, Arthur P., and Betty V. H. Schneider. *Industrial Relations in the California Aircraft Industry.* Berkeley: Institute of Industrial Relations, University of California, 1956.

Anderson, Fred. *Northrop: An Aeronautical History.* Los Angeles: Northrop Corp., 1976.

Anderson, John D., Jr. *A History of Aerodynamics and Its Impact on Flying Machines.* Cambridge: Cambridge University Press, 1997.

Avila, Eric. *Popular Culture in the Age of White Flight: Fear and Fantasy in Suburban Los Angeles.* Berkeley: University of California Press, 2004.

Banham, Reyner. *Los Angeles: The Architecture of Four Ecologies.* New York: Harper & Row, 1971.

Barlett, Donald L., and James B. Steele. *Empire: The Life, Legend, and Madness of Howard Hughes.* New York: Norton, 1979.

Beard, Edmund. *Developing the ICBM: A Study in Bureaucratic Politics.* New York: Columbia University Press, 1976.

Beers, David. *Blue Sky Dream: A Memoir of America's Fall from Grace.* New York: Doubleday, 1996.

Benford, Gregory. "Sunshine Technopolis: Southern California's Dimming Future." *Futures* 36 (2004): 939–42.

Biddle, Wayne. *Barons of the Sky: From Early Flight to Strategic Warfare, the Story of the American Aerospace Industry.* New York: Simon & Schuster, 1991.

Bilstein, Roger E. *Flight in America: From the Wrights to the Astronauts.* Rev. ed. Baltimore: Johns Hopkins University Press, 1994.

———. *Stages to Saturn: A Technological History of the Apollo/Saturn Launch Vehicles.* Washington, D.C.: NASA History Office, 1996.

Blackburn, Gerald A. *Downey's Aerospace History, 1947–1999.* Charleston, S.C.: Arcadia Publishing, 2009.

Bloch, Robin. "Studies in the Development of the United States Aerospace Industry." UCLA Graduate School of Architecture and Urban Planning, Discussion Paper D875, 1987.

Boyne, Walter J. *Beyond the Horizons: The Lockheed Story*. New York: St. Martin's Press, 1998.

Bright, Charles D. *The Jet Makers: The Aerospace Industry from 1945 to 1972*. Lawrence: Regents Press of Kansas, 1978.

Bromberg, Joan Lisa. *NASA and the Space Industry*. Baltimore: Johns Hopkins University Press, 1999.

Castells, Manuel, and Peter Hall. *Technopoles of the World: The Making of 21st-Century Industrial Complexes*. New York: Routledge, 1994.

Chapman, John L. *Atlas: The Story of a Missile*. New York: Harper, 1960.

Cochran, Chris. "The Aerospace Industry in California." California Department of Commerce report, August 1988.

Collins, Martin J. *Cold War Laboratory: RAND, the Air Force, and the American State, 1945–1950*. Washington, D.C.: Smithsonian Institution, 2002.

Cooke, Philip, and Kevin Morgan. *The Associational Economy: Firms, Regions, and Innovation*. Oxford: Oxford University Press, 1998.

Corn, Joseph J. *The Winged Gospel: America's Romance with Aviation, 1900–1950*. Oxford: Oxford University Press, 1983.

Courtwright, David T. *Sky as Frontier: Adventure, Aviation, and Empire*. College Station: Texas A&M University Press, 2005.

Culick, F. E. C., ed. *Guggenheim Aeronautical Laboratory at the California Institute of Technology: The First Fifty Years*. San Francisco: San Francisco Press, 1983.

Cunningham, Frank. *Sky Master: The Story of Donald Douglas*. Philadelphia: Dorrance and Co., 1943.

Cunningham, William Glenn. *The Aircraft Industry: A Study in Industrial Location*. Los Angeles: L. L. Morrison, 1951.

Davis, Mike. *City of Quartz: Excavating the Future in Los Angeles*. New York: Verso, 1990.

Dear, Michael J., ed. *From Chicago to L.A.: Making Sense of Urban Theory*. Thousand Oaks, Calif.: Sage Publications, 2001.

Deverell, William. *Whitewashed Adobe: The Rise of Los Angeles and the Remaking of Its Mexican Past*. Berkeley: University of California Press, 2004.

Deverell, William, and Greg Hise, eds. *Land of Sunshine: An Environmental History of Metropolitan Los Angeles*. Pittsburgh: University of Pittsburgh Press, 2005.

Didion, Joan. *Slouching towards Bethlehem*. New York: Farrar, Straus, & Giroux, 1968.

———. *Where I Was From*. New York: Knopf, 2003.

Dyer, Davis. *TRW: Pioneering Technology and Innovation since 1900*. Boston: Harvard Business School Press, 1998.

Engel, Jeffrey A. *Cold War at 30,000 Feet: The Anglo-American Fight for Aviation Supremacy*. Cambridge, Mass.: Harvard University Press, 2007.

Ferguson, Robert G. "Airframe Manufacture and Engineering Exchange." In *Atmospheric Flight in the Twentieth Century*, edited by Peter Galison and Alex Roland, 257–86. Dordrecht and Boston: Kluwer, 2000.

———. "Technology and Cooperation in American Aircraft Manufacture during World War II." PhD diss., University of Minnesota, 1996.

Fernlund, Kevin J., ed. *The Cold War American West, 1945–1989.* Albuquerque: University of New Mexico Press, 1998.

Fox, William L. *Aereality: Essays on the World from Above.* Berkeley, Calif.: Counterpoint, 2009.

Galison, Peter. "Removing Knowledge." *Critical Inquiry* 31 (2004): 229–43.

Galison, Peter, and Alex Roland, eds. *Atmospheric Flight in the Twentieth Century.* Dordrecht and Boston: Kluwer, 2000.

Gauthier, Donald J. "The Aircraft Industry and the Emergence of a Regional Production System in Southern California." Master's thesis, UCLA, 1993.

Gavaghan, Helen. *Something New under the Sun: Satellites and the Beginning of the Space Age.* New York: Copernicus, 1998.

Gluck, Sherna Berger. *Rosie the Riveter Revisited: Women, the War, and Social Change.* Boston: Twayne Publishers, 1987.

Gordon, Robert, et al. *Aerojet: The Creative Company.* Los Angeles: Aerojet History Group, 1995.

Graham, Richard H. *SR-71 Revealed: The Inside Story.* New York: Zenith Press, 1996.

Gray, Mike. *Angle of Attack: Harrison Storms and the Race to the Moon.* New York: W. W. Norton, 1992.

Gregory, James N. *American Exodus: The Dust Bowl Migration and Okie Culture in California.* New York: Oxford University Press, 1989.

Guillen, Reynal. "The Air Force, Missiles, and the Rise of the Los Angeles Aerospace Technopole." *Journal of the West* 36 (1997): 60–66.

Hallion, Richard P. "The Impact of the California Institute of Technology on American Air Transport and Aeronautical Development, 1926–41," appendix 1 in *Legacy of Flight: The Guggenheim Contribution to American Aviation.* Seattle: University of Washington Press, 1977.

Hallion, Richard P., and Michael H. Gorn. *On the Frontier: Experimental Flight at NASA Dryden.* Rev. ed. Washington, D.C.: Smithsonian Books, 2010.

Hise, Greg. *Magnetic Los Angeles: Planning the Twentieth-Century Metropolis.* Baltimore: Johns Hopkins University Press, 1997.

Jardini, David. "Out of the Blue Yonder: The RAND Corporation's Diversification into Social Welfare Research, 1946–1968." PhD diss., Carnegie-Mellon University, 1996.

Johnson, Clarence L. *Kelly: More Than My Share of It All.* Washington, D.C.: Smithsonian Institution Press, 1985.

Johnson, Stephen B. *The Secret of Apollo: Systems Management in American and European Space Programs.* Baltimore: Johns Hopkins University Press, 2002.

Kargon, Robert, Stuart W. Leslie, and Erica Schoenberger. "Far Beyond Big Science: Science Regions and the Organization of Research and Development." In *Big Science: The Growth of Large-Scale Research,* edited by Peter Galison and Bruce Hevly, 334–54. Stanford, Calif.: Stanford University Press, 1992.

Kasarda, John D., and Greg Lindsay. *Aerotropolis: The Way We'll Live Next.* New York: Farrar, Straus, and Giroux, 2011.

Kelly, Shawna. *Aviators in Early Hollywood.* Charleston, S.C.: Arcadia Publishing, 2008.

Kessler, Lauren. *The Happy Bottom Riding Club: The Life and Times of Pancho Barnes.* New York: Random House, 2000.

Kling, Rob, Spencer Olin, and Mark Poster, eds. *Postsuburban California: The Transformation of Orange County since World War II.* Berkeley: University of California Press, 1991.

Koppes, Clayton R. *JPL and the American Space Program.* New Haven, Conn.: Yale University Press, 1982.

Kraemer, Robert S. *Rocketdyne: Powering Humans Into Space.* Reston, Va.: American Institute of Aeronautics and Astronautics, 2006.

La Chapelle, Peter. *Proud to be an Okie: Cultural Politics, Country Music, and Migration to Southern California.* Berkeley: University of California Press, 2007.

Law, John. *Aircraft Stories: Decentering the Object in Technoscience.* Durham, N.C.: Duke University Press, 2002.

Lécuyer, Christophe. *Making Silicon Valley: Innovation and the Growth of High Tech, 1930–1970.* Cambridge, Mass.: MIT Press, 2006.

Libby, Joseph Edward. "To Build Wings for the Angels: Los Angeles and Its Aircraft Industry, 1890–1936." PhD diss., University of California, Riverside, 1990.

Livingstone, David. *Putting Science in Its Place: Geographies of Scientific Knowledge.* Chicago: University of Chicago Press, 2003.

Lord, M. G. *Astro Turf: The Private Life of Rocket Science.* New York: Walker, 2005.

Lotchin, Roger W. "California Cities and the Hurricane of Change: World War II in the San Francisco, Los Angeles, and San Diego Metropolitan Areas." *Pacific Historical Review* 63 (1994): 393–420.

———. *Fortress California, 1910–1961: From Warfare to Welfare.* New York: Oxford University Press, 1992.

Mack, Pamela E. "What Difference Has Feminism Made to Engineering in the Twentieth Century?" In *Feminism in Twentieth-Century Science, Technology, and Medicine,* edited by Angela N. H. Creager, Elizabeth A. Lunbeck, and Londa Schiebinger, 149–68. Chicago: University of Chicago Press, 2001.

Markusen, Ann, et al. *The Rise of the Gunbelt: The Military Remapping of Industrial America.* New York: Oxford University Press, 1991.

Markusen, Ann, and Joel Yudken. *Dismantling the Cold War Economy.* New York: Basic Books, 1992.

Marrett, George J. *Contrails over the Mojave: The Golden Age of Jet Flight Testing at Edwards Air Force Base.* Annapolis, Md.: Naval Institute Press, 2008.

———. *Howard Hughes: Aviator.* Annapolis, Md.: Naval Institute Press, 2004.

Mattingly, Doreen. "Local Labor Market Dynamics of Production Workers in a Southern California Aircraft Plant." Master's thesis, UCLA, 1991.

Maynard, Crosby. *Flight Plan for Tomorrow: The Douglas Story, a Condensed History.* Santa Monica, Calif.: Douglas Aircraft, 1962.

McGirr, Lisa. *Suburban Warriors: The Origins of the New American Right.* Princeton, N.J.: Princeton University Press, 2001.

McWilliams, Carey. *Southern California Country: An Island on the Land.* New York: Duell, Sloan, & Pearce, 1946.

Mettler, Ruben F. *The Little Brown Hen That Could: The Growth Story of TRW Inc.* New York: Newcomen Society in North America, 1982.

Miller, D. W. "The New Urban Studies." *Chronicle of Higher Education*, 18 August 2000, A15–16.

Miller, Jay. *Lockheed Martin's Skunk Works: The Official History.* Leicester, U.K.: Midland, 1995.

———. *The X-Planes.* Arlington, Texas: Aerofax, 1988.

Molotch, Harvey. "LA as Design Product: How Art Works in a Regional Economy." In *The City: Los Angeles and Urban Theory at the End of the Twentieth Century*, edited by Allen J. Scott and Edward W. Soja, 225–75. Berkeley: University of California Press, 1996.

Nash, Gerald D. *The American West Transformed: The Impact of the Second World War.* Bloomington: Indiana University Press, 1985.

Olszowka, John. "From Shop Floor to Flight: Work and Labor in the Aircraft Industry, 1908–1945." PhD diss., SUNY-Binghamton, 2000.

O'Mara, Margaret Pugh. *Cities of Knowledge: Cold War Science and the Search for the Next Silicon Valley.* Princeton, N.J.: Princeton University Press, 2005.

Orr, Verne. "Developing Strategic Weaponry and the Political Process: The B1-B Bomber, from Drawing Board to Flight." PhD diss., Claremont Graduate University, 2005.

Paris, Michael. *From the Wright Brothers to Top Gun: Aviation, Nationalism, and Popular Cinema.* Manchester, U.K.: Manchester University Press, 1995.

Paschal, Huston, and Linda Johnson Dougherty. *Defying Gravity: Contemporary Art and Flight.* Raleigh: North Carolina Museum of Art, 2003.

Pattillo, Donald M. *Pushing the Envelope: The American Aircraft Industry.* Ann Arbor: University of Michigan Press, 1998.

Pendo, Stephen. *Aviation in the Cinema.* Metuchen, N.J.: Scarecrow Press, 1985.

Pisano, Dominick A., ed. *The Airplane in American Culture.* Ann Arbor: University of Michigan Press, 2003.

Pynchon, Thomas. "Togetherness." *Aerospace Safety* 16 (1960): 6–8.

Rae, John B. *Climb to Greatness: The American Aircraft Industry, 1920–1960.* Cambridge, Mass.: MIT Press, 1968.

———. "Financial Problems of the American Aircraft Industry, 1906–1940." *Business History Review* 39 (1965): 99–114.

Ramo, Simon. *The Business of Science: Winning and Losing in the High-Tech Age.* New York: Hill and Wang, 1988.

Rand, Christopher. "The Ultimate City, I–III." *The New Yorker*, October 1, 8, and 15, 1966.

Rich, Ben R., and Leo Janos. *Skunk Works: A Personal Memoir of My Years at Lockheed*. Boston: Little, Brown, 1994.

Richardson, D. Kenneth. *Hughes after Howard: The Story of Hughes Aircraft Company*. Santa Barbara: Sea Hill Press, 2011.

Rossiter, Margaret W. *Women Scientists in America: Before Affirmative Action 1940–1972*. Baltimore: Johns Hopkins University Press, 1995.

Rust, Daniel. *Flying Across America: The Airline Passenger Experience*. Norman: University of Oklahoma Press, 2009.

Saxenian, AnnaLee. *Regional Advantage: Culture and Competition in Silicon Valley and Route 128*. Cambridge, Mass.: Harvard University Press, 1994.

Schatzberg, Eric. *Wings of Wood, Wings of Metal: Culture and Technical Choice in American Airplane Materials, 1914–1945*. Princeton, N.J.: Princeton University Press, 1999.

Schoneberger, William A. *California Wings: A History of Aviation in the Golden State*. Woodland Hills, Calif.: Windsor Publications, 1984.

Schoneberger, William A., and Ethyl Pattison. *Los Angeles International Airport*. San Francisco: Arcadia Publishing, 2007.

Scott, Allen J. *Technopolis: High-Technology Industry and Regional Development in Southern California*. Berkeley and Los Angeles: University of California Press, 1993.

Scott, Allen J., and Edward W. Soja, eds. *The City: Los Angeles and Urban Theory at the End of the Twentieth Century*. Berkeley: University of California Press, 1996.

Sell, T. M. *Wings of Power: Boeing and the Politics of Growth in the Northwest*. Seattle: University of Washington Press, 2001.

Shapin, Steven, "Who is the Industrial Scientist? Commentary from Academic Sociology and from the Shop-Floor in the United States, ca. 1900–ca. 1970." In *The Science–Industry Nexus: History, Policy, Implications*, edited by Karl Grandin, Nina Wormbs, and Sven Widmalm, 337–63. Canton, Mass.: Science History Publications, 2004.

Sides, Josh. *L. A. City Limits: African American Los Angeles from the Great Depression to the Present*. Berkeley: University of California Press, 2003.

Simonson, G. R., ed. *The History of the American Aircraft Industry*. Cambridge, Mass.: MIT Press, 1968.

Smith, Bruce L. R. *The Rand Corporation: Case Study of a Nonprofit Advisory Corporation*. Cambridge, Mass.: Harvard University Press, 1966.

Sobel, Robert. *The Entrepreneurs: Explorations within the American Business Tradition*. New York: Weybright & Talley, 1974.

Springer, Anthony M. *Aerospace Design: Aircraft, Spacecraft, and the Art of Modern Flight*. New York: Merrell, 2003.

Starr, Kevin. *Coast of Dreams: California on the Edge, 1990–2003*. New York: Knopf, 2004.

———. *The Dream Endures: California Enters the 1940s*. New York: Oxford University Press, 1997.

———. *Embattled Dreams: California in War and Peace, 1940–1950*. New York: Oxford University Press, 2002.

———. *Endangered Dreams: The Great Depression in California*. New York: Oxford University Press, 1996.

———. *Golden Dreams: California in an Age of Abundance, 1950–1963*. Oxford: Oxford University Press, 2009.

———. *Material Dreams: Southern California through the 1920s*. New York: Oxford University Press, 1990.

Stekler, Herman O. *The Structure and Performance of the Aerospace Industry*. Berkeley: University of California Press, 1965.

Taylor, Frank J., and Lawton Wright. *Democracy's Air Arsenal*. New York: Duell, Sloan, and Pearce, 1947.

Vander Meulen, Jacob A. *The Politics of Aircraft: Building an American Military Industry*. Lawrence: University Press of Kansas, 1991.

Verge, Arthur C. *Paradise Transformed: Los Angeles during the Second World War*. Dubuque, Ia.: Kendall/Hunt Publishing, 1993.

Vincenti, Walter G. *What Engineers Know and How They Know It: Analytical Studies from Aeronautical History*. Baltimore: Johns Hopkins University Press, 1990.

Wakeman, Rosemary. "Dreaming the New Atlantis: Science and the Planning of Technopolis, 1955–1985." *Osiris* 18 (2003): 255–70.

Waldie, D. J. *Holy Land: A Suburban Memoir*. New York: St. Martin's Press, 1996.

Weems, Jason. "Barnstorming the Prairies: Flight, Aerial Views, and the Idea of the Midwest, 1920–1940." PhD diss., Stanford, 2003.

Weschler, Lawrence. *Seeing is Forgetting the Name of the Thing One Sees: A Life of Contemporary Artist Robert Irwin*. Berkeley: University of California Press, 1982.

Westwick, Peter J. *Into the Black: JPL and the American Space Program, 1976–2004*. New Haven, Conn.: Yale University Press, 2007.

———. "The Jet Propulsion Laboratory and Southern California." In *Societal Impact of Spaceflight*, edited by Steven J. Dick and Roger D. Launius, 467–81. Washington, D.C.: NASA History Division, 2007.

Wilburn, James R. "Social and Economic Aspects of the Aircraft Industry in Metropolitan Los Angeles during World War II." PhD diss., UCLA, 1971.

Wild, Mark. *Street Meeting: Multiethnic Neighborhoods in Early Twentieth-Century Los Angeles*. Berkeley: University of California Press, 2005.

Wohl, Robert. *The Spectacle of Flight: Aviation and the Western Imagination, 1920–1950*. New Haven, Conn.: Yale University Press, 2005.

Wolfe, Tom. *The Right Stuff*. New York: Farrar, Straus, and Giroux, 1979.

CONTRIBUTORS

Peter J. Westwick is an assistant research professor in history at USC and director of the Aerospace History Project at the Huntington-USC Institute on California and the West. He received his BA in physics and his PhD in history from Berkeley. He is the author of *Into the Black: JPL and the American Space Program, 1976–2004* (2006) and *The National Labs: Science in an American System, 1947–1974* (2003). He is working on a history of the Strategic Defense Initiative and a history of surfing.

Glenn E. Bugos is a historian with the NASA Ames Research Center, in the heart of Silicon Valley. He has written a history of the center, *Atmosphere of Freedom* (2010), and several articles on various topics in aerospace history. He received his PhD in the history of technology and business from the University of Pennsylvania, and he is also president of Moment LLC, a corporate history consultancy.

Dwayne A. Day is a senior program officer with the Aeronautics and Space Engineering Board of the National Research Council. He has directed numerous studies for the Air Force and NASA and served as an investigator on the Columbia Accident Investigation Board. He holds a PhD in political science from George Washington University. He has written a history of the Air Force Chief Scientist's Office, and has edited several books and written numerous articles on space history.

Wade Graham is the author of a social history of gardens in America, *American Eden: From Monticello to Central Park to Our Back Yards, What Our Gardens Tell Us About Who We Are* (2011). He has a PhD in American history and teaches urban and environmental policy at the School of Public Policy at Pepperdine University.

Stuart W. Leslie teaches the history of science and technology at Johns Hopkins University. The essay on William Pereira in this volume is part of a larger study of laboratory and health-care design, forthcoming as *The Architects of Modern Science* from the University of Pittsburgh Press. He also writes about corporate architecture, most recently an article in *Enterprise and Society*, "The Strategy of Structure: Architectural and Managerial Style at Alcoa and Owens Corning." He is the Lindbergh Chair at the National Air and Space Museum for 2012–13.

M. G. Lord is a cultural critic and journalist. She is the author of *Astro Turf: The Private Life of Rocket Science* (2005), a family memoir about Cold War aerospace culture, *Forever Barbie: The Unauthorized Biography of a Real Doll* (1994), and *The Accidental Feminist: How Elizabeth Taylor Raised Our Consciousness and We Were Too Distracted by Her Beauty to Notice* (2012). She teaches in the Master of Professional Writing Program at USC.

W. Patrick McCray is a professor in the department of history at the University of California, Santa Barbara. He is the author of four books, including *Giant Telescopes: Astronomical Ambition and the Promise of Technology* (2004) and *Keep Watching the Skies: The Story of Operation Moonwatch and the Dawn of the Space Age* (2008). His book *Limitless: From Space Colonies to Nanotechnologies in Pursuit of the Future* is forthcoming.

Sherman N. Mullin, an aerospace engineer and executive, retired as president of Lockheed Advanced Development Company, the Skunk Works, in 1994. He is a Fellow of the American Institute of Aeronautics and Astronautics. A book collector, he has 3,000 volumes in his library, primarily literary and military biography.

Mihir Pandya is completing a dissertation in cultural anthropology at the University of Chicago. His dissertation is a historical ethnography of Cold War–era Stealth airplane projects. He will be joining USC as a postdoctoral associate with the Science, Technology, and Society Research Cluster. His areas of interest include science and technology studies, the anthropology of security and secrecy, and the history of the Cold War.

Philip Scranton is University Board of Governors Professor, History of Industry and Technology, at Rutgers University. He has authored numerous volumes, most recently *The Second Wave: Southern Industrialization from the 1940s to the 1970s* (2001) and *Endless Novelty: Specialty Production and American Industrialization, 1865–1925* (1997). His edited volumes include *Beauty and Business: Commerce, Gender, and Culture in Modern America* (2000) and *The Rise of Marketing and Market Research* (forthcoming), with Hartmut Berghoff and Uwe Spiekerman.

Anita Seth is a doctoral candidate at Yale University and a labor organizer with UNITE HERE, which represents five thousand workers at Yale along with hospitality workers across the United States and Canada. Her dissertation compares the social and economic consequences of Cold War defense industry build-up in Los Angeles and in the Russian city of Novosibirsk.

D. J. Waldie is the author of *Holy Land: a Suburban Memoir* (1996) and other books about Los Angeles and Southern California. He is a contributing editor for the *Los Angeles Times*.

Zuoyue Wang is a professor of history at the California State Polytechnic University, Pomona. Born in China and originally trained in physics, he received his PhD in the history of science from the University of California, Santa Barbara. Author of *In Sputnik's Shadow: The President's Science Advisory Committee and Cold War America* (2008), he is currently studying the history of Chinese American scientists and engineers with partial support of a grant from the National Science Foundation.

Index